'Funny, emotional ... anyone wanting to ...

'Hilarious.' *Refinery*

'Tender, courageou... make us all braver.'

'I loved it! Such a w... and the book lives ... Nigella Lawson

'Painfully hilarious.' *Red*

'*Sorry I'm Late* follows the author's year of gregarious challenges with painful hilarity. In our world of JOMO (joy of missing out), this book might make us all try (and sometimes fail) to be that little bit braver.' *Suitcase Magazine*

'Relatable, moving, and fantastically funny. One Asian-American woman with a low centre of gravity has thrown herself into a personality experiment most of us would never dare. Introverts everywhere will be cheering – and then wondering who they are.' Rhik Samadder

'A chronicle of Pan's hilarious and painful year of being an extrovert.' *Stylist*

'In a world of self-care and nights in, this book will inspire and remind you to do some things that scare you every so often.' Emma Gannon

'Excellent, warm, hilarious.' Nik...

'Beautifully written, fascinating and so, so funny. Had me properly guffawing on the bus.' Lauren Bravo

'You will laugh and laugh while reading this.' *Sun*

'Hilarious, unexpected and ultimately life-affirming.' Will Storr

'Absolutely bloody great. As a textbook, concrete, public changing, foghorn extrovert, I find Pan's descriptions of introversion and shyness fascinating and she is very funny.' Nell Frizzell

'*Sorry I'm Late* is much more personal, colloquial and intimate than other books in this bashful little genre.' *Guardian*

'*Sorry I'm Late, I Didn't Want to Come* achieves what so many books claim (but then frankly fail) to do: making you laugh, while at the same time managing to inspire. Pan is a gem, and her introvert's exploration of extroversion is all at once delightful and deftly rendered.' Sara Barron

SORRY
I'M LATE
I didn't want to come

Jessica Pan

BLACK SWAN

TRANSWORLD PUBLISHERS
61–63 Uxbridge Road, London W5 5SA
www.penguin.co.uk

Transworld is part of the Penguin Random House group of companies
whose addresses can be found at global.penguinrandomhouse.com

First published in Great Britain in 2019 by Doubleday
an imprint of Transworld Publishers
Black Swan edition published 2020

Parts of Chapter 2, 'Talking to Strangers', originally appeared in the *Guardian*.
Quotation on pp. 163–4 from *How to Own the Room* by Viv Groskop
reproduced by permission of the author and Penguin Random House.

Every effort has been made to obtain the necessary permissions with
reference to copyright material, both illustrative and quoted. We apologize
for any omissions in this respect and will be pleased to make the
appropriate acknowledgements in any future edition.

A CIP catalogue record for this book
is available from the British Library.

ISBN
9781784164157

For Ian –
Wǒ ài nǐ

CONTENTS

AUTHOR'S NOTE

Let's be clear: I don't think anybody – introvert, extrovert or otherwise – needs to be cured. But I was, for a while, an unhappy introvert and I wanted to see how my life might change if I spent a year undertaking daunting new experiences. This book is about what happened next. Please enjoy my nightmares.

INTRODUCTION

There are two types of people in this world: those who watch Glastonbury on TV as though it's a horror movie, peering over the top of the blanket as they bear witness to the muddy hell-hole. They sigh from relief at the sheer joy of missing out, because they are so happy to be on their sofas and not there, surrounded by thousands of swaying, loud, drunk people with full bladders and greasy hair.

And then there are those who choose to go to Glastonbury. I am not one of those people.

My friends at university threw me a surprise party in my bedroom for my twenty-second birthday. As soon as everyone jumped out of the dark, I burst into tears. People at the party thought I was touched. Actually, I was horrified. For the first time in months, the tears weren't because I was in unrequited love with my Spanish language tutor. Good friends, family and some vague acquaintances were sitting on my bed – which was incidentally the very place I usually went to escape from those good friends, family and vague acquaintances.

I had nowhere to hide. They were here for a party. How long until they left?

Eventually, I just turned on all the lights and waited for everyone to take the hint.

If you're like me, then you, too, know what it feels like to dread your own birthday parties. You fear giving speeches, team bonding exercises and every single New Year's Eve.

I feel this way because I'm an introvert. Actually, I'm a shy introvert (more on this later), and any shy introvert worth their salt has invariably done the following: thrown a ringing phone across the room, faked being sick, walked into a networking event and immediately backed out, and pretended not to speak English when approached in a bar. That last one is advanced level, but the most effective method of all. The rest are necessary survival skills. We are also gifted at avoiding eye contact to deter people from saying hello with a technique I like to call 'dead robot eyes'.

I would say 90 per cent of my acquaintances don't even know that I'm an introvert because I take such pains to hide it. After-work drinks? Sorry, I'm very busy. Lunch at the pub? Can't, I have plans (eating ramen alone in blissful solitude). Co-workers just think that inside the office I'm distracted, and that outside the office I have both a full social calendar and debilitating face blindness.

Now that I'm older and wiser, on the morning of every birthday I gently wake up my husband Sam and whisper in his ear, 'If you throw me a party, I will murder you.' He always nods obligingly, half-asleep. Except he doesn't really get it, because he's a different breed altogether – a quiet person who likes going to a busy pub and hanging out at festivals. But he's grown used to most of our nights out ending with my hissing, 'Get my coat and meet me by the lifts!'

while I sprint towards the back exit to escape an approaching tipsy hen party that has just arrived at the bar.

Sam goes along with it, but the depths of my neuroses are a foreign country to him. He doesn't understand why, for example, I prefer dogs to people. But that's easy. Dogs don't require small talk, they don't judge you, and they don't hum near your desk while you're trying to work. They don't ask when you're going to have kids. Or cough on you. But to Sam, dogs have wild eyes, might put their dirty paws all over you and are ready to strike at any moment, which is exactly how I feel about humans.

I assumed that life as a shy introvert would go on this way for me forever. But then, something unusual happened: I found myself roasting in a sauna, clutching a copy of *Men's Health*, wearing a black tracksuit and weeping as I yelled profanities at a spa employee.

And something had to change.

That's the short version.

Some people are great at talking to strangers, building new relationships and making friends at parties. I'm really good at other things, like loitering palely in dark doorways. Disappearing into sofa corners. Leaving early. Feigning sleep on public transport.

Nearly a third of the population (at least, depending on which study you consult) identifies as introvert, so it's likely that this could describe you, too. If we'd, say, met at a party that neither of us had flaked on, we could bond over this while hiding in the kitchen near the cheeseboard.

There are a lot of heated debates about what defines an introvert or an extrovert. The main accepted definition is that introverts get their energy from being alone, whereas extroverts get their energy from being around other people. But psychologists often discuss two other related parameters: shy versus outgoing. I always assumed that all introverts were shy, but apparently some introverts can be ultra-confident in groups, or capable of smoothly delivering presentations. What makes them introverts is that they just can't take stimulation and large crowds for extended periods of time.*

But I am shy: I'm afraid of making contact with strangers, being the centre of attention, but I also need time to recharge after being around a lot of people and loathe large crowds. I am, as one article defined it, a 'socially awkward introvert'. A shy introvert or *shintrovert*, as I shall henceforth refer to myself (which is also a pervert who is very into lower legs).

I don't know if shintroverts are born or made, but for me, my tendencies began to show very early on. I grew up in a small town in Texas where I skipped birthday parties, faked illnesses to avoid school presentations and spent many nights journaling about a parallel universe where interacting with multiple people and occasionally being the centre of attention wasn't my worst nightmare.

As a kid, I didn't understand why I felt so differently about life from my extroverted immediate family. My father is Chinese and my mother is Jewish–American and they both love two things deeply: Chinese food and chatting to new

---

* For more on this, please see A Note on Introversion on p. 329.

people. Meanwhile, my two older brothers were always inviting big groups of their friends over to our house, where they'd linger for hours. I originally thought they were all just better at pretending to like the things I hated. Later, I was confounded: why did they love meeting big groups of new people and socializing for hours and throwing big birthday parties when I didn't? I thought that there was something deeply wrong with me.

Still, growing up in a small town, I dreamt of a bigger life full of new experiences. But it wasn't a life I could envisage for myself there. I wanted an entirely clean slate. A new place where I could reinvent myself, free from anyone who knew me. I tried Beijing, then Australia, and eventually London, where I live now.

But one thing remained constant during these travels: no matter how far-flung the lands, I remained essentially the same. A shintrovert. Dumplings, shrimp on the barbie, scones and cream. Shintrovert eating in the corner. The Forbidden City, Sydney Opera House, Tower of London. Shintrovert hovering in doorways. I'd thought that maybe foreign lands would shake the introversion out of me but, like my eczema, it thrived in all climates.

And then came the 'Quiet Revolution', sparked by Susan Cain's bestselling book in 2012. Within its pages, I read that one out of every two or three people is an introvert. That there was nothing wrong with us. That introverts, to paraphrase, concentrate well, relish solitude, *dislike small talk, love one-on-one conversations, avoid public speaking.* Shy, sensitive homebody, you say? Damn right I am!

I was enormously relieved to read these things and decided to embrace this side of myself. This is who I was. Rather than beating myself up for the person I wasn't, I chose to celebrate the person I was. After all, my disposition is one reason I became a writer, and it meant that I had very close relationships with my small group of friends during this time.

Then in the space of a year, it all went wrong. I became unemployed and my closest friends moved away. My career had stagnated, I was lonely, I lost the desire to run; I had no idea what to do next in my life. In truth, I wanted to pull my old trick and hop on a plane and begin a new life, perhaps this time as someone named Francesca de Lussy. But it was abundantly clear that I didn't have the personality, confidence or hat collection to pull this off.

I had a lot of time to sit around and ponder: what did I really want from life? Really, I wanted a job, some new friends who I felt truly connected to and more confidence. Was that so much to ask? Surely not. So what were other people out there with jobs and close friends and rich, fulfilling lives doing that I wasn't? Eventually, and with mounting fear, I realized: they were having new experiences, taking risks, making new connections. They were actually out there, living in the world instead of staring out at it.

I once overheard my former colleague Willow talking about her trip to New York. Willow had stopped to pet a woman's dog in Prospect Park: she ended up spending the day with the woman, going to a jazz club with her until 4 a.m. and later landing her dream job through one of her new friend's connections. She'd met her boyfriend in a queue for the toilet at a festival. She discovered she had hypoglycaemia by talking to a doctor at a party. Her entire life has been shaped by these random encounters. All because she chooses to talk and listen to people she has just met, rather than run away from them at full-speed muttering, 'I don't speak English!'

What might happen if I flung open the doors of my life? Would it change for the better?

Although I had accepted who I was, at this juncture in my life it was not making me happy. I had taken my introvert status as a licence to wall myself off from others.

Although I savoured my introvert world, part of me wondered what I might be missing out on. When you define something or someone, you inevitably limit it. Or her. The way I saw myself became a self-fulfilling prophecy: 'Speeches? I don't give speeches' or, 'Parties? I don't throw parties.' I accepted who I was but I was also too scared to challenge my fears, go out and have the experiences that I craved.

During my bachelor's degree in psychology, I took a neuroscience course, partly because I was so interested in the interplay between nature and nurture. But now that I was an adult, how much could I change as a result of new experiences?

The famous Shakespeare quote is, 'To thine own self be true'. Yes. But I didn't want to be tethered to my insecurities and anxieties for eternity. I didn't want to stay stunted. We're humans. We have the capacity for growth and change.

And once I realized that, a small voice inside me said, 'Screw this bullshit!' I'd been using the introvert label as an excuse to hide from the world.

Up until that point, I'd been clinging to my shintrovert status, and it had made it almost impossible for me to have those things I secretly yearned for – a career I cared about, new meaningful relationships, filled-with-laughter friendships and experiences that I hadn't planned out in excruciating detail.

I was an introvert in a hole, not in a hole *because* I was an introvert. There are plenty of happy introverts, who are living their best lives, but I wanted to emerge from that hole – I believed a larger life than the one I currently had would ultimately make me happier.

But to do that? Something had to change.

Question: What would happen if a shy introvert lived like a gregarious extrovert for one year? If she knowingly and willingly put herself in perilous social situations that she'd normally avoid at all costs?

Would it offer up a world of life-changing experiences?

Or would she wind up in the woods, eating weeds and only communing with wolves until she died of malnutrition, alone but kind of happy that she never had to engage in small talk about Bitcoin ever again?

Here goes nothing.

THE SAUNA,
A STORY
or
rock bottom

I met my husband, an Englishman, in Beijing, where we fell in love the most probable way two shy people can: at work, flirting on instant messenger, two desks apart, never making eye contact. Sam and I both worked at the same magazine and it was the first time I'd ever felt completely and totally at ease with someone who I was also attracted to. After eventually speaking to each other in person, we moved to Australia together and then eventually got married and moved to a tiny flat in Islington, north London.

I'd spent nearly three years getting used to Beijing, a city where the locals always tell you what they think about you. The local teahouse owner? He thought I was too fat. My landlady? She thought I was too thin. My fruitseller? He thought I did not drink enough hot water. Actually, they all thought that.

Locals would also ask how much money I made as a magazine editor (not very much), or why I wore flimsy flip-flops in a big dirty city (I was young and stupid), or why I was looking so haggard (have you seen Beijing's pollution records lately?). But at least I always knew where I stood.

After that, I assumed it would be a breeze to assimilate in England, a country without a language barrier. Plus, I had a few old friends there, and I'd be with Sam. After the chaos of my three years in China, I was in awe of London: all the green space! The orderly queues! The toilets with toilet seats! I stared at all the types of chocolate bars and crisps in a big Sainsbury's and felt pure euphoria. I wanted to walk around the city with open arms. I wanted London to love me the way that I loved it.

London did not love me.

Instead, London (well, a Londoner) stole my wallet and my visa and thus my right to work in the UK. If London was trying to punish me, it was doing it in a really passive-aggressive way, because not having my visa also meant that I couldn't leave the country. It had imprisoned me but it would not let me work.

And that was just the beginning. A woman would thank me on the train for moving my bag and I was almost certain that what she was really saying was 'Too fucking right.' A man would squeeze by me on the escalator, and the pitch of his 'May I . . . ?' would nearly reduce me to tears. People would ask me if I wanted to do something and I had no idea if it was an order, a helpful suggestion or sarcasm.

And friends? I'd struggle to make new friends in the easiest of places, never mind in London. People prefer to keep to themselves, especially in public. This was wonderful at first. No one ever approached me to chat. I was left alone. I once tripped and fell in a crowded street in broad daylight. I began the 'I'm fine, I'm fine, honestly' protest. But no one had stopped. I lay on the ground, impressed. These people were better introverts than I was!

Because I couldn't work without my UK visa, I spent my days partaking of Britain's best cultural invention – TV marathons of *Come Dine With Me*, where I was excited to learn that most British dinner parties end with a poached pear and everyone secretly bad-mouthing the host while perched on the edge of her bed.

After a few months, I got my visa back and did the mature thing and got a job at a marketing agency writing blog posts for a shoe brand. My specialty was writing guides for what shoes to wear in what weather – the kind of decision most people have mastered by age seven.

Before I knew it, Sam and I had spent a few years in London. And during that time, all the friends I did have in London left. You may think that's an exaggeration. It is not. Rachel, my best friend from university, moved to Paris. Ellie, a good friend from China, moved back to Beijing. English colleagues I bonded with scattered to the countryside or the suburbs. London became an increasingly lonely place. The streets had become familiar, but they were, as ever, filled with strangers. I buried myself at work, under blog posts and client meetings and shoes.

Then, one fateful night, I attended an awards ceremony at work. The bosses introduced the award for the person who stayed the latest; the person who spent their weekends at the office. The person who had 'sold their soul for the job', they explained. It was dubbed the Midnight Oil Award. They opened the envelope and called out my name. As I made my way towards the makeshift stage, various male colleagues slapped me on the back and congratulated me for having no life. I gritted my teeth, forced a smile and accepted the award.

It was engraved with my name. Later, as I carried it home, it felt like a cursed artefact, like Frodo's ring, except less all-powerful and shiny and more a weight, a symbol of my failure. Failure, because I was so not interested in my job or what I was doing with my life. Failure to be the sort of person I admired, someone who tried new things and took chances and who avoided the easy option.

Also like Frodo's ring, the trophy was impossible to destroy by dumping it in the bin or a fire. I'd seen the film trailers – I assumed it would just find me again. I placed it in the least dignified place I could think of. 'Fuck you,' I whispered softly to the trophy as I closed it in a cabinet, leaving it to rot next to half a dozen bags-for-life and a bottle of drain cleaner.

Back at work the next day, I learned that a colleague named Dave had won the Midnight Oil Award the previous year. Here's the thing about Dave: he always looked miserable. He ate the same sandwich every single day. At the office Christmas party, both of us sitting in a corner, he'd drunkenly confessed to me that he'd do anything to leave, if he only knew how.

I studied Dave. And then I did something really stupid that felt really, really good. I quit my job.

With no back-up position, I began to call myself a free-lancer. In my case, 'freelancer' was a euphemism for wandering around the flat in my pyjamas and becoming overly excited when I spotted cats in the garden. I was still writing blog posts about shoes, but now I was doing it for less money while sitting on our sunken blue sofa. As I watched people going by on their morning commutes, it struck me that I lived in a city of nine million people and only spoke to two every day: Sam and a barista.

The barista wasn't a chatty guy. And Sam had his own life outside the four walls of our home: a job he liked, colleagues he bonded with, an evening running club and best friends that he met up with to watch football. He had a separate world and I only had him. Every morning when he left for work, I'd slide my head under the covers, not wanting to face another grey day completely alone. No one was expecting me anywhere. My brother texted me: 'I haven't heard from you in a while – I have no idea what's going on with you. Are you happy?'

This last question shattered me. I couldn't tell my family, who were so far away, that I was in a deep hole and I didn't know how to get out. I couldn't even admit it to Sam. Or myself.

On a cold wintry day, I woke up at 11 a.m. after spending the previous night googling 'black holes', 'do I have attention deficit disorder' and 'were Mick Jagger and David Bowie friends?' until the small hours. I had also emailed Rachel, who now lived across the Channel, to confess that I definitely probably might have attention deficit hyperactivity disorder because I seemed to flit from one task to another, yet things never seemed to get done. I was messy, I was forgetful, I had trouble concentrating.

Rachel wrote back saying, 'I don't know . . . everything you've said sounds a lot more like depression to me. Inability to concentrate is actually one of the symptoms of depression. Maybe you should talk to someone . . .'

What did she mean, *everything I'd said*? I glanced back at my previous email. My sign-off was, 'I look forward to nothing.'

I quickly closed my computer.

When we're young, we think our lives will be creative and vibrant and full. But little by little, I was backing myself into a corner and my only way forward increasingly felt like a long, dark hallway with all the doors slammed shut. Except, of course, in the age of unfettered social media access, they were actually glass doors and I could peer inside at every one of my glamorous contemporaries living their best photogenic lives with fifteen to twenty of their closest friends.

I had essentially created a fortress around myself, stacked high with books and a sign on the wall that said, 'I DON'T NEED YOU ANYWAY!'

But I did. Rachel could see it. I needed to see it, too. The time had come to break free of my increasingly uncomfortable comfort zone. I knew that I wasn't depressed because of being an introvert. I was an introvert who happened to be depressed. I hated who I had become. I wanted to start over.

So I joined a gym.

That may not sound like a solution to the problem I actually had, and before you start thinking that this is a story about how losing weight changed my life, cured my depression and made me a millionaire, I should probably warn you that it's not. It's a story about my first, tentative steps into the outside world. To slowly rejoin society. To get out of the house. The first steps I would take as a shintrovert trying not to shintrovert any more. But it's also a story about something far more important: subterfuge. And some light planking.

I was lured in because the gym offered free membership if you attended three fitness classes a week and won their in-house fitness and weight-loss challenge. Looking around, I saw that the women in this gym were super fit. They had sleek ponytails. They seemed satisfied. Women who had probably fulfilled their own parents' dreams by becoming doctor-lawyer-bankers, not women whose arses had melded to fit the shape of their sofa cushions as they wrote blog posts about different ways to lace your boots. Not women who celebrated clean hair days.

If I completed and won the gym challenge, I'd have free membership and immediately join a group of people who seemed to have their lives together. Maybe even make a friend or two. I'd also be fitter and possibly happier (endorphins, better at lifting furniture, fancy shampoo in the changing rooms, etc.).

I was confident about winning the competition, because it's easy to win things like this when you have nothing else going on in your life. And I was right. Week by week, the competition pool shrunk as people dropped out, failing to attend the requisite three classes.

And by the final week, it came down to two possible winners. Me and a woman named Portia.

Regrettably, I developed a deep resentment of Portia.

I had pinned my entire future on this stupid contest and now I had to beat her. I began to ponder the cold, hard facts: the final weigh-in was in one week. The contest was based only on percentage of body weight lost. What determines how much we weigh, when you get right down to it? Fat, muscle, bone. And water.

Here is another, totally normal fact that I came across during one of my nocturnal googling sprees: wrestlers and boxers regularly drop 10–15 pounds of water in a few days to 'make weight' in their categories.

I promptly tumbled down a black hole of wrestling and boxing blogs, written exclusively by and for guys named Brandon. These blogs provided detailed how-tos on dropping water-weight fast. There were simple tricks, like drinking black coffee (a diuretic), and slightly more extreme things, like taking caffeine pills and mainlining dandelion tea. But I could drink coffee, right? *Normal* people do that. I drank coffee every day already.

Since the very first time I'd flopped on to the sofa in despair about Portia, Sam had been patient with me and my mission. This lasted right up to the day before the final weigh-in, when I was explaining how showering the day of the competition was a rookie mistake because the body absorbs water through the skin. That could lead to gaining a kilo. That shower could be the difference between victory and failure.

'You signed up for this contest to get healthy and happy and now all you're talking about is vanquishing someone named Portia, the benefits of caffeine pills and why you're not going to *shower any more*.'

'I'm just not going to shower *tomorrow*!' I shouted back. 'And I didn't end up buying caffeine pills. *That* would be lunacy.'

I went back to my wrestling blogs, where I discovered the most universally endorsed strategy: the sauna.

But this wasn't to be some toxin-flushing, Scandinavian, feel-good spa trip. The sauna served one purpose: to roast that water out of your body. To maximize the sweat, the Brandons advised staying fully clothed.

I like saunas. I could go to the sauna. Couldn't a woman just go to the sauna without it being a crime? Couldn't a woman drink black coffee and not shower *and* go to the sauna? *Of course!* I told myself. Of course she could. A woman could easily do all of these things on a totally normal day.

Clearly, Sam had been right. I'd forgotten about why I'd joined, too consumed with beating Portia. I mean, part of me knew it was shady as hell to do these things. I didn't like who I was becoming – but I'd felt like a loser for more than a year and was desperate for a win. I was reaching for rock bottom.

The day of the final weigh-in, I stepped into the sauna. I took a seat on the hot wooden planks, fully dressed in a black long-sleeve T-shirt, black sweat pants and woolly socks. The dry heat engulfed my body. Outfitted like a ninja who is really into self-care, I closed my eyes and leaned back.

I thought about the wrestling blogs that had led me here. Just like me, my amateur wrestler heroes knew how to sacrifice to get what they wanted. I thought about how they would completely understand that sitting in a sauna and sweating for a few minutes was worth it if it meant getting your life back on track and saving money on your gym membership.

It was getting pretty unbearable inside the sauna, but I had already done the hard part – choosing to be a duplicitous motherfucker. All I had to do now was endure fifteen minutes of heat. Just close my eyes and wait it out. I could do this. I could be stoic in this heat, like a desert beetle.

It was hard to be too Zen, though, because the receptionist was not living up to my high hopes. She kept coming to check on me, deeply suspicious of my behaviour. She'd fling open the sauna door, letting out all my hot air, and I kept jumping up and slamming it shut again, indicating with my hands that we could talk to each other through the thin glass pane. We repeated this routine a few times – her opening the door, me slamming it shut in her face to keep the heat in.

'Why are you wearing clothes? That's crazy! You should take off your clothes!' she shouted at me through the glass. By this point, my clothes were drenched in sweat.

'No. This is what I want!' I said to her, offering no further explanation. I crossed my arms. The third time, I finally shouted, 'Jesus Christ! Please just go away!' Dumbfounded, she left me in peace.

I settled down again. My mouth was parched. I couldn't drink water, because that would defeat the purpose of this visit, but I was already so thirsty. I checked the clock every thirty seconds. Five minutes passed; it felt like an hour. I reached for the magazines in the corner to distract myself, only to find that every single one was about men's fitness.

I flipped lethargically through the pages of one and landed on a summer feature about how to stay safe during outdoor hikes. I absent-mindedly skimmed a fact box about heat stroke: 'Brought on by over-sweating, dehydration and over-heating, heat stroke can cause brain damage and/or death.' Uh, what was that?

My mouth went even drier than it already was. I hadn't had any water that day. I was sweating profusely inside a very hot sauna. I had created the perfect conditions for heat stroke. *On purpose.* Was I going to give myself heat stroke? Was I having a heat stroke right now? What *is* heat stroke?

I panicked. I was going to die in this sauna. I instantly saw my obituary: 'She gave herself heat stroke while trying to win free gym membership in north London.' They would tell my parents that I had died dressed like an assassin, reading a guide to 8-minute abs.

I was still slow-cooking, but something deep inside me went cold. I had completely lost it. I wasn't losing my marbles; my marbles were long gone.

I opened the sauna door.

Later, at a cafe drinking water, I stared listlessly into space. I drank more water. I went home and lay on my sofa, because that's all I had the energy to do.

What had happened to me? Jobless, friendless and now sanity-less.*

The fact that my Come-to-Jesus, rock bottom moment was in a sauna reading *Men's Health* isn't really something I'm proud of. I had completely lost perspective. I no longer knew where my natural introversion ended and my depression and loneliness began. After all, I had once been a happy introvert, but I had managed to wedge myself into a hole, through fear, insecurity and stagnation.

That day, I took stock of the facts: my life was small, and I wanted to see if I enjoyed it being bigger. And bigger, I knew deep down, meant opening my world up, specifically to other people. Lots of them. I had read so many articles about how hard it is to make friends in your thirties, and I knew it would probably be even worse for people like me. My modus operandi in friendship was either a) you're my best friend and I tell you all of my intimate secrets, or b) you're a stranger, dangerous and unknown, ready to strike at any moment.

I looked out of the cafe window at the world rolling by without me. I missed my friends, dispersed across the world. I missed feeling excited about things. The reality of it was this: I felt that my life was passing me by.

I knew what I had to do.

I would talk to new people – not small talk, but real 'and how did your father feel about that' chats. I would give

---

* Yes, of course I won the weight-loss challenge. Portia was not deranged enough to go to those lengths. Only me and the Brandons of the world are.

speeches. I would travel alone and make new friends on the road, I would say yes to social invitations, I would go along to parties, and I would not be the first to leave.

And if I survived all of that, I would attempt the Everest of shy person trials: I would perform stand-up. Instead of a 'choose your own adventure' journey, this is a choose your own nightmare.

Finally, to fully atone for turning those lights on early at my twenty-second birthday party surprise, I'd throw a dinner party and invite some of the people I met along the way and *not* kick them all out after an hour. I would entertain, I would small talk, I would celebrate.

It would be like jogging: very sweaty and uncomfortable, with moments of heart-pounding agony, but possibly good for me in the long term.

In other words, I would extrovert.

I gave myself a year.

TALKING TO
STRANGERS

or

new people

The man sitting next to me is good-looking. Tall, dark and handsome. Kind, blue eyes. Plaid shirt. Jeans, rolled up.

We glance sideways towards each other and lock eyes. I take a deep breath.

'I live far away from my parents, and they think I'm happier than I am, and I can't bear for them to know that sometimes I literally don't know what I'm doing with my life,' I say to him.

He blinks. And then says, 'I haven't seen my family in ten months, and I just realized that I don't miss them and I'm afraid that makes me a bad person.'

My turn again.

'I fear I'll never make enough money,' I say. 'No matter what, it seems like after I pay my tax bill, I have no money left over. Ever. I fear I'll always struggle with this.'

Your turn, buddy.

'I feel inferior to my wife because she earns considerably more money than I do,' he says.

He was really going for it.

'All of my closest friends have moved away or we've grown apart and I'm afraid I'm never going to have a new close friend that I can tell anything to and it makes me sad,' I say, my voice slightly shaking.

'I find it very difficult to make new, genuine friends. That's why I've come tonight. I told my wife I had a work thing – she doesn't know I'm here.'

A bell rings.

Chris and I both signed up for the same workshop. The advertisement promised the class would teach us how to make better connections with other people. Neither of us knew this meant confessing humiliating, personal secrets to strangers. They didn't mention that in the brochure.

'If what you're saying makes you feel like a loser, you're doing it right!' shouts our group leader Mark encouragingly.

Chris and I nod at each other in agreement, as we sink lower into our seats.

Nailed it.

A defining feature of extroverts is that they like being around other people. And presumably, interacting with them. Talking to them, even. It's a lot to take in.

If, like me, you only know a handful of people, then it stands to reason that most of these 'other people' you interact with will be strangers. And so here's the first massive stumbling block in my year of extroverting: I am afraid of talking to strangers.

In London, I learned quickly that if you talk to a stranger in public, they look at you like you've slapped them in the face: shocked and aggrieved. Betrayed as well, because you have broken the social contract that we all agreed to follow in public: no one exists but you. More than one British person has told me that only Americans and unhinged people talk to strangers. Or, given the reputation of northerners, the whole of Yorkshire. But then, of course, there is still the excruciating hell of everyone eavesdropping on your awkward conversation.

A few years ago, I found a box of badges at my local cafe in London. I picked one up. It read: 'I Talk to Strangers'. I chucked it back immediately, afraid someone had seen me holding it. It might as well have said: 'I Eat Spiders'.

For me, talking to strangers is something you do as a last resort: lost in an unfamiliar neighbourhood, dead phone, broken leg, typhoon – and really, only if these things happen all at once.

I know it's not only me who feels this way. During rush hour in cities, we all stand squashed on public transport, essentially spooning, in total silence. Sure, I'll shove my face into your armpit, but talk to you? Never.

I went back for one of those 'I Talk to Strangers' badges, though. It occurred to me that 'chatty tourist' would be a great Halloween costume with which to frighten Londoners.

Anyway, I forgot about the badge for years, until I read an article that surprised me: apparently, when people are forced to talk to strangers, it makes them happier.

Around that time, on a flight from New York to London, I found myself sitting in a three-person row with two men. I immediately went into default shut-off mode: I put on my head-phones and stared straight ahead. *Don't talk to me, I'm not here.* And it seemed to work, because they turned to each other instead. Pretty soon, they were exchanging barbecue recipes, then pouring out their souls and showing each other family pictures on their phones. By the time we touched down at Heathrow, one had invited the other to his birthday party that Friday.

This was astonishing to me. If that's what had come of a six-hour flight, how much was I missing by ignoring the dozens, if not hundreds, of strangers I saw every day? Was I missing out on life-changing recipes, birthday parties and sympathetic shoulders to cry on?

Extroverts like spending time with other people, so my first step is to try and get comfortable talking to those other people. The mere idea makes my palms start itching.

And what if I was very bad at it?

Would I be ostracized from English society for ever and banished to an island full of the unhinged and the chatty: Americans, those people outside Oxford Street station trying to save your soul, car salesmen, seven-year-old children and men in bars with lethally high confidence levels?

Because that seems unfair: I really don't want to go there, either.

On day one, I decide it's best to start as I mean to go on: face-planting straight into my first potentially life-ruining experiment.

With a deep breath, I walk purposefully up to a woman at the bus stop at 8 a.m. She immediately turns away. I take a seat on the upper deck with the other morning commuters. The woman next to me is immersed in her phone, playing *Candy Crush*. No one else on the bus is talking. My heart is racing as I practise various opening lines about candy, but then the woman notices me staring at her phone, and I feel as if she just caught me looking down her shirt. I abort the mission.

Deflated from my bus failures, I decide to go for some low-hanging fruit. I walk up to an unfamiliar barista at a local cafe. I can do this, right? I'm just talking to the nice man with the coffee.

'You're new!' I say, confident that he has to answer because being friendly to customers is part of his job.

'I've worked here for three years,' he replies.

The customer next to me laughs.

A small part of me dies.

I'd read that being lonely or isolated is a risk factor for early mortality, which means that, by some stretch, maybe talking to strangers will save my life. Though at the moment it feels like it's actually knocking a big chunk of years off it. I'm going to need help. Of the professional variety. But who?

The next day, while holding my 'I Talk to Strangers' button in my hand for whatever the opposite of comfort is, I realize that I will need others along the way to guide me through this year of unknown territory. Experts. Gurus. Mentors. People who will prevent me from extroverting straight off a cliff.

After some quick research, I decide to call Stefan G. Hofmann, director of the psychotherapy and emotion research laboratory at Boston University – he regularly coaches people through their fear of interacting with others. In a light German accent, he tells me that, 'Social anxiety is a completely normal experience. We are social animals. We want to be accepted by our peer groups and we do not want to be rejected. If people do not have any social anxiety, something is seriously wrong with them.'

So that's something.

I ask Stefan if he thinks talking to strangers would be easier outside of England, which seems particularly tricky to me. By the time I'm done humiliating myself in this green and pleasant land, I may need to migrate somewhere else.

'I think it depends on the city. For instance, Boston is harder than New York, where they are chattier. And I'm from Germany, where we're very tied up. You can barely talk to a German. But we are very helpful once you get our attention,' he says.

His experience has shown that an effective treatment for social anxiety is a form of exposure therapy: to put people in their worst-case scenario, where they are guaranteed to be repeatedly rejected. For instance, he might instruct a patient to stand on the side of the road and sing really loudly. Or he'll have another patient approach one hundred strangers on the Tube and ask them for £400. Or have someone spill a cup of coffee all over themselves at a very public place, every day.

Just, you know: your basic NIGHTMARES.

But, Stefan explains, 'No one is going to fire you or divorce you or arrest you if you do these things.' He has an 80 per cent response rate in alleviating anxiety. So, there may be method in his madness.

'What . . . what would you prescribe me?' I have to ask.

'Well, what are you afraid of?'

An impromptu therapy session ensues during which, after some probing, I confess that I'm most scared that a stranger will think I'm weird and stupid.

'Then it would be best if we constructed a conversation where you go up to a stranger and say something completely stupid,' Stefan suggests. 'I would have you ask a stranger, "Excuse me, I just forgot. Does England have a queen and, if so, what's her name?" You would have to say these exact words and nothing else.'

My heart starts to beat very quickly. But he doesn't stop talking.

'You also shouldn't just pick nice old ladies to ask or friendly-looking people. And you can't say, "I'm so sorry, I kind of forgot who the Queen is . . ." because that is safety behaviour and it will prevent you from getting over your fear,' Stefan adds.

'Great,' I say. I'd rather break both my legs in a violent typhoon in a scary, unfamiliar neighbourhood than ask strangers in London the dumbest question I can think of.

'What do you think the consequences would be if you did this?'

I tell him I think the stranger would think I was lying, playing a prank or suffering from amnesia. Or, most likely and – for me – most damning, think I'm an idiot.

'Yes, and then what would happen? Picture it.'

I close my eyes.

'They would roll their eyes and walk away. Or, if it's on the Tube, everybody will look at me and think I'm stupid and weird.'

'Excellent. Excellent,' Stefan says. 'What you're describing is a realistic scenario we could all live with: you ask someone, they roll their eyes and they walk away. So the person thinks you're stupid and that's the end. Life goes on. There are millions of people living in the world, there will be some who think that we're stupid and that's fine.'

'I'm finding just the thought of this very stressful,' I say to him.

'Well, you know what I think?' says Stefan.

'What?' I ask.

'How about you try it?'

I laugh nervously. Stefan laughs at my reaction. We laugh. And laugh.

I hang up the phone.

I glance at my sofa and then back to my phone. And at the badge in my hand.

'I Talk to Strangers'.

I stand up and grab my coat.

I'm so nervous that I think I might get arrested. I probably *should* be arrested for what I'm about to do: disorderly conduct and disturbing the peace. (Is it emotional abuse? I think it may also be emotional abuse.)

A man walks towards me on an underground platform. He's in his early forties, wearing a navy blue suit and he looks like he's in a rush. He's getting closer. And closer.

I wave a hand in front of his face as he passes. He abruptly stops in his tracks and looks at me, surprised.

'Excuse me, I forgot . . .' I say, trailing off.

He looks at me expectantly.

'Uh, is there a queen of England? And, if so, what's her name?' I splutter.

'The queen of England?' he repeats, disbelieving, eyebrows raised.

'Yes. Is there one? Who . . . who is she?' I ask.

'It's Victoria,' he says.

Of all the scenarios I had imagined, this wasn't one of them.

'Victoria?' I ask.

'Yep.'

'So you're saying the queen of England is called Victoria?' Now I'm the disbelieving one.

'Yes,' he says, and hops on to the train. I'm so confused, I immediately flag down the next person I see: another man, this one in his twenties, at least six feet tall, dressed in a tracksuit and carrying a gym bag. I ask him the question quickly and he stares at me with bemused contempt.

'It's Victoria,' he says and walks off.

OK, extrovert experiment aside – does *no one* know who the queen of England is?

Do *I* even know who the queen of England is?

Dazed, I stop four women in a row and each of them tells me, 'Elizabeth'. Some laugh in shock, some pause fearfully, and all of them look at me as if I am very slow. One asks if I'm OK. But not one of them calls the police.

And I don't die.

Stefan was right.

Sure, I now have serious doubts about the average British person's grasp of history and/or current affairs. But me? I am fine. Better than fine. I am downright giddy after traversing that gauntlet. I practically skip home, kicking leaves up in the air with joy.

Some people say there is no such thing as a stupid question, but by asking the stupidest of questions I had finally faced my fear of talking to random strangers.

My confidence was dangerously high. Like, tall-American-men-after-four-beers high. Maybe I could really do this.

The next day, I'm eating alone at a sushi bar, enjoying my lunchtime solitude. Just as I take a bite of spicy tuna, I sneeze violently and spray sushi all over my black jeans. And at that moment I hear a man's voice over my shoulder.

'Do you mind if I sit here?'

My mouth full of food, my nose running, rice bits everywhere, and a businessman in a suit looking expectantly at me. Oh no. This is terrible. This is horrifying. For both of us.

To the man, I gesture at the chair, nod and say lamely behind a napkin, 'I sneezed. I'm sorry.'

He takes a seat.

I realize there's nothing I can say that was worse than that sneeze: it's only up from here. I take a deep breath.

When he finally looks up from his phone, I pounce.

'Where are you from?' I ask.

I'd detected an accent. He's French. He smiles, then seems to gesture as if to say he's going to get back to his lunch, but I will not be defeated this easily.

'But where in France? Are you . . . offended by Brexit?' It's not my best work, but the conversation rolls along nicely enough. (And, yes, he does feel offended by Brexit.)

In the coming days, I discuss the sudden cold weather seven times. 'Do you think we'll get snow this year?' I ask strangers.

No one knows.

'I need coffee,' I say to a woman in her fifties in the queue at Pret.

'Yes,' she says. 'Coffee is good.'

Everyone in earshot wants to die as well.

It turns out, it's very hard to get past the small talk.

I pet many dogs and pretend it's an excuse to talk to their owners. I strike up a conversation with the woman next to me at a storytelling event and we chat about the weather. On the bus, I sit behind a child and her grandmother playing twenty questions. I suddenly interject, 'Is it a fox?' They stare at me bewildered, but gradually accept my participation (it was a raccoon).

I feel like a kindly village idiot wandering the city. But try as I might, I can't get past the mundane. Stefan helped me make contact with strangers. Now I needed someone to help me *connect* with them.

So I decide to call up my next expert: Nicholas Epley, a professor of behavioural science at the Chicago Booth School of Business. He's the psychologist who had started me on this whole adventure when he discovered that when people talk to strangers during their commutes, it makes them happier. I tell him how odd this sounds to me: you're saying that people actually like talking to each other on the bus or Tube? Is that not the WORST place to talk to people?

'Well, it seems like the easiest place to me,' he says. 'Other places are spots where people are doing other things already. On the Tube or on the bus, they're just sitting there, doing nothing.' Or playing *Candy Crush*.

Nick says that the silent train coaches of London are probably a result of pluralistic ignorance: everyone is actually willing to talk but thinks everyone *else* is unwilling. The train could be full of people who want to strike up a conversation, but it remains silent nonetheless.

So he tested this back in Chicago. Subjects consistently thought they were more interested in talking to their neighbour than their neighbour was in talking to them.

'We polled people and asked: what percentage of people do you think would be willing to talk to you if you talked to them first? People on trains estimated 42 per cent would and 43 per cent would on the buses.'

They were wrong. The actual percentage of people who would be willing to engage with you in conversation is almost 100 per cent. Basically everyone but Morrissey, who, popular legend has it, once sat alone in an empty room at a bustling Hollywood house party drinking a cup of tea in silence.

'Obviously, there are people who don't talk back,' Nick says, 'but that wasn't a common experience.'

I'm taken aback by how Nick talks about this with such confidence.

'So you're saying that you could come to London and just talk to strangers up and down the Tube all day long?' I ask.

'Absolutely,' he says.

Arrest this man.

OK, fine, maybe he could do this, but what about introverts who might want to be left alone on their commute? Did his research compare the reactions of introverts and extroverts?

'We have introverts and extroverts in our experiments. We measure personality in our experiments – and it's not the case that extroverts are happier talking to strangers than introverts.'

This surprises me. And gives me a little bit of hope about the rest of the year.

I bring up the problem I've been having: I can't seem to get past small talk. I'm not having any of those amazing connections: it's just the weather, or what's your dog's name, or what do you do. Or who's the Queen.

'Just the weather?' Nick sounds disappointed. 'Can you do it better?' he asks.

Of course I *could* do it better. If I were someone else. But I'm abysmal at this – I don't know *how* to do it better.

'You need to self-disclose more. Share more about yourself. Ask them personal questions.'

As Nick coaches me through meaningful conversation topics – what do you like about your job, tell me about your family, where's the most interesting place you've been to this year – I realize that I'm a grown woman having a lesson on how to have a conversation.

I also realize that I did not know how to have a conversation with new people.

But if you think about it, no one teaches us how to do this. OK, technically life does, but I've come across so many people who are also pretty bad at this: they ask no questions, they ramble, they don't listen, they interrupt, or they ask too many questions and offer up nothing of themselves.

Talking is what bonds us to other people the most and we are supposed to learn this through experience out in the real world. I'd spent that time hibernating with a book.

All of this 'offering up something personal' made me feel the old clammy twinge of fear of rejection.

Then Nick reminds me that social life is governed by reciprocity.

'A few years ago, I was driving through a remote part of Ethiopia and I kept passing all these mothers and children outside of their mud huts. Everybody I passed stared at me like I was dead: totally blank facial expressions. It was the most uncomfortable I'd ever felt in my life.

'But then it occurred to me, while I was sitting there, I was looking at *them* in exactly the same way they're looking at *me*. So I started smiling and waving as I went by – and it was like I flipped a switch. As soon as I started smiling, waving and looking friendly, they started waving from their windows, grinning at me and running out their houses to give me high fives.

'That's the truth of the world, Jessica,' he says, casually full-naming me to let me know something big is coming. 'Nobody waves – but *everybody* waves back.'

I hear his mic drop all the way from Chicago.

Later that week, as I'm walking through my neighbourhood, I see a man painting on the street. I remember that I need to be the first to wave. I tell myself that he has kind eyes to pump myself up for the encounter. Once I say hello, he puts down his paintbrush and we chitchat about the area (I chitchat these days), then he surprises me. He invites me to a private art show at someone's house the following week. And that's how, a few days later, I end up in an enormous house: three storeys tall, high ceilings, Picasso prints on the walls; my entire flat would fit in the kitchen. I make a vow to myself: I will get past small talk. Tonight, I will learn from these people. Tonight, I will self-disclose.

I walk with purpose through the halls and see a well-dressed, intimidating man in his sixties, alone. I'm nervous about talking to him, so I hover near him and he keeps walking past me. Finally, I decide to bite the bullet. I jump out of the corner at him like a nightmare.

'Hi, I'm Jess,' I say. 'Where do you live?' Suddenly, hearing my voice aloud, I'm aware this is both a basic thing to say and also – depending on how you hear it – a terrifying thing to say.

It turns out that Malcolm lives on a beautiful quiet square that I run by most days.

Disclose something about yourself, I hear Nick's voice in my ear. *Ask him what you really want to know.*

'I peek into the windows of those houses nearly every day,' I say. 'With the massive kitchens that extend into courtyards and the amazing gardens at the back. I pretend to live there sometimes. I've always wanted to know, is that the best place to live in the entire world?'

'It is,' he says.

He walks away.

No one said this would be easy.

I scour the house for my next victim, and meet a fifty-year-old named Dave who's been reinventing himself as a stand-up comedian. He initiates conversation first when we are both standing in front of an abstract painting that looks like a sick walrus. We trade tips on fighting writer's block, which he tells me is cured by drinking red wine and listening to Rod Stewart. So far, so good.

I keep circulating (I circulate these days), and near the end of the night end up in a conversation with the artist from the street, Roger, who invited me. He steers the conversation towards his paintings.

'Art is the only thing that makes sense to me,' he says. 'It's light, texture and . . .'

No. No no no. I do not want to talk about the virtues of art at this art show. I think: what do I really want to know about this gentle, soft-spoken man?

'Roger, what's the worst thing you've ever done?' I ask. I can't believe I've just asked that. I briefly wonder if he's going to laugh in my face.

Instead, he thinks for a moment, contemplating with his glass of wine. 'Well, I burned down the art department at my school when I was a teenager.'

Bingo.

In my past life, I would have walked straight past this man. Now, here I am at the fanciest party I've ever been to, discovering his past felonies, and all because I stopped to say hello. And the research is right: it brings me joy. I mean, it's not as fun as re-reading *I Capture the Castle* by a fire in a log cabin, but it's not the worst.

The party inspires me to keep going. This doesn't mean that I stop feeling nervous before each encounter – I do. But it's like ripping off a plaster. Take a breath, and after the initial shock, the painful part is over. On the train home one night that week, I'm sitting next to a man and trying to get up my nerve to talk to him. But I also don't want him to think I'm hitting on him.

'Hi,' I finally say. 'Where'd you get that blazer? My husband is looking for one just like it.' Subtle AF.

At first, he recoils in surprise and clutches his bag close to his chest. Then he recovers. 'Finland,' he tells me. This is not useful information, but the plaster is now off.

After his initial shock, the Finnish man starts asking me questions. He tells me he's lived in London for five years; we discover we both love the TV show *30 Rock*. Talking to him on a cold, rainy night is much better than sitting in stony silence carefully avoiding eye contact. It isn't the deepest of conversations, but as he stands up to get off at his stop, he turns to me and says, 'What a nice surprise it was to meet you tonight.'

I'm left sitting there, with the other passengers who had been staring at us like we were a science experiment.

And we are. We are *my* science experiment. And I think it might be going quite well.

Back in the classroom, I steal a glance at the man in the plaid shirt and rolled-up jeans as the instructor Mark sets up the next slide in his presentation.

Mark points to a slide of an Edward Hopper painting of a forlorn woman staring out of the window.

'As people, we are extremely vulnerable. We are tiny insignificant little things on this big planet, hurtling through space, in a big galaxy. We are so vulnerable that if a branch from a tree falls on to our head, it will kill us.'

I lower my body in my seat and touch the back of my neck protectively.

'We need allies to survive, hence the need for sociability. We all seek deep connections with other people but as we get older, loneliness is an unavoidable part of life,' he says, gesturing to the Hopper painting again.

The class is called 'How to Be Sociable', at the School of Life, the brainchild of bestselling author Alain de Botton.

I didn't know what to expect at a class that promises to teach you how to be sociable. When I was twelve, my mother made me attend one evening at a cotillion class, an etiquette programme popular in the South in the States for teaching manners. I think it may have also been an effort to make me less shy. I spent the night scared that the teacher, a dainty woman called Mrs Flowers, who prowled the room in kitten heels with a microphone, was going to call on me. Then she put her mic down and I spent the rest of the night catatonic while being forced to dance the foxtrot with a twelve-year-old boy with sweaty hands. It was mortifying and it set me back years. I hoped this night would not be similar.

The evening class takes place in a basement and there are about forty people of all ages here. Our instructor Mark is jocular and confident as he stares out at us and we, the good people of Russell Square, stare back at him.

I don't know what brought these thirty-nine other people to this class, but Britain was recently dubbed the loneliness capital of Europe so I'm assuming one factor is loneliness. A recent study says that staring at our phones and ignoring people has become our new normal, which is probably also why we have forgotten how to be around our own species.

Loneliness has been declared a health epidemic, and spending time with each other is the obvious cure. To do so, Mark tells us, we need to talk to each other. But, he stressed, that doesn't just mean everyday small talk, but deep, meaningful conversation that makes us feel connected to another person. Which is exactly what Nick had told me. I think back to his advice about trying to have more personal conversations, which I applied at the gallery house party – that guy really seemed to know what he was talking about.

Honestly, I'm kind of happy to have permission to dive right into more interesting territory because I have a very real allergy to small talk. I don't want to discuss jobs and weather and how people's commutes are. Introverts tend to hate chit-chat (it's an awkward social interaction, but also meaningless and unrewarding), but this kind of enriching conversation that Mark is referring to is incredibly rare and hard to come by, something I had already found out on the streets of London.

We're told that we can engineer conversations to be more emotional and interesting by understanding that we all have a 'Surface Self' and a 'Deep Self'. The Surface Self talks about the weather, facts, what we had for dinner, our plans for the weekend. The Deep Self talks about what these things actually mean to us and how we feel about them.

Deep Self holds on to our fears, our hopes, our loves, our insecurities, our dreams. Surface Self is preoccupied with logistics, facts, details, admin. Deep Self is the wedding vows, Surface Self is the wedding planner. Deep Self likes to stare into your eyes talking about your secret desires, while Surface Self keeps checking out of the conversation to plan their shopping list. I prefer to understand it like this: Destiny's Child's *The Writing's on the Wall* is Surface Self ('Jumpin' Jumpin'', 'Bug A Boo', 'Bills, Bills, Bills'). Beyoncé's *Lemonade* is Deep Self ('Pray You Catch Me', 'Daddy Lessons', 'Don't Hurt Yourself'). Got it?

Mark shows us a short video of a dinner party. In it, a man describes his commute in detail, before asking the woman across from him what she studied at university and going on about what he majored in. Then she begins talking about her favourite vegetarian recipes. This is an example of 'shallow conversation'. It feels eerily familiar to every (rare) dinner party I have attended.

In another clip, a different man mentions the death of his mother, before he brushes it off and swiftly moves on to football. Then he's abruptly interrupted by a woman, who asks him how he feels about the death of his mother, given that it was so soon after her divorce from his father. How was he coping with both those things happening at once? The woman is kind in the video, but she also feels slightly invasive.

Mark stops the video. 'You might think, "Maybe he didn't want to talk about his mother and it was rude of her to ask", but he's the one who brought her up. He *did* want to talk about it, but he couldn't find a way in,' he says. 'People are usually very happy to answer personal questions if they feel the person asking them is genuine and kind.'

A woman in front of me 'uh huhs' in audible agreement.

A man in his thirties raises his hand. 'But people don't always want to share their personal feelings and life, right? Some people might hate that.'

Mark turns to him. He tells him, sure, maybe, but the fear of being intrusive is hugely exaggerated. The more important point is this: what we should actually fear is being boring and dying having never connected with anyone.

Then he stares at all of us, meaningfully, and says it again, slowly. 'The fear and bleak reality of being boring and dying having never connected with anyone is *vastly underestimated*.'

Mark then claps his hands and asks half of the class to turn to the stranger sitting to our right and offer them a fact about us or something going on in our lives. It's up to the other person to make sure to steer the conversation away from the superficial and into the deep, emotional, rewarding territory.

I turn to the woman sitting to the right of me. Her name is Lindsay. American. She's from Alabama. She's wearing pearls and a black cashmere jumper.

I bait her. 'I'm going to Texas soon to visit my family,' I say. God, she could go anywhere with this. Family. Tensions with family. A return to America fraught with anxiety or possible longing and regret.

'Oh . . . that's a long flight. How long is that flight?' Lindsay asks.

'Eleven hours,' I say. *Too surface, Lindsay*.

'Wait, let me try again. Are you . . . um . . . are you going to go shopping? Damn it!' she says.

Like a wise guru, I silently gesture for her to try again.

'Are you looking forward to sunny weather?' she ventures.

Lindsay cannot do this. She cannot ask a deep question. I had thought that Americans might be better at this than Brits.

Come on, Lindsay. Ask me about my family. Ask me if sometimes I lie awake wondering why I moved so far away from them when every year I miss them more. Is it really just because London has good plays and nice cafes and newspapers I'd like to write for? Ask me something real, Lindsay.

The conversations between the pairs around us are swirling, deep and intimate, but Lindsay is now asking me if I'm looking forward to eating Mexican food in Texas. I can't hide my disappointment. The bell rings, indicating that it's my turn to dig deep into Lindsay's psyche.

But first she has to state a fact about herself. She takes a breath. And says nothing.

She can't think of anything to say about herself. Fair enough. Maybe she was nervous. I decide to take the lead.

'How long have you lived in England for?' I ask.

'Five years,' she says.

'What brought you here?' I ask. I'm still staying shallow, but need something to work with.

'My husband's work transferred him here.'

I nod, looking into her brown eyes.

'How do you spend your days?'

'Usually just at home with the kids.'

I'm gonna do it. I'm gonna go deep.

'Are you in this class because you're finding it hard to make friends?' I say, jumping straight in.

'I just thought it might be interesting,' she says.

She's deflecting. She's not going deep. She's staying on the surface. I have leaped into the cold, deep water and she is standing on the shore, clutching her pearls, not even putting her swimsuit on.

'Oh, well, I just thought . . .' I begin. But no. Screw it. The point is to get to the vulnerable.

'Are you lonely, Lindsay?' I ask, gently.

'LONELY? I am *not* lonely,' she bellows.

'It's OK if you are,' I say.

'I am not lonely,' she repeats again, a little more quietly.

You are, I think. We all are. I think back to that Edward Hopper painting. We're all going to die alone, especially Lindsay.

All right, FINE, maybe that wasn't the intended message. And yes, OK, sure, I only spent five minutes with Lindsay and we were complete strangers, but I was looking for that lightning bolt of connection. On second thoughts, though, Lindsay would have aced Mrs Flowers' cotillion course where we were told dinner conversations were to always be polite and pleasant. Seeing as she was from Alabama, maybe she'd taken the course herself.

The bell rings and I face forward again.

For the second part of class, Mark tells us that sharing our vulnerabilities and insecurities is the quickest way to make a real connection with someone. Most people want to boast about their lives, but this leaves people feeling jealous or resentful.

'It's not that we want others to fail, but we need to know that our own sorrows have echoes in other people's lives. That's what connects us. Strength may be impressive, but it's vulnerability that builds friendships,' Mark says.

I think back to when I really bonded with my childhood best friend, Jori. We'd known each other since we were ten, but we became true best friends when we were fourteen, perhaps the most fragile moment of adolescence. Jori was refreshingly open and vulnerable to me about so many things: her crushes, her flaws, who she was jealous of in school, how her first kiss was with a very handsome French boy in Paris on a school trip (who stole her digital camera and gave her a nasty stomach virus). Her unflinching honesty made me feel like I could tell her anything without judgement, and we became fiercely close.

I switch seats and am paired with a second girl, this one in ballet flats and black tights who is so lithe that she could be twelve, but is probably twenty-two. On a screen, Mark posts a list of questions to help spark vulnerable conversations. I read one off the screen to her.

'Tell me about one of your regrets,' I ask her.

'I don't have any regrets,' she says.

'You have zero regrets?'

'Yep,' she says.

'None? Really?'

'Well, I am really happy with my life so if I changed anything, then it wouldn't have turned out this way, would it?'

Oh, come on. This wasn't some 'butterfly effect' question where just talking about one change throws off the entire course of your life – this was a conversation of hypotheticals. Besides, this is boasting! Blatant boasting! Boasting is illegal here – I briefly consider reporting her to Mark.

Mercifully, the bell rings and I return to my seat. Maybe I am the one who is doing this all wrong. I'd been paired with two women who weren't exactly naturals at the deep talk, but maybe I was expecting too much.

And then comes the kicker: 'vulnerability tennis'.

Mark, in his now slightly know-it-all tone, tells us, 'We think to be interesting we have to be impressive – but sharing our failure connects us more than sharing our success.'

For our next exercise, we are to face a new partner and bat our insecurities and fears and emotions back and forth, like Serena and Venus Williams, except instead of volleys and serves flying at 120mph, it's deep confessions and secrets, which actually hurt about the same as getting pegged by a tennis ball straight in the boob.

The only rules in this game are that we can't comment on the other person's statements. Our only response is an equally embarrassing confession. Like a loser-off.

And that's how I meet Chris.

'Sometimes I think I just want to have a baby because I'm afraid of dying alone,' I say to him.

He takes this in, his face giving away nothing.

'I feel inferior to my colleagues at my job and have regrets about not going to university,' he says. 'Actually I'm not sure I'm smart enough to have gone to university.'

See, *this* is something I can work with.

Compared to Lindsay and the woman with zero regrets, Chris is a worthy opponent.

And as Mark had predicted, I feel a connection with Chris after our 'tennis match'. We've just been through a brutal series of personal revelations and have crawled out on the other side, exhausted but filled with endorphins. It feels like the relief that comes after a really good cry. The shared emotional turmoil means that despite having only just met, I feel a kinship with Chris, especially because he was so willing, honest and non-judgemental. During the exercise, we were both aware of how ridiculous this scenario was, and before each of us said our statements of truth we both did a weak little laugh, so it sounded something like, 'Hahaha, here goes my deepest, darkest secret that I truly hate about myself – enjoy! Haha . . . sometimes I cry myself to sleep at night so hard it wakes up my neighbours . . . Hahaha . . .'

But, awkward laugh or not, it was so much easier to say these things to a total stranger. Someone who knows nothing about you can't judge you properly or tell your secrets to anyone that you know. It's liberating. It's also surprising what they're willing to tell you, too. If you saw Chris on the street, you would assume he had everything. He's good-looking, has a respectable job, he's married to a successful woman and he supports a football team that consistently performs well.

Yet, he is just as lonely and lost as any of us.

As we are leaving, Mark says that we should think about what we've learned next time we are with our friends or meeting someone new. 'Think about a dinner party,' he says. 'We take so much time cleaning our house, cooking the food, but then we just let conversations run rampant and stay shallow. But we can go deep. We can edit. We can alter the course of the conversations and make connections for life.'

At the end of the class, there's a sigh of relief. It has been a very heightened emotional rollercoaster. The class lasted two and a half hours, and I am going home with a treasure trove of secrets to take with me to the grave. But I feel like I've been given a new outlook on life. It's OK to go deep. It's OK to share our worst failings. In fact, it's encouraged – and it feels kind of great.

Most people in the class seem to feel the same way, our faces looking slightly shell-shocked as we are filing out the door. I suddenly stop Chris on the way out.

'Do you want be friends?' I ask him. All normal social etiquette is out the window.

'Sure,' he says and writes down his email on a piece of paper.

I walk home, elated. I picture us meeting up as new future best friends and having long, fulfilling conversations over Sunday lunch. It could be the beginning of something beautiful.

The next morning, in the cold light of day, reality creeps in. What was I thinking? Chris and I could never be friends in real life. I know too much! He lied to his wife about where he was. I know he is ashamed to make less money than she does. We both know the most humiliating things about each other – and literally nothing else. In fact, if he knew he'd see me again, I'm sure he never would have told me any of his secrets.

I send him an email saying it was nice to meet him, but he doesn't reply and I'm relieved. Chris knows it could never work as well. We had a moment, a strange tennis match of fears and secrets in the middle of the classroom, one that I will remember forever, and it was special and it made us both feel less alone. But that's all it could be. I'm starting to really understand the saying, 'I could tell you, but then I'd have to kill you.' Our budding friendship is a victim of our coerced over-sharing; we can never meet again.

So this means that Chris is out there in the world, just walking around knowing my deepest insecurities. Knowing that I fret about being broke, inferior and childless.

What have I done?

A few weeks after the class, I board the Eurostar to Paris to visit Rachel. My window seat is next to an older French man in his seventies. After the relentless chattiness of the past month, I'd planned to just stare out the window or read during the journey, but the peace is being brutally violated by an extremely loud woman in her twenties shouting at her friend.

'Will's embarrassed by me because I'm so loud. He thinks I'm mean and rude. But I'm hilarious!' she says, roaring at her friend, who seems to be struck dumb by the verbal onslaught coming at her.

I search frantically in my bag for my headphones.

'You know, if Will died I might be sad, but definitely not as sad as if my ex Steve died. If Steve died, I would be devastated! But if Will died, I'd be fine,' she shouts.

I turn my bag over and empty all the contents on my folddown table, still searching for my headphones.

'Will's always like, "Don't shout so much in public – it's about how the people around you feel."' At this point, she starts gesturing around the carriage and I can't help but think that poor Will sounds like a nice guy. 'I do not give *a fuck* about these people!' she concludes.

I think back to Stefan saying, 'People who lack social anxiety: it's a sign of psychopathy.'

Everyone else on the train is studiously staring into dead space, listening to this woman slag us off. I *know* we can all hear her: I've no doubt Queen Victoria can hear her from the afterlife.

'Turkey is a *great* place for tanning!' she declares to her friend as I realize I left my headphones on my kitchen table. I may cry.

I glance at the older man sitting next to me. He's looking at his tray table, also frozen by the inane conversation dominating our air space.

'Me and Will had sex in the kitchen last night, but he's still too femme for me,' she says. I'm not sure her friend has said a single word in response.

I risk another look at my neighbour: we are both in hell. If I don't talk to him, we're going to have to endure this for the entirety of the journey from London to Paris. I have to save us from that.

I have to be the hero this train carriage needs.

I mean, I'm not gonna tell her to keep it down. *God no*. I'm not a superhero. But I could save one person.

This time I look properly at the man sitting next to me. Stacked on top of his tray table are four books, most of them about Kafka. He's wearing an old-fashioned, beige trench coat. What can I say to him? Going straight into, 'What tensions do you have with your mother?' feels a little forward. After about five minutes of agonizing on an opener, I turn to him.

'Are you a professor?' I ask him. Sure, I am stereotyping, but something about his serious coat and smooth hands looked like he struggled more with philosophical dilemmas than laying bricks. He turns to me, surprised.

'I was,' he says, in heavily accented French.

I gesture towards his stack of books.

'Are you a writer?' I ask.

'Yes, I am tired,' he says. 'You could tell?'

Flustered at the misunderstanding, I nod.

We fall back into silence. Then I repeat my last question again more clearly and he tells me that yes, he is a writer. His name is Claude, and Claude writes about art and art criticism. We keep talking and he tells me about all the countries he's lived in: Spain, Brazil, Japan. He travels all over the world to curate exhibitions. He speaks excellent English, but his accent is thick, so I have to concentrate hard to hear him over the blustering conversation in front of us.

I can't help looking at his left hand. On his pinky, there's a delicate ring with a red jewel. Just looking at it makes me sad. It doesn't look like it was originally his. Something about it makes me think that there's sorrow behind it.

Somehow, we do alight on the tensions with his mother, but unintentionally. He starts talking about her when I ask him where he grew up. Then he stops. I wait.

'The thing about my mother is . . .' He pauses and looks at me. Then deems me worthy to be told. 'Well,' he says. 'This . . . this is a story!' and he punctuates the air with his finger.

He tells me that he didn't know his mother was Jewish, that she kept it a secret during the war because she was afraid of the Nazis, and he only found out that he was Jewish after she died. He doesn't know who his father is.

Holy shit.

Claude and I talk non-stop for the entire train journey to Paris. He tells me about how he met his wife in Italy, many years ago. He is friendly and he laughs a lot, telling me about where to go in Paris and how Bordeaux is beautiful but too bourgeois to live in.

We disembark together and walk along the platform. I can see Rachel waiting for me near the turnstiles, and I see her face as she clocks that I am walking towards her with a seventy-something man. I stare at her, as if to say, 'Be cool.' Her eyes widen as we approach her together.

'Claude, meet my friend Rachel,' I say. They shake hands and speak a little French to each other before Claude bids us good day and disappears into the train station.

Rachel looks at me, confused.

'I've started talking to strangers,' I tell her.

'OK, but do you have to talk to *French* strangers? Jesus Christ. That's next level,' Rachel says.

As we walk out of the station, I feel overcome with that excited rush that comes from reuniting with a close friend you haven't seen in months. It's a relief not to have to try so hard or worry about what to say because you're talking so quickly to catch up on everything you've both missed.

Ten minutes later, Rachel is shushing me on the Metro for being too loud.

I'm told that the older we get, the easier talking to strangers will become. With age, we grow more confident and less involved with what other people think of us. On a crowded bus one day, an older woman sitting down near me smacks my elbow and barks, 'Open the window – I'm hot!'

I'm giddy just imagining the shit I'll get up to when I'm eighty.

On the phone, Nick Epley had told me that he thinks that society, in which individuals are more isolated than ever before, would be happier if people talked to each other and made small connections when it's easy to. When you're both waiting in the same queue for twenty minutes; when the plane is delayed, you're stuck at the gate, you've already listened to four podcasts and you're admiring the shoes of the woman sitting next to you and want to tell her about something you just heard on Radio 4 but feel weird about it; when you want to ask the person eating lunch on a park bench where they got their delicious-smelling curry – maybe just do it. Most people will enjoy it.

And if you're game to really talk, head into Deep Self territory. But don't, say, grab a book out of someone's hands and ask, 'So, when was the last time you cried in front of someone else?' (Trust me on that one. Although this question has been tested by Nick and will get you into fertile Deep Talk territory *real* fast.)

I had spoken with people I never imagined I could. Strangers. French people. I mingled at parties where I knew no one. Talked to painters on the street. I could play *and win* vulnerability tennis. I had humiliated myself on the underground. Crucially (and slightly anti-progress) I feel stronger for knowing you don't have to talk to everyone (threatening people at bus stops, anyone who makes you uncomfortable, people who think Turkey is mainly good for tanning, etc). But mostly, I can't believe how differently all these encounters actually went compared with how I imagined they would go in my mind.

I'm not completely cured of social anxiety, but at least I now know I can talk to people if I really want to or need to. It is no longer impossible.

I'm also shocked to discover that talking to strangers turns out to be one of the cheapest, easiest ways to feel good and get a hit of dopamine when you're feeling low, invisible or lost in your own world. When Claude and I parted ways at the Gare du Nord he said, 'I never do this, but I wish I did. This journey passed like a dream.' (He's French, so he's allowed to say things like this.)

Although, when I tell people how I asked strangers on the Tube who the Queen is, they look visibly upset: at me (for asking the question), at being forced to hear about the excruciating awkwardness I put other people through (angry at me, again), and at those men, subjects of Queen Victoria. Were they time travellers or just idiots? Or were they taking the piss? On that, no one is certain.

We all have stories from the past that we don't tell other people, usually about embarrassing jobs or awful room-mates, or terrible people we slept with in low moments. High school boyfriends who secretly thought they were were-wolves (that one might be just me but Andy, I'll never forget you). Humiliating crushes we had (Arnold Schwarzenegger, Prince Eric in the *Little Mermaid*). That spell when we took up playing the harp. *Honestly, what were we thinking?* we ask ourselves now, with the clarity of hindsight.

I rarely talk about my time as a TV reporter, and when I do it often sounds like I was in prison: 'I got out but please don't ask anything about what happened or how I got there.'

That's because not only was I really, really bad at my job, I was also terrified of it.

The broadcasting company I worked for was brand new and short of reporters who spoke English. I had limited life skills, but I *did* speak English. My only other qualification was that I'd just graduated from journalism school (it was in Australia, but I still think it counts). I'd always wanted to travel and write and experience new things, and journalism seemed like the best way in – even if it meant I'd have to interview strangers, talk on the phone and push myself out of my comfort zone a lot of the time. If I had to do something for my job that gave me anxiety, I could usually make myself do it – I think nearly everyone in the world has experienced that. But my shyness was suited to the part where I got to sit down and write my articles.

But now I was going for TV. I had secret hopes of making a live show called *Chinese Desert Island Discs* in a not-so-subtle effort to become the Kirsty Young of North-East Asia.

That is not what happened.

When I accepted the job, I wilfully ignored the fact that I had shied away from every single opportunity to be in the spotlight in my life: I faked being sick for school plays, avoided anything that involved presentations, refused to raise my hand in class, even when I knew the answer. Always.

While many people might be fine with raising their hand in an average-sized class, standing in the spotlight in front of a larger audience is daunting for a lot of us. Public speaking is an incredibly common fear – though introverts are significantly more likely than extroverts to suffer. Typically we are more sensitive to new stimuli and to our environments, so when faced with an unnerving task like speaking in front of a large group of others, introverts are more likely to have a faster heart rate or increased blood pressure.

But whatever! That was Old Jess. She didn't have a blazer. She wasn't living in Beijing. New Jess wanted to be a TV reporter and, by God, she would.

Except I would metaphorically black out whenever that little red light showed the camera was on. I'd break out into a cold sweat. My heart would pound loudly in my ears. My brain would stall and I would become an anxious, self-conscious mess of nerves. I'd start speaking so fast that I stuttered. Sophia would yell at me in my ear piece from behind the camera: you're talking too fast, stop moving your hands, why are you nodding your head like you're a rapper, stop looking so scared, don't cry because your make-up will run . . . OK, we need more make-up.

Can you give yourself PTSD from watching yourself on camera? If so, I was well on my way. From what I've seen, I looked like I'd been kidnapped, dipped in a vat of bronzer and made to read from a teleprompter at gunpoint.

Despite my efforts to practice more, I just couldn't seem to get better. I froze all the time. I was too nervous. I was too sweaty. I lacked motor skills. I became a deer in headlights, except they were studio lights and people were yelling at me to stay in front of them, instead of safely scurrying off into the forest.

All the other reporters or news anchors there seemed to be ultra-confident, beautiful naturals on camera. They exemplified the idea that your vocation should match your natural skill-set. Not me, who had found a job I was apparently genetically predisposed to screw up at every opportunity.

To get through the days, I would shove all these doubts and miseries down into a mental box called 'Fodder for Therapy', but there were cracks in that box. There always are. You think you're fine until you're sitting on the steps behind work, watching old Beijing locals dancing in the square across the street, and Coldplay's 'Fix You' comes on shuffle and suddenly you're crying.

After living together in Australia, both of our visas had expired, so Sam moved back to London, and I moved back to Beijing. We were dating long-distance, which was terrible. My colleagues were talented, natural performers who I couldn't relate to, and I lived with a girl I barely knew and her cat, who I was allergic to. With no one to talk to, I'd listen to podcasts instead. My favourite was *The Moth*, true stories told live by regular humans like me. I liked that they weren't seasoned performers. They were just onstage, telling their true story. It was my coping mechanism: lying in bed laughing and crying while listening to these strangers' stories.

Back at work, my anxiety on camera meant I was unnatural and awkward, but while I was trying to get better I'd get yelled at, which made me even more nervous. The fear came from the spotlight, even if the spotlight was just a camera. It was something about staring down the barrel and knowing my face would be projected into people's homes, people who would also be wondering why I was so bad at this. I wanted to be good at this job, but I walked into the office with deep dread every single day.

Eventually, I quit my job at the TV station. The day I left, I ran out of the studio, clutching the five blazers I kept at my desk. It was exactly how I imagined a real prison break would feel. I moved to London and married Sam, trying to forget about the whole ordeal.

I vowed never to put myself in the spotlight again. This is healthy, I told myself: we mature and realize we cannot be all the things we had hoped we would be.

Soon after the sauna 'incident', Sam and I decided to move flats in London.

Our noisy upstairs neighbours drove us out of our previous home. I blame their daughter for most of the noise. I know you aren't supposed to say that you hate a child. I also know that if you met this eight-year-old child, this tiny, leaden-footed girl, you would hate her, too. You would.

Maybe she'll grow up and be the next Millie Bobbie Brown or Malala or Malia, I don't know. But at eight, she was stomping, yelling and throwing shit on to the floor above our heads with wild abandon, even when she was happy. It's hard enough to say to your neighbours, 'Please be quieter,' but it's even harder to say, 'Your child's mirth makes me want to die.' When she took up the violin, Sam and I knew the jig was up.

Unpacking boxes in our new place down the road, I am sorting through piles of business cards. Magazines. Books. Fliers.

And then I find it. The *Moth* programme, hidden in a pile of books and magazines. I study the programme and find the name of a director. Meg.

A few years earlier, I'd finally attended a live Moth event at Union Chapel, a working church by day and a famous music and comedy venue by night. That evening, I had been spellbound by the storytellers, standing under the spotlight, beneath the colourful stained glass windows, performing for an audience of nine hundred people. I had felt a steady thrum of anxiety, awe and sympathy for them.

I walk by Union Chapel most days, as I live in the same neighbourhood. In fact, the private art show I'd attended with Roger, the painter I'd met on the street, was two doors down from the chapel. Today, I pause, holding the programme in my hands, thinking about what to do next.

I'd been doing my best to extrovert. I was chatting to strangers, I was saying yes to more social engagements, but this, this was my psychological nemesis, the one thing I couldn't imagine myself ever being able to do. My story. Onstage. Under a spotlight. No notes.

My time in TV reporter jail and my lightning-quick exit was a source of such embarrassment and shame because I had run away from my fear rather than facing it head on. And I know, deep down, that what scares you, owns you. I don't want to be owned by my fear any more.

There's no question – I have stage fright. Still, this doesn't feel like a valid excuse to not try. Other shy introverts step up and conquer this fear every day. Why not me this time?

Emboldened by finding the programme, I compose an email to Meg about a story I could tell. Their mainstage story-tellers are usually very accomplished, like astronauts or famous novelists, or someone who has lived through very unusual circumstances like finding out about a surprise twin. But occasionally they have a story from a normal person who finds themselves in a curious situation – like asking random people on the Tube who the Queen is. This is a story I could try to tell, and one Meg might be interested in, especially because it had happened locally, right near Union Chapel. I type up a quick summary and hit send before I can change my mind. Before I can actually picture myself onstage in front of nine hundred people watching from the darkness. Before I can imagine the stakes of signing up for this kind of event. Then I immediately go for a walk and try to suppress the urge to scream into the ether out of sheer fear and regret.

*

'So just tell me the full story,' Meg says.

She's on the phone, calling from Sweden. I'm sitting in my new flat in London.

Meg is warm, her voice hearty. I've probably heard it on the *Moth* podcast a dozen times before. I quickly tell her about my foray into talking to strangers, and Meg is delighted by my experience of how skittish British people are when you talk to them out of the blue.

'You know, people in London are much friendlier than in my village in Sweden. People never talk to each other here, but they do stare at you.' Meg had relocated to Sweden from New York a few years ago, but visits London regularly for work.

'I feel like people here avoid eye contact, too,' I say.

'Not compared to Sweden,' she says. 'Everything is very insular. I throw an annual Christmas party, and invite everyone I know, and people here cannot fathom that I combine friend groups. They think it's so strange.'

I don't tell Meg that the idea of throwing a big Christmas party for everyone I know sounds like a nightmare and that I'm gonna have to side with the Swedes on this one.

As we wrap up the call, Meg says she's not sure if she can include my story in her programme.

'I'll be in touch in a few weeks,' she says.

I hang up, my heart beating fast, half hoping I never hear from her again.

But it is not to be. Meg follows up to say she wants to cast me in the next show. In one month.

What? I can't be ready for this kind of mammoth task in one month. I thought I had multiple months to prepare, maybe with hypnosis, maybe with a lobotomy, maybe with a well-timed religious miracle.

I tell Meg I'm not ready – but could I be in the show in six months' time? She tells me no – she's already organizing the other stories to fit in around mine.

In my year of extroverting, I'd hoped this challenge would come last. Public speaking is my biggest fear and I wanted to work up to it. Also, delaying it increased the odds that some entirely unpredictable calamity would occur before the date and I wouldn't actually have to do it at all (see, again, 'well-timed religious miracle').

I don't say these things to Meg. I ignore the frantic chaotic catastrophizing going on in my brain and quickly give her a tentative yes before I can fully process the reality of what I'm doing.

And then I immediately start googling ways to combat stage fright. The first article I land on recommends taking beta-blockers to inhibit the body's response to adrenaline.

Part of me feels very tempted to do this. But I also know it is a shortcut. It isn't facing the beast. It is sedating the beast and tip-toeing around it.

Realizing I am mere weeks away from the *Moth* performance, I am white-knuckle terrified. When I think of being onstage in front of all of those people, with no notes, no backup, no nothing, I break into a cold sweat. I want to curl up in a ball and hide. I want to flee my current life and start a new one. Preferably somewhere warm. It will not involve public speaking. It will involve lots of carbs. Maybe I could be a baker. No, I hate early starts. Whatever. New me will figure it out.

That night, Sam burns cheese on toast on the grill and I scream, 'WHAT IS WRONG WITH YOU?'

He stares at me, aghast. Notices my shaking hands.

'Jess, you're going to be fine,' he says.

'No, I'm not,' I say. Inside, I'm screaming, 'Don't you know it is THE END of days?'

I know he wants to understand, but I also know he can't. He doesn't have the fear the way I do.

Seventy-five per cent of people fear public speaking more than they fear death. Sociobiologists trace this fear back to our ancestors: singling yourself out from a group is inviting them to attack you. Or ostracize you. Which in modern life means wandering alone until you die of exposure and starvation, still clutching your PowerPoint notes.

I will have to fight a deep, ingrained evolutionary instinct to get on to that stage.

Talking to strangers on the street was hard. Now, compared to talking to nine hundred strangers at the same time, it seems like a piece of piss.

In a classic self-defeating move, the extent of my fear means I'm doing nothing to prepare because I'm petrified to even try. Meg wants me to rewrite my story to adapt it for the stage: I am definitely not doing this. I'm also not practising it, not rehearsing it, not getting hypnotized to become a different person who is capable of doing it.

I am also not sleeping. I lie awake, staring into the darkness, my mind whirring. I download various relaxation apps. Too antsy for meditation, I opt for listening to bedtime stories instead to lull me to sleep. Somehow, I had made it through my childhood without hearing the story of the Velveteen Rabbit and, let me tell you, I'm grateful for it. Did we all know that the creepy rabbit has feelings but he's not real? What *is* that? He has buttons for eyes? This is horrifying. How is this soothing?

Almost nightly, sleep evades me until dawn, when my brain, exhausted and fried, finally gives in to slumber. An hour later I'm jolted awake by a woman yelling at full-volume from my phone, '"I am Real!" said the little Rabbit. "I am Real!"'

'I don't know if I can do this,' I say to my friend. She has just flown in from Berlin (remember, I have no friends in London), as we make our way through Hampstead Heath towards the swimming ponds.

'You aren't yet the person you are going to be at the end of this,' she says. 'You're going to change to fit the challenge. It's going to be great.'

We slip out of our jeans, boots and coats in the outdoor dressing room. She gets into the cold water first. We are both half-Chinese and named Jessica, but she is great at public speaking and talking to strangers. We're the precise inverse of each other.

She's already halfway across the pond while I'm slowly submerging myself. The water is so cold that it prickles my skin and shocks my body.

Forty-five seconds later, I climb out and am sunning myself on the deck when a woman in her sixties, Jane, comes over to say hello. She and Jessica are old friends because Jessica used to live in London, and also she is friends with everyone.

When she is done talking to us, Jane turns and dives into the pond headfirst. When she emerges, I say, 'I can't believe you got your hair wet when it's so cold!'

'Oh, I always have to get my head wet. It just deletes everything that's weighing on you. It completely clears your mind,' Jane says.

I stare at the murky surface. I am afraid of the cold, dark water, but I might have to jump straight into it, like Jane did. I want to delete everything, too.

Eleven days before my performance, I climb out of bed after another sleepless night. To conquer this fear, I need help. Real help. I come across an online forum about cures for public speaking. Some of the recommendations: hypnotherapy, lots of practice, imagine John Humphrys in his underwear (does this work?), apps, breathing exercises, wrapping yourself in a brightly coloured shawl for confidence.

Then, someone named Julia recommends a voice coach and speech therapist who, Julia says, 'changed my life' and 'cured me completely'. The voice coach is named Alice. I take out my phone.

'Hi, I have stage fright and a big event in eleven days, can you help me?' I blurt out as soon as a woman answers.

'What's your issue?' Alice asks.

Neuroticism, acute self-consciousness, intermittent stutter, insecurity, crippling anxiety, bad back, bad at languages, fear of spiders, shorter than I'd like to be, slow metabolism.

'I blank in public, I get scared, I talk too fast and I forget what I'm supposed to say.'

Alice picks up on my urgency.

'Come to my house on Tuesday at two p.m.'

Finally, an adult who can handle this situation. I think I've found my next mentor.

Alice lives in south London. On the overground, I start feeling excited. I'm going to finally conquer this. This is going to happen. I've sent Alice my story, and now she's going to give me tea and set me on a sofa, listen to me and soothe me, possibly swaddle me. It's a cool, grey day. I wrap my black trench coat snugly around my body as I walk from the train station to her house.

I ring the bell and, a moment later, Alice answers. She has white hair, pulled back in a neat ponytail with a tidy fringe. She's petite, slim and well-dressed in a way that makes her look very clean and wealthy. She could be anywhere between forty-five and seventy-five. I honestly have no idea.

'Come in,' she says, motioning me in to her deceptively enormous house, settling in her large kitchen with French doors.

Alice sits across from me at her kitchen table and begins with a few simple questions. Her demeanour is a little cold, and I feel under interrogation. As she probes me about my shyness and stage fright, I become defensive. This doesn't feel like sinking into a warm bath. Embarrassed by my fear, I find it hard to talk about it to her without feeling judged.

'So tell me the story you're going to tell on the night,' she says. She looks so expectant. It's time to perform, and even though it's just for her my hands go hot. I swallow.

'So I was in this cafe and I found this badge . . .' I say to Alice. Alice holds my stare as I talk to her, and it's unnerving. I lose my place in the story.

I start again. I begin for a few sentences, telling her about moving to London and how I sometimes pet strangers' dogs, but my mouth is dry and my heart is racing. And then – my brain does its thing. It kind of flicks off. It goes black. And then there's nothing there. Literally, nothing.

'I've forgotten my story,' I say to Alice, stunned. I mean, it's just an anecdote. She's not quizzing me on *The Canterbury Tales* or the oral history of Mongolia – it's literally something that happened in my life. I've been struck with temporary amnesia. I can't remember the next part.

I picture the stage at Union Chapel. The spotlight and the darkness and hundreds of faces looking at me and me standing there going, 'I had badges . . . my badges . . . badges?' It would be so humiliating. Everyone would stare at me, wondering what was wrong with me. I'd always be this fucked up person who couldn't pull herself together to do this one simple thing.

Try. *Think, Jessica. Think about your story. What happens in your story next.*

As Alice watches me, unmoved, I feel hot. Ridiculous tears prick the back of my eyes and start to stream down my face.

She pushes some paper towards me. 'Write it down,' she says. I take the paper, barely seeing it through hot tears. I take the pen.

'I can't,' I say. 'I don't remember.' I once read that torturing criminals leads to false confessions. It makes sense to me. I was five minutes away from confessing I was Banksy if it would get Alice to stop staring at me with her piercing blue eyes.

'It's the segues,' she says. 'It's that turn in the story, that doesn't feel natural, that's what's messed you up.'

She tells me to draw out my story in pictures. I am unable to do even this. So she gets out a piece of paper and begins to do it for me.

'OK, so you have a badge' – she draws a badge and then she draws a cat.

'Why did you draw a cat?' I ask.

'You said you were petting people's dogs when you talk to strangers.'

Exactly, I think. *Dogs.*

She draws an aeroplane. Poorly. I do not see how this is helpful at all. I do not talk about aeroplanes in my story. Alice is drawing up a timeline and filling it with nonsense hieroglyphics, including one of the Union Jack flag to represent me coming to England, a cat to represent me petting dogs and some spectacles to represent . . . ?

'What are those?'

'That's your professor you speak to.'

What? My story looks like a children's scavenger hunt.

This is just going to confuse my mushy brain. She draws a crown to represent the Queen, but my personal hieroglyphic signifier for the Queen would obviously not be a crown, it would be two crossed ankles, in that way that Claire Foy always sits in *The Crown*.

I pretend to go along with it, knowing this won't work.

'Now tell me the story again,' she says. 'You've cried, you've had your little emotional bit and now tell me the story.'

What? False. The emotional bit was not over. I have a lot of good, hard crying left in me, Alice. At this point, I'm still holding my emotion in – there hasn't been that satisfying release of heavy, fast tears and shaky breathing. After ten to fifteen minutes of that then, *then*, I'll be done.

But we don't have time for that.

I run upstairs to the bathroom to grab some tissues. I sit on the edge of her enormous bathtub trying to pull myself together. Alice is clearly a tough love kind of person. She is not going to indulge me with the swaddling I'd imagined. This is going to be hard work. But I didn't come here to cry in a stranger's bathroom – I came here to conquer this fear.

I come back downstairs, sit back across from Alice and she moves on, as if nothing has happened.

She is saying a lot of words, but they aren't sinking in. It takes me a minute to hear them.

'You really aren't special,' she tells me. 'You're not the centre of the universe.'

Jesus.

I think I know what Alice is doing. She's telling me that no one is actually obsessed with my performance the way I am. Which I know is true. She's right. But while I do over-think the audience's reactions and my imperfections, I also constantly feel unspecial. That's part of the problem. I don't feel worthy enough to stand onstage and command an audience's attention, so to have her say that I'm not special is just reinforcing that fear – that I'm an imposter, that I'm not good enough, that I don't belong there, that I'm going to fail.

'Nobody cares if you fail,' Alice says.

I don't agree. Meg will care. The audience will care. I will care, for ever. There are stakes to *me*.

At this point, I just want to leave. I want to walk out of that house and keep walking for ever.

And I do. I say I have to go; I leave Alice at the front door, and I walk and walk and walk. I'm five streets away when I realize I've left my coat in her house and that I've gone in the opposite direction from the station.

I stand on the unfamiliar street. It's cold and windy. I start to shiver in my light T-shirt as it, naturally, begins to rain. I'm in a part of London I've never been to before and I have 9 per cent battery life left on my phone.

I close my eyes.

Julia, the woman from the online forum, had said that Alice changed her life. She didn't mean that she just abandoned her old life and started a new one, right? Because that was looking like a pretty good idea to me right now.

I finally find my way to the station, coat-less, and while on the train, I relive the scene again and again. Me sitting across from Alice being interrogated. 'TELL ME THE STORY,' she says, and me, blubbering, 'I have these badges and I just can't remember,' sounding like every disturbed witness ever to be harangued on *Law and Order*.

I wish I could explain to others why I started crying in that ordinary moment, just talking to a well-groomed woman in a very nice house. It's hard to even comprehend it myself afterwards. But in those kinds of moments, under scrutiny, I become sick with nerves, irrational, not myself. Maybe it was taking me back to those fraught months in Beijing when I felt too exposed and too seen.

Under the pressure of Alice's gaze, imagining the magnitude of being onstage, and carrying the anxiety from my past performance failures, my body released the fight-or-flight hormone adrenaline. With so many things to worry about (Do I sound OK? Am I saying this right? Do I look weird? Did I get that detail wrong? Does she hate me?), I had become overstimulated, jittery and easily distracted – the very opposite of focused and Zen, the state you want to be in when you are performing. Research shows that when we are stressed our bodies also release cortisol, which interferes with our attention and short-term memory.

In short, my brain had briefly short-circuited. While I couldn't control my reaction to this fear, I could rationalize it. Despite what my brain thinks, I'm not actually being chased by sabre-tooth tigers onstage. I don't have to view my failure as a TV reporter as indicative of how I will always be.

66

I could try to let go of my entangled web of past anxieties around public speaking.

But it was very deep within me. It was going to take a lot to dig it out.

I go back to the swimming ponds, this time by myself. Before I can talk myself out of it, I dunk my head in the water and get my hair wet. *Delete everything*, I command the water as I dip under the silky brown surface. It's still bracingly cold but it shocks my body into a state of euphoria and then calm. Swimming in the water, hidden behind the trees, staring up at the sky, my worries feel far away.

After I dry off and change into my jeans and jumper, I wander through the Heath, walking under the trees, and get lost in thought. I resolve to at least try. I need to fight through the anxiety and see what happens. I can't keep crying in bathrooms. I took a vow this year to be braver and not give in to my natural inclination to run and hide. I can't give up so quickly. But crucially, I want to be free of this. Free of this fear that has been haunting me for more than thirty years. Here is my chance to exorcise it. I do not want to waste it. Deep in thought, I get so lost on the Heath that I walk for over an hour before finding the right train station.

When I get home, subdued from the water and my walk, I force myself to practice my story aloud in the flat, alone. I go through the entire thing twice. Unpleasant, but necessary medicine.

*

I go back to Alice for a second session. I have no other options – I'm not cured but I also haven't found another cure. Besides, she still has my coat.

This time, she leads me to a different room with a piano and a beautiful original fireplace.

Alice sets up two chairs and we once again sit across from each other, our feet flat on the ground and our knees about three inches apart.

She demonstrates a breathing exercise, where you close off one nostril with a finger to breathe in through the other nostril and then you switch. She has me do this twenty times. We do it together.

I don't know where to look, and it lasts an eternity.

Then Alice leans forward, sitting with her legs splayed. 'Try to be masculine, take up a lot of space, make your body loose,' she says. I imitate her movements; it feels good.

Then we stand facing each other.

'Sometimes we lose our voices because there's no oxygen going through the vocal cords. When this happens, we need to do the "sniffy mother-in-law".' Alice does a snotty 'hmmph' through her nose.

'Now you do it,' Alice says.

'Hmmph!' I faux-sniff in the air, pushing air out as my voice vibrates in the back of my throat.

'Good!' she says. I'm starting to relax. 'This will bring your voice back if you lose it.'

Then she has me stand and put my hand on my diaphragm. I'm supposed to feel it contracting or something. I don't feel it, but pretend to.

'OK, now I'm going to lead you through some vocal warm-ups. Just imitate me,' Alice says. I nod.

'Ba-ba-ba-baa,' she belts.

'Ba-ba-ba-baa,' I belt back.

'MmmyyyYYyyy!' Alice belts, her voice undulating.

'MmmyyyYYyyy!' I echo.

'Good!' Alice says.

I like this praise for easy tasks. This I can do.

'MyyYYyy mummy is marrrrrvellous!' Alice shouts.

I pause.

'Just say it like I did,' Alice says. She repeats, 'Myy mummmmmy'sss mmmmarrvellous!'

But Alice says this in a British accent. I have a hybrid accent that is best described as American-who-hasn't-lived-in-America-for-ten-years-and-lives-in-London-but-also-I-married-a-man-from-Sunderland-who-used-to-live-in-Australia.

'Do you want me to say it . . . *just* like you?'

Alice nods, exasperatedly.

It hits me. I am Colin Firth in *The King's Speech* and she is my wily, bulldogged Geoffrey Rush. I look into Alice's eyes. She looks into mine. Yes. This is it. The go-ahead I've been waiting for since the day I moved to England.

'My mummy's marvellous!' I bellow in a haughty British accent. I sound exactly like one of the children in *Mary Poppins*.

'MY mummy's marvellous!' Alice shouts back at me, encouragingly.

'MY mummy's marvellous!' I shout back at her, delighted, now sounding like Hermione Granger. What would someone think if they walked in on this scene? That we are psychotic. And that we are both enormously proud of our marvellous mummies.

The bellowing goes on for a bit. Probably too long.

Alice says, 'Great, now I'm going to sit down and you're going to tell me your story.'

Oh.

Alice takes a seat in the back of the room. I go into the hallway. She calls out my name, 'Please welcome to the stage . . . Jessica Pan!'

I jump out from the hallway. She is sitting in a chair, her small thin legs crossed. I don't look at her. I look at the nice crown moulding above her. (This house!)

But then I focus. I begin the story, standing about ten feet in front of her. And I finally, finally make it through the entire thing. I don't stop. I don't flounder. At the end, Alice claps.

Before I can bask in the glow, Alice says, 'Now you're going to say it again and I'm going to heckle you. Because people might be drunk on the night. They might be loud. They might shout at you.'

I really don't want to tell her the story again. It makes me feel so dumb to repeat myself. But she calls out my name again and again as a one-woman rowdy crowd, so finally I jump out of the hallway again and tell the story. This time Alice is on her phone and purposely laughing loudly at the wrong parts. She yells, 'WHO CARES?' when I'm about thirty seconds in. I ignore her and keep going.

Alice. The tiny heckler who might just save me from myself. I manage to finish the story again. When I leave her house, everything feels different. Better.

I see Alice one more time. She has me go through the story twice more and each time I become calmer. My voice grows steady. My mind is clear. I'm starting to believe I can do this. Me! Perform! In front of real people! Just as I'm wrapping the story up for the second time, I see something out the corner of my eye. A spider mission impossibles his way down from the ceiling, dangerously close to touching me, and I back away into a corner, suppressing a scream.

Today's lesson: always stay on your toes.

As I am gathering up my things to go, Alice tells me, 'I want you to remember why you are telling this story. You have to *want* to tell your story. There needs to be that desire. When you are struggling with nerves, try to remember why you want to do this.'

Straight from Alice's house, I head to the *Moth* rehearsal. The performance is tomorrow, but tonight I'm going to meet the other four storytellers who will share the stage.

There's Daz, an Australian documentary maker with blonde pixie hair; Ingrid, a former academic turned writer; David, an American who has just flown in from Washington, DC; and me. There's a fifth storyteller who couldn't come because his daughter is sick, but I don't catch his name. Probably because I've just found out that David was one of Barack Obama's speechwriters at the White House.

I'm sorry, what? I'm going to be performing with the man who helped write Obama's speeches? I'm going onstage after *this* guy? I can't follow him!

But then I realize: Who else could give me better advice? Who else but a man who has helped the greatest orator alive? If anyone could give me advice about public speaking, it would be this guy. Well, it would be Obama, but this guy is a close second. I corner him.

'So do you think Obama gets stage fright or do you think . . .'

'I think he had other things to worry about,' David says.

'Right,' I nod.

David tells me that he and Obama both rehearse a lot, which is reassuring. For some reason, I hadn't imagined Obama rehearsing. I thought people like him were just born articulate, calm and graceful.

'I also think it's good to remember that Beyoncé gets stage fright,' David says.

I like David but this means nothing to me. People always say things like this, but I am not Beyoncé. Not even a little bit. At the end of the day, she's still Beyoncé, and I'm me, which is why she will almost definitely do well and for me, all bets are off.

Once during a live Grammy's performance, Adele stopped midway through, swore, rolled her head back and said, 'I'm sorry for swearing, can we start again?' I am much more Adele than Beyoncé.

'Do you think . . . David, do you think I'm going to be able to do this?' I ask.

'I do,' he says. My own personal Obama cheerleader. I try to trust him, the way Obama must have. (Obama and I? We are the same.)

Meg gathers all of us around a table and the four speakers take turns telling our stories in front of the others. Ingrid, tentative at first, tells the most moving and animated story. She's transformed as she talks about nursing her mother as she died of breast cancer and then dealing with her own son being bullied at school. You can tell she's still grieving over her mother, but Ingrid somehow manages to be funny and poignant at the same time.

I love listening to everyone else's stories, to see them moved with emotion as they revisit an important, defining moment in their lives. But what I really like about the story-tellers is how they all seem terrified. It's kind of the best thing ever. Their collective terror comforts me. I'm not insane. I'm not alone. I'm just like them. Meg is like our den mother, high energy and constantly assuring us that, despite our stage fright, it's going to be OK. None of us believes her.

I don't sleep that night.

It's hot. So hot. I am unable to do anything all day because I have no attention span. As the evening draws nearer, finally, I take a shower. Sam irons my shirt. I am dressed exactly like Sharon Horgan was when I saw her at Union Chapel at a Letters Live event: button-down light blue men's shirt, black jeans, grey boots, hair down, big jade earrings to ward off evil spirits.

When I arrive, I already see a short queue of people at the door. The audience had always been 'in theory' to me, but now they are real, lined up, and some of them are looking at me. I stand outside, frozen in fear, when the door slides open and one of the producers pokes her head out and motions me to come in. Then she reminds me of the rules of performance at *The Moth*: stories last twelve minutes. Once we hit the twelve-minute mark, a violinist will play a series of threatening violin notes to let us know we're out of time. And we definitely cannot go over fifteen minutes.

I'm only half listening to her. I walk tentatively into the chapel, looking at all the empty seats, and find the other storytellers practising using the mic. During my turn, I hop up onstage, sick with adrenaline. I say a few words and am thrown off by how strange I sound. Curveball. I do not need a curveball at this point.

'The thing no one tells you is that once people fill up the room and sit down, it's much less echoey,' a man standing near the stage says. 'It won't sound so weird when you're actually up there telling the story.' The other, final, rogue storyteller has just arrived straight from a literary festival. He introduces himself as Nikesh, but I don't hear him properly. His full name is Nikesh Shukla, and what I don't know at the time is that he is the guy who edited *The Good Immigrant* and I have read two of his books. I'm too distracted in the moment to enquire further, so to me he is just another person out on the battlefield.

He is dressed in pineapple shorts and a pineapple shirt.

'You don't seem nervous,' I say suspiciously.

'I am,' he says. 'Why do you think I wore this? So that everyone is looking at the pineapples instead of at me.'

We're waiting in the Green Room, milling around. Daz, the Australian, keeps running away and coming back. She is even more flighty than I am, the effect accentuated by the long flowing coat she wears that acts as a cape as she strides across the room. I know without asking that this is her armour for the night.

She bursts back into the Green Room, sits down at the piano and starts pounding the keys.

'This relaxes me!' Daz says, the piano melody drowning out the rest of the noise in the room. An elfin, brunette woman, introduced as our time-keeper, takes out her violin, riffing off the piano. It's discombobulating, all this loud, erratic music, as if I've stepped into an avant-garde film just as the protagonist loses their mind.

Meanwhile, Meg and another producer are talking loudly over the music. David is pacing back and forth in his black blazer. I stand in the corner, watching. The whole scene makes me feel like my brain has been turned on to its side and shaken.

I run out of the room and through a hallway to peer past the large black curtain. The lights are dimming, the sun is setting, and people have just started taking their seats.

There's so much adrenaline in my body that I could lift off. Half an hour before showtime.

'Where is Jess?' I hear Meg call out in the room. The piano music abruptly stops. I have been flagged as a flight risk.

Rightly so, because I am pulling my hair back into a pony-tail and adjusting my socks. I'm wearing ankle boots with a heel, but I know how to run in them. In fact, I'm pretty fast in these boots: I could just run away and never return.

I hear a voice behind me and turn around to see David.

He is looking at me imploringly.

'Can you take me somewhere to—' he begins.

I look into his eyes, puzzled.

To start a new life? To head out to sea? To find Obama? Honestly, where is he?

'. . . buy an iced coffee?' he asks.

I sigh.

'I'm low energy,' he says. 'I need it before I go on.'

An excuse to escape. I lead him as we weave through the aisles of Union Chapel, past the producers and the stage crew, and the people queuing up outside.

There is now a huge queue out the door.

'It's the paparazzi!' I say, in a stupor of fear.

'That's not what paparazzi is,' David says.

'I know!' I say, waving him away, staring at the crowd.

They are here. They are here. The people are here.

'Where are we going?' he asks.

'It's Sunday night in London and you want an iced coffee, David,' I say. 'We're going to Starbucks.'

As we cross the street and walk, I can't really feel my body. Or think. David is talking, but I can't really respond. He's saying something about how English people don't like him because he's too chatty and he once put his dirty toothpick back in the wrong pile at a food market or something.

'Uh huh,' I say.

David continues talking all the way back to the Chapel with his coffee. I take a seat in the front row to wait for when the lights dim, and we are on.

David sits down next to me, sipping his iced coffee.

'I get very chatty when I'm nervous,' he says. He launches into the history of Icelandic democracy and Vikings.

I'm beginning to appreciate why the British hate David.

'David, I can't talk right now,' I finally say.

'OK,' he nods, and he drinks his iced coffee, muttering about the Icelandic government system to himself.

Five minutes to go. I run off to go do my Alice breathing exercises.

It's always like this. There is so much time and then there is NO TIME. THERE. IS. NO. TIME.

I go into the bathroom quickly to do my calming nostril breathing. Why, oh why God, do I have to do this in a bathroom? 'Sharon Horgan has used this bathroom,' I tell myself. 'And Damien Rice.' More calm breathing.

'Lily Allen has been here. Amy Winehouse. Elton John.' THINK OF ALL THE DRUGS THAT HAVE BEEN DONE HERE. No, brain, FOCUS.

I get back to my breathing. I lean forward in the way Alice taught me. Yes. That feels better.

Someone comes in to the bathroom. I feel my heart beating extra fast. I stare at the wall, and I recite my story to myself very quietly. Just me and the urine trails of Damien Rice and Elton John.

I close my eyes and think about what Alice had said – that there had to be a desire to tell this story. I think about how I want to share my story with the audience. How this is my chance to perform on a large stage for the first time in my life, and how far I have had to come even to get here.

I exit the stall and look at myself. Red lipstick. Ironed shirt. I stare at my reflection in the mirror and lean forward.

There is only one thing that comes to my brain at this moment in time.

'My mummy's marvellous,' I say to myself.

'Please welcome to the stage, Jessica Pan!'

I can't feel my legs. Or my face.

I step through the black curtain and up the stairs. The host hugs me, I walk across the stage and adjust the mic, trying to ignore the fact that hundreds of people are watching me. Meg is sitting right below me but I don't look at her, because it'll throw me off.

All I see is the spotlight, surrounded by vast darkness. The light is blinding.

It's time.

And I begin, no preamble, just straight into the story as is custom for these nights.

'I went to get a cup of coffee and I found these badges . . .'

I knew the story so well. I knew every beat. And then, in the right place, I hear laughter. But I cannot enjoy it because I need to concentrate on the story and a part of my brain is still going, 'AHH YOU ARE DOING THIS DON'T MESS UP ISN'T IT CRAZY THAT WE'RE DOING THIS THAT'S SO CRAZY DON'T FUCK UP THOUGH DON'T STUTTER KEEP GOING.'

In a cathedral with bright lights and vast darkness, it feels like I am telling a funny story to God and God is giving occasional feedback through celestial applause.

Am I dying? Is this death? In a church? Just telling a funny story?

And finally, finally I feel the end coming. I say the final line: no stutter, no blanks.

Before I step off stage, I giggle into the mic, once, out of sheer, colossal relief.

There's applause and whooping. I run off stage and throw my body into the first row of pews.

Ingrid puts an arm on mine and beams at me. I am floating, grinning in the darkness.

Nikesh takes the stage. I forget about myself completely as he tells a story about his mother, and how when she died he felt so lost he decided to learn how to cook her specialities. I'm transported to his kitchen. The sorrow in his story hits me hard and I feel tears spring to my eyes. I sense that Ingrid is crying next to me.

I love them both. I don't know them, but I love them. They were total strangers two days ago but now it feels like we've shared such intimate moments, straight into Deep Talk territory from day one.

Then before I know it, the show is over.

And I survived.

I stay out late that night with the other storytellers. We have been into battle, and we are celebrating victory. Sam congratulates me, equally stunned and thrilled that I have pulled this off. He heads home to bed, but I stay out until the bar closes. Meg has a flight back to Sweden in the morning. David is flying to Washington, DC. Nikesh has already taken a train back to Bristol. Ingrid buses back to Muswell Hill. We hug and cheek-kiss goodbye. I can't believe we've only just met, given how close I feel to them tonight.

I walk home in the dark, warm night.

When you believe something about yourself for so long, but then finally challenge it, everything feels different. I want to dance. I want to run. I feel like knocking on all the doors and shouting, 'I am a REAL rabbit! I AM REAL!' because I'm delusional with relief and happiness. I have done something that I have *never, ever* thought possible.

When I get home, I can't sleep. My body is buzzing from the exhilaration of taking a big risk and from the joy of it paying off. At the beginning of my story onstage, I had started off quick and scared, but as I went on, I had grown in confidence. I'd cracked open the shell of that fear.

My fear was performing in front of others, and by performing in front of Alice I had slowly chipped away at it. If I'd hopped onstage without performing it for anyone else, I'm positive my mind would have blanked again and I would have cried.

But by practising in front of others (Alice, and also Meg and the other storytellers), feeling their eyes on me, my fear, while still there, had greatly subsided, and in its place I'd started to believe I could do it.

My solemn vow to keep off the public stage had been smashed and I was elated. Fear and anxiety had dominated my life for weeks, and a less potent strain had dominated my life for the preceding thirty-two years, all the way to China and back again. But that night, blinking into the lights, feeling my heart pound, I'd stood onstage and performed for an audience. I had shaken off the constraints of the fear and crossed over to the other side.

I didn't know how long it would last, but for approximately twelve minutes I was free.

HEART PROBLEMS

a real-life interlude

With phase two over, I feel ready for more. Except I'd forgotten the painful truth of that old Yiddish proverb: make plans and God laughs.

I'd committed to a year of pushing myself well outside my comfort zone, but because I'd set my own parameters there was still some semblance of safety in it. But of course, real life does not care about any of this. Real life does not have any regard for your lists, or your plans, or your lofty dreams.

Just days later, still delighted after my performance, I get the text at midnight, as I'm climbing into bed.

It's my dad: 'Can we talk?'

Something is wrong. He calls and tells me he's been having heart palpitations. He's had a scan, and they've discovered that he has a tumour. On his heart. Which is a very bad place to have a tumour.

I knew that he'd been having heart palpitations, but there hadn't seemed to be a real reason to be concerned.

He's going to have open-heart surgery in Los Angeles, because it's an experimental surgery they don't perform in our town in Texas. A last-minute spot has just opened up: they're operating on his heart in three days.

My dad. Is having open-heart surgery. In three days.

All thoughts of talking to strangers, of extroverting, of changing my small and lonely life, fly out of my head.

I am not ready to deal with this. No one is.

I book a flight to Los Angeles for the next day. I don't know when I'll be back. I don't know if or how my father will recover. I don't know anything – I can't think about what might happen. I just know that I have to get halfway across the world as soon as possible.

I love my parents. I do. But not to go too Philip Larkin, we're all a little fucked up by our parents after all, but sometimes I wonder if part of my shintroversion is a direct result of how enthusiastically my parents will extrovert on a daily basis. For starters, they'll talk to anyone: flight seatmates, waiters, people in the queue with them, passing postmen, people eating at the table next to them. I'm still haunted by their most recent visit to London in which my father had the following conversation with our Uber driver:

> Dad: Where are you from? Eastern Europe? Russia?
> Uber driver: I'm Georgian.
> *Long pause*
> Dad: Stalin was from Georgia . . .

My father is the most unpredictable: I've seen him hit the ground in hotel lobbies, showing doormen how to improve their press-up form, ask a Polish waitress if she missed her family deeply and regretted moving to London, and discuss circumcision rates in the US vs the UK *at my own wedding breakfast*. With my new British in-laws. Whom he'd met the night before.

'Your dad can talk to anyone,' my mom likes to say.

Yes, OK, but *should* he?

Before my dad's surgery, we have one 'normal' day to spend together. Whenever I visit LA, I always stay with my grandparents, who are now both ninety years old. The night before my dad's surgery, my parents and my grandparents and I go out for Chinese food at Hop Li, our regular Chinese restaurant haunt. As we eat crunchy Hong Kong-style noodles, garlic eggplant and egg foo-young, my grandparents try to get my parents to eat egg drop soup and my parents refuse, just like they always do. It all feels so normal – too normal. But there's a pall over the evening.

As the fortune cookies hit the table, my mother doesn't take one. She visibly turns her head away from them. I know that she is afraid she will get a bad fortune, and she can't take any risks when it comes to what tomorrow will bring. I don't take one either. We eat the sliced oranges on the table instead.

Before bed that night, before my dad and I say goodnight to each other again and again, he does twenty press-ups on the floor to prove to me that he's strong. *Don't think, don't think, don't think if this is the last time he will ever do this.* He's in high spirits: he's been dreading the surgery, but now he's actually excited to just get it over with.

In my grandparents' kitchen, he uses a pair of kitchen tongs to demonstrate the surgery. He repeatedly refers to the tumour on his heart as a 'truffle'. In an echo video scan of his heart, the tumour flutters back and forth as blood flows through his heart. It looks so innocuous, as if it's just a small mushroom blowing in the breeze of his bloodstream. 'We go in, take out the truffle and we're done,' he says, with a little too much relish. 'Simple.'

Except he leaves out the part where the surgeons put him under, put his body on a pump and cut straight through his heart to reach the truffle, stitch his heart back up and restart it. He leaves out the part where they put his body back together again.

I haven't spent much time in hospitals. Most of what I expect comes from a few episodes of *Gilmore Girls*, the one TV show my parents and I could bear to watch together. It's the right amount of funny and the right amount of sex scenes (nearly zero) to make for ideal parent–child viewing.

In the show, Richard, the grandfather, has a heart scare and, later, a heart attack. During these scenes, Lorelai and her daughter Rory are constantly pacing the white hospital hallways in search of coffee and junk food in between comforting each other. There are always vending machines and stressed-out nurses, kind doctors and endless cups of bad coffee in paper cups. Is the world really like that?

Once, while we were watching an episode of the show, my dad said to my mother and me, 'Don't you two wish you were like Lorelai and Rory? Best friends?'

It was an uncomfortable moment because our relationship wasn't like theirs at all. Rory was sixteen and Lorelai was thirty-two. When I was sixteen, my mom was fifty-one. We fought a lot when I was growing up. We did not meet everyday at the diner for coffee after school. I certainly did not tell her about my first kiss or the night I lost my virginity. We just didn't have that kind of relationship.

We are very different from each other. As a kid, I would sit beside her in silence while she would chat to strangers multiple times a day. We loved each other but were so different that we just weren't best friends.

On the day of my dad's heart surgery, my parents and I wake up at 5 a.m. to head to the hospital. We're told that despite arriving early we could be waiting for hours before the procedure due to delays.

It's still dark when we park the car. My dad takes off his watch and hands it to me. I put it on, clicking the silver clips into place. The weight is heavy on my wrist. We walk through the hospital, and he signs himself in.

My mom and I sit next to him while a hospital employee has him sign a few more forms. Then the man says, 'OK, I'm going to take you upstairs now so you can change into your hospital gown and they can put your IV in.'

My mom and I both stand up.

The man says, 'Only one visitor is allowed.'

And that's it. That's the moment.

I thought we had a few more minutes together, but it hits me that this could be the last time I see my dad alive. I start crying, and I hug my dad hard and I say that I love him. I don't know what else you are supposed to say in these moments, but when I had pneumonia when I was four, I remember what he told me. 'I know you're strong,' I say to him and hug him one more time.

Alone in the waiting room, sitting as far away from everyone else as possible, I start crying quietly. I don't have tissues to cry into and am using my shirt; and at that moment I realize that I have also just gotten my period. I am bitterly half-laughing, half-crying at this when a woman walks up to me.

'They want you to go upstairs,' she says. Only five minutes have passed. I look at her confused, but the woman gives me directions and a new visitor's pass; I fly towards the lifts and up into a crowded hospital floor. I sprint down a hallway, searching for the correct room number.

Then I hear it.

My mom's voice, loud and clear.

'Mom?' I call out tentatively.

She calls back, 'We're in here!' and pulls back a curtain. My dad, now in his gown, IV in, is propped up on the bed and I run to him to hug him again, because I can, not caring about why I'm suddenly allowed up here or how long I have before I need to buy some tampons.

A steady stream of doctors and nurses comes in – an anaesthesiologist, the heart surgeon's assistant, another anaesthesiologist and then another nurse – speaking so quickly with such big words about what happens next. They talk about all the medications they are slowly feeding him, about stopping his heart and cutting through its walls before restarting it. It makes me dizzy with fear.

Twenty minutes later, it's finally time for him to go into the operating room. I start to panic. I feel like I need a bargaining chip to persuade him that he has to come back, to make sure his heart will definitely start up again. Bribing has always been key in our family.

'A grandchild from me by 2020 if you make it out of this, OK?' I blurt out at him, right before he goes.

His eyes light up. 'Can I get that in writing?'

The man has five grandsons already but he's intent on having a full football team.

But now it really is time. The nurses and doctors come, and they wheel his bed out and down the hallway. He disappears from view.

My mom and I walk towards the lift and get inside. 'Let's have breakfast,' she says. 'I'm hungry.' It's odd how mundane life carries on in the shadow of the most dramatic moments.

We walk through the lobby to the dining hall.

'How did you get me upstairs?' I ask. 'They said only one visitor was allowed.'

'Last time we were here for preliminary tests, we had this really nice Ugandan nurse. We chatted a lot about his family. Just now, he came up to me and said, "I'd know that smile anywhere" and I told him that I was so scared and that you were all alone in the waiting room and that we really needed to be together right now. He smiled and said, "Let me see what I can do."'

I'm so moved by this and sort of shaken because my mom just worked a goddamn miracle with her chattiness.

By sharing her wish with the nurse that she had befriended a few weeks ago, my mother had managed, in all of this chaos, to teach me a little about extroverting.

We get in line at the canteen and then sit down across from each other at a table in the enormous dining hall. We've both opted for a cherry Danish and strong coffee. My dad's watch still feels heavy on my arm, and I'm trying to ignore it and why it's there and focus on my pastry instead. The cherry Danish tastes better than it should under these circumstances. My mom takes a sip of her coffee, her hands around the paper cup, elbows on the table, and looks around the canteen at all the doctors and nurses.

'Do you think they've all had sex in a broom closet upstairs?' she asks.

'What?'

'You know, like in *Grey's Anatomy*. There's not a broom closet in that show that hasn't had doctors and nurses getting busy. It must be very stressful for the janitors here,' she says.

And I laugh, loudly, for what feels like the first time in years.

Maybe we aren't Rory and Lorelai, but in that moment it feels like we kind of got there in the end. It's just that I had to be the one who was thirty-two, not her.

Still, when I mention that I've just gotten my period, my mom is up out of her chair, off to find a pharmacy to buy tampons for me. And I am officially sixteen again.

Hours later, we get word from a nurse that my dad is out of surgery. Later, the cardiothoracic surgeon stops by to tell us that he's successfully removed the mass from Dad's heart and repaired a hole in it that we hadn't known was there. We should be able to see him in a few hours.

When we're finally allowed through to the ward, my dad is still unconscious and on a ventilator. It looks like he's in a coma. My mother grabs my hand. We have a new ICU nurse, Pete, who comes over to us and tells us that everything went great, not to worry. He has a kind smile and he's very gentle and slightly rotund. I immediately love him. He feels like a young Chinese Santa with a California accent, which is exactly the kind of nurse I didn't know I needed in my life.

Slowly my dad begins to stir ever so slightly. My mom and I study every minuscule movement he makes with rapt attention.

Pete turns on the radio to cut the tension in the room. Just as Rod Stewart's song 'Maggie May' starts to play, my dad's eyes open. He stares at us groggily. Then Pete slowly takes him off the ventilator, and my dad starts talking. Just like that, he is back.

So many things scare me in my daily life – talking to strangers, driving on the freeway, public speaking – but losing a parent will leave such a massive, gaping hole in my heart and life that I can't even bear to think about it realistically for more than thirty seconds without losing it. There's a clarity that comes with seeing everything in such sharp relief. In this moment, as my father has just come to after open-heart surgery, I am so elated I'm practically manic.

I will need to hold on to this feeling very tightly because over the next few days we spend most daylight hours in the hospital, keeping my dad company while he recovers in the ICU. This means I am with my mother for about seventeen hours a day, an experience we haven't endured since I was, say, seven, and I'm pretty sure that back then I was allowed to watch more TV alone.

My dad is resting. But my mom doesn't know how to do this – instead, she is filling the silences.

What I had not anticipated about flying into LA to be there for my dad is that I'd inadvertently enrolled in extroverting boot camp, with my mother as Team Leader.

It is a fast and furious baptism by fire. My mother talks to people in the hospital lift, joining their ongoing conversations with a frightening lack of constraint. 'The actress you are talking about is Alicia Vikander,' she says to one group. 'And she is *beautiful*.' She chats to doormen, she stops a man putting cream in his coffee at Starbucks to ask how long the route is to Wilshere Boulevard, even though I know she knows the way. She chats to women in the bathroom about the pros and cons of Weight Watchers.

The woman waves to people while we walk around a nearby park.

Twice in one day she joins conversations as she's passing by. Two nurses, a good thirty feet away, are talking about a movie that they can't remember the name of. '*WHIPLASH*,' she shouts across the ICU, and then adds, 'I HAVEN'T EVEN SEEN IT!'

And serving as the baseline for all this chatter, the type of small talk that sets my teeth on edge, my mom also talks to the nurse Pete a lot. But this is good chat. This is 'Take your mind off the fact that your loved one is still attached to many tubes' chat and I am grateful to her for making it. We find out that Pete's Chinese grandparents are from the same village as my dad's parents, that they came over in 1948, that he grew up in San Francisco, that he knows where to get the best Korean food in LA (he makes a list of places for us). In turn, my mother tells him about where she and my dad have been in China, where they used to live in San Francisco and their own favourite restaurants in LA.

Meanwhile, my dad gets slowly better and stronger in the ICU.

Five days in and Pete tells us that we probably won't see him again, because he has a couple of days off and my dad will likely be released before he starts his next shift.

My heart jolts. Pete is leaving? Our Pete? I've become so attached to him. So has my mother.

'I really like Pete,' 'Me too,' is a daily incantation that we make in the car park as we leave each night.

Pete has seen us all sob and cry and fight. He's drawn my dad's blood, given him medicine, made sure he was eating the right food. He's also seen me wrestle my mother as I pried her iPhone out of her hands so I could turn off the sound on her typing and message notifications. Every. Single. Day.

Honestly, the man knows too much. But his warmth, his willingness to chat and to be disarmingly open with perfect strangers, has made this hellish experience bearable. He has made me want to make an effort to extrovert more: I want to be someone's Pete one day.

After a week in the ICU, my dad is finally released, and the LA apartment feels crowded with semi-invalids. I lie on the couch watching *The Crown*, between my grandma and my dad, who both happen to be on the same heart medication: her for being ninety, him for recovering from heart surgery.

Time stands still in this apartment. At lunch my mother says, 'Does anyone want a sandwich?' and we all exclaim, 'Yes, please!' without taking our eyes off the television.

This begins to feel like a new, strange normal. I've just accepted my new life: no past, no future, just limbo for ever in this Los Angeles apartment full of pastries, good sandwiches, Netflix and ninety-year-olds.

But I know I can't stay for ever. I need to get back to my real life in England, to my husband, to my job, to my vomit-inducing social experiments waiting patiently for me back home. There was a lot about the trip that I hadn't anticipated – the whole goddamned thing, really – but now I'd seen first-hand how talking and being open through tense moments can transform them. How the right stranger can become your personal hero.

Verbose extroverts like my mom and Pete can sometimes be maddening. But they also can make uncomfortable moments in life more bearable. They convince nurses to sneak you in to see your father in the hospital. They make your father feel better.

In a surprise extroverting lesson from the universe, which I had somehow endured, miraculously, my mother and I only had one small fight which ended when we bonded over how attractive a certain anaesthesiologist was and how maybe he should be on *Grey's Anatomy* because he would look great shirtless in a broom closet.

My parents order a cab for me, insist on making sure I physically get into it, and demand a text from the airport gate. I am sixteen again, possibly for the last time ever. I fasten my dad's watch back on to his wrist. I wave goodbye to my parents and slip on my backpack and board my flight to England.

I land in London in the early morning. On the underground on my way back home from Heathrow, I ponder the strangers around me in the train carriage. I wonder if that moment in the hospital with my father waking up from surgery will stay at the forefront of my mind. That reminder that my fears and problems are inconsequential when it comes to actual life and death. That everything is really small stuff compared to what I'd just been through.

And then I remember that I promised my dad a grandchild by 2020. I should probably talk to Sam about that.

IN SEARCH
OF THE ONE
or
friend-dating

'Are you going on holiday?' the woman asks me as she spreads hot, liquid wax on my bikini line.

'Um, not really,' I say.

'Is it a special date?'

I pause, wincing in anticipation of the imminent, searing pain.

She pauses, too, hovering over me, waiting for my answer.

'Sure,' I say. Accurate enough.

She rips out a chunk of pubic hair. I stifle my yelp into my hands.

I'm not having a bikini wax because I'm going away to Ibiza or because I have a romantic weekend planned. I'm getting a wax because I have an imminent 'friend-date' with a relative stranger and it involves swimming and I cannot let this potential best friend see me in my wild, natural state. Not yet. It's too soon. I can't scare her off.

Some research says that we have the most friends we'll ever have when we are twenty-nine, while other studies say we start to lose friends after the age of twenty-five. When we are in our thirties, our social circles decline and continue to do so for the rest of our lives. I had read this research before, but I didn't realize that when I was in my thirties I would be the poster girl for that statistic. (The poster reads: 'Beware: this woman talks to strangers and is therefore a danger to herself and others.')

For the *Moth* performance, Sam had been in the audience to see me, but at the end of the night, I saw big groups of friends and family mob the other storytellers as they walked off stage. Even though I was still on a high after the performance, I'd watched this with a twinge of sadness. I didn't have that. And after holding my mother's hand in the waiting room, I'd briefly wondered what would happen if I had sudden major surgery, with my parents on the other side of the world. I didn't want Sam to be sat there alone in the waiting room. And so, for so many reasons, I want to find more close friends who live in the same city.

Since I turned thirty, all of my closest friends in London had moved away, had babies, or moved away *and* had babies. Introverts tend to value quality over quantity when it comes to relationships, and after this exodus I was left with no friends. I had not thought to stockpile them in case of a drought.

Where do you go to make friends when you're an adult?

No, honestly, I'm asking, where do you do this? There are no more late-night study sessions or university social events. And while meeting friends at work is the obvious answer, your options are very limited if you don't click with your colleagues or if you're self-employed. (Also, if you're only friends with people at work, who do you complain about your colleagues to?)

I don't volunteer. I don't participate in organized religion. I don't play team sports.

Where do selfish, godless, lazy people go to make friends? That's where I need to be.

Nearly all of my closest friends have been assigned to me: either via seating charts at school, university roommates, or desk buddies at work. After taking stock, I realize that most of my friends were forced to sit one metre away from me for several hours at a time. I've never actively reached out to make a new friend who wasn't within touching distance.

With no helpful administrators, just how do we go about making friends as adults? Is it possible to cultivate that intense closeness without the heady combination of naivety, endless hours of free time on hand and lack of youthful inhibitions? Or is that lost for ever after we hit thirty?

Loneliness, on the other hand, has no age bracket. I used to think that exciting countries could keep you happy and warm on novelty alone. Now I know: you can move to Paris, delight in the city, drink your café au lait, but no matter how pretty the buildings and balconies are, eventually you're going to find yourself hugging lamp posts for company like you're in *Les Misérables*.

And so I would have to go out and find new friends.

I feel embarrassed to want them. I don't even want to say it aloud because it sounds desperate and sad. So I seek out a friendship mentor. Rachel Bertsche went on fifty-two friend-dates in one year and detailed it in her bestselling book, *MWF Seeks BFF*. She understands my fear of looking pathetic.

'I would say to people, "I'm looking for new friends" and people would hear, "*I have no friends*",' Rachel B tells me over the phone from Chicago. 'I had friends – just none in my current city. We feel desperate or weird reaching out for friendship, but we shouldn't. It's important.'

True. Friends listen to you, laugh with you, give you advice, encourage you, inspire you, fill your life with joy. A big source of my loneliness is not having a close friend I can call and meet for coffee at a moment's notice and share everything that's been happening in my life. Or a group of friends to go out with. Nothing big. Not too showy. A small coven I could count on to cast spells on my enemies. Brené Brown calls these friends 'move a body' friends. You know. The people you call when you accidentally murder somebody.

And all of mine were abroad.

Surely it wasn't just me who was struggling to find friends in London? One day on Twitter, I see a tweet that resonates.

A writer named A.N. Devers who moved to London two years ago tweets:

> Well, since making friends in this fucking country is so hard, I became a rare book dealer instead . . . FUCK THIS PLACE. All I wanted was a little tiny social life. LOOK AT THE LENGTHS I HAVE TO GO TO TO GET IT.

My first thought is: do rare book dealers have lots of friends? This is a solution I haven't considered. But that tweet garnered a large response, with many people jumping in saying age was to blame, and busyness, but also how London could be a particularly frosty place. A few people, including myself, reply to her tweet, saying we'd love to meet up.

She replies saying that now she's too busy, but maybe later.

I delete my tweet in a panic of shame.

Studies show that we're spending more time online than ever before, scrolling through our social media accounts, liking photos of strangers' cats and dinner plates, reading twenty-four-hour news, watching the latest Twitter meltdown of our world leaders unfold, but all of this connectivity can leave us isolated.

While the internet creates a space for introverts to find like-minded people and online communities, it has its limits. It seems like everyone is relying so much on technology and social media for our interactions, and while we can write witty tweets or heartfelt Instagram comments, we don't know how to say hello to the cashier at the grocery store without breaking into a sweat. We're at risk of losing our ability to interact with other humans in person.

Social media is a huge part of the loneliness problem (we've stopped meeting up with our existing friends in person, we struggle to meaningfully talk with each other), but maybe technology can also be the solution. At least, that's what Instagram keeps trying to tell me. Bumble, the dating app, now has a 'BFF' feature, which matches you with new friends (or, new best friends for ever). These days, it's the norm to meet new romantic partners via apps on their phones. If people were finding love via matchmaking apps, could I use them to find my new best friend?

And why stop at a new best friend? What about an entire squad? I wanted to be able to write things on Instagram like, 'The gang's all here!' and not just have it be a photo of me with a dozen blueberry muffins and a Sally Rooney novel.

Sam's friend Shaun shudders when I mention signing up for apps to make new friends. 'What, so you're going to meet up with a bunch of weirdos?' he asks me, when I casually mention it in conversation. A promising start.

'No,' I say, slowly. 'I don't think they're weirdos. I think they're . . . just like me . . .'

Despite having met his fiancée on Tinder, he can't bear the idea of doing the same for friends.

Why the stigma? Well, for one it's hard to admit you want friends and research says men are less likely than women to publicly do so, but given that studies also say that it's harder for men to make new friends, maybe they need these apps more than we do: 2.5 million British men have no close friends. I download Bumble BFF and Hey Vina!, two friend-ship apps, on to my phone. What if Shaun is right? What if there *are* a bunch of weirdos out there? People who like country music or are into ventriloquists. People who queue up to go to Madame Tussauds. People who like dancing in public. People who say 'soz'.

And what am I supposed to put on my bio?

I seek advice from one of Sam's close friends, John, who has been using the dating apps for a few years.

He has plenty of thoughts: 'It's good to be specific. People usually try to be as broadly appealing as possible, but I think it's important to discourage people you won't like and encourage people with similar interests. Having said that, I would avoid overtly naming things you don't like as it looks negative.'

First and foremost, I want to discourage people who live far away. I already have my fill of long-distance friends. At a Christmas party I once attended, I spent the majority of the party petting a friendly brown dog with a woman who seemed similarly eager to ignore the other guests for the duration of the evening. We laughed together easily. I was pretty sure I had found her. The one. But near the end of the party, we discovered that she lived and worked an hour-and-a-half Tube journey away from me. We didn't bother to exchange numbers, because we both knew – it was over before it had even begun.

A kindred spirit, lost to the depths of south-east London. As she put on her coat and left the party, I watched the door close behind her and whispered, 'Goodbye, for ever.'

I wanted to avoid that kind of heartache in the future. London was a big city; surely I had a few soulmates somewhere in North London. I was not travelling to Greenwich for anybody.

So, I write that I like seeing live comedy and plays, eating spicy food, going to good cafes and reading good books. This is all true. I don't add that I have no friends in London. Announcing that fact feels like saying, 'No one else wants me – maybe you will?' Best to spring it on them later.

I choose my profile photos carefully. Something that says 'fun' and 'cute' but not too serious. Me, smiling, alone, in front of a food truck. Me, hiking with no make-up in very flattering sunset-y light on top of a mountain. Something that says, 'Look how normal and fun I am.' None of me weeping on the sofa.

And just like that, I'm in. My profile is active and I'm swiping on potential new best friends.

I study faces and bios of other women. Are you the one? Are you the one? Could you be the one? I contemplate smiling profile shots. What about this nice woman in a pea coat petting a dog? Or this lady with purple hair petting a dog? Or this blonde woman in shorts . . . petting a dog?

After a few minutes on the app, I realize that nearly every photo is a variation of three things: women posing with dogs, women holding glasses of Prosecco and women standing on top of mountains (guilty). A disproportionate number of women are petting elephants (Sri Lanka is very in this year). This is the female-friend 'come hither' equivalent of single men posing near tigers on Tinder.

I come across a photo of a woman holding a surfboard on a beach. 'Could I curl up in bed with you and watch TV? Could we travel together? Will you make me laugh on my darkest days? Will you be forgiving of my cellulite?' I ask her photo.

Her bio says, 'I went to Paris for lunch once and I regret nothing.' I love her instantly. Though I am also intimidated by her. Perhaps she will be my new extrovert guide.

The app works like all the others: you swipe right on the people you want to meet (people with pets, people eating tacos) and swipe left on people you'd rather skip (people at Glastonbury). I start off tentatively, trying to give attention to each woman, but soon become a callous lothario from swiping fatigue. Snapchat filters that transform you into cute animals in every photo? Next! Interests include spirituality and mindfulness? Next! Only kissy selfies? Next!

The app is designed for reciprocity. You swipe right on the people you're interested in but if they don't swipe back, poof, you'll never get the chance to talk. And apparently, the woman who lunches in Paris and regrets nothing doesn't want to talk to me. Which is fine. That's her right. Whatever. I'm fine. (I hope she regrets it.)

When you have a match, there's a ding (such a rush) and the app encourages you to send a message to 'your future BFF'.

Crucially, after you've matched, you only have twenty-four hours to message each other before your potential friendship expires. And if they don't reply to your message within twenty-four hours, they disappear for ever. There are so many areas for rejection on this app.

A woman named Elizabeth appears. Her bio reads: 'I'm into cooking, trying restaurants, trash TV, theatre, reading, travelling and exploring. Love a girls' night in as much as a night out. Lived in New York for a few years. Looking for friends to explore the city with or maybe start or join a feminist book club.'

Yes! Yes, Elizabeth, yes! I send her a message about how I'd be up for her feminist book club and trying new restaurants. Safe. Solid. Not groundbreaking, but friendly enough.

Elizabeth doesn't reply.

'Elizabeth, don't do this to us!' I yell at her photo. I watch the time dwindle away.

And then, before we have even begun, our time is up. Her profile photo fades to grey, like she's dead. Which she is. To me.

I don't have time to mourn her. There are plenty more fish in the sea, plenty more women petting elephants to meet.

I match with another woman. Her name is Ellen. She looks nice. Kind eyes. She asks me if I intend to stay in London. I admire this upfront attitude. Why invest in me if I'm only here temporarily? That's how we all got here in the first place. We made friends, put in the hours, shared all of our best anecdotes – and for what? For them to up and leave for Athens.

Then she asks me my star sign.

'Aries,' I reply.

I'm chopping onions for the chilli I'm making for dinner when Ellen sends another message. I lean over the counter to read it.

'Oh no! Aries are THE WORST! It's a massive clash! It's always, "ME ME ME" and they're so moody and stubborn. And obsessed with having a man in their lives.'

I blink at this message. OK, Ellen. Calm down. I might be an Aries, aka THE WORST, but if you prick me, do I not bleed? (And then retaliate swiftly, as me and my star sign compatriots are wont to do.) But Ellen, do I not need friends, too? Do all Aries deserve to die alone?

I can't resist asking, 'What sign are you?'

'It's in my profile,' she replies.

I check her profile. She's a Gemini. I decide to try to rise above this. Her profile says that she's from Carlisle and she loves football. 'What football team do you support? Carlisle?' I ask her, trying to climb on to more neutral territory.

'It was, but now I support Arsenal because I moved to London.'

Ditch her, Sam's voice says in my head. *Ditch her now.*

See, Sam is not very discerning with his friends (I'd go as far as to say he could afford to be a little *more* discerning). But he comes down hard on people who abandon their home football teams for shinier, more fashionable alternatives (he supports Sunderland, a team who have been on an unprecedented downward spiral in recent years). Loyalty to your team is a sign of basic decency. People who ditch theirs are fairweather fans and fairweather friends. It's an unspoken truth that they are not really to be trusted.

Probably because they are snakes. Two-faced Gemini snakes.

'I think it's the end of the road for us, Ellen,' I say out loud, while chopping the onions extra hard. I finish making dinner, and neither of us messages the other again.

This was already so much more complicated than I had imagined. I was being eliminated as a friend based on my birth month. And I had rejected a woman because of her chosen football team. Truly, does this app turn everyone into arseholes?

Well, at least we don't start out that way. Each match sends a friendly message, followed by a smiley face. The smiley face with red cheeks, to be precise. Everyone uses this emoji. It says, 'I'm a nice person, I want to get to know you, I have good intentions, I'm not a murderer.' It's scary how effective it is. How reassuring. As if, by law, we all know murderers are obliged to use the murder emoji (skull, I'm assuming) as an opening gambit to give us a fair heads-up.

Most women say they like: brunch, yoga, wine, gigs, dancing, watching movies. Same goes for art galleries and exhibitions. We just want to be television ads showing off perfect all-inclusive holidays to Tenerife.

I send a few messages like, 'I like comedy, too!' and 'What's your favourite kind of ice cream?'

Within a few hours, I begin to finally understand the widely discussed app fatigue. A colleague once told me that she had rejected 15,000 men on Bumble and was done with apps, and I had responded, 'But the next match could be someone amazing!' I'd gone into this wide-eyed, hopeful: you could meet anyone! So many different, interesting exciting people, just sitting in the palm of your hand, waiting to be met! Adventures to be had!

An hour later, I'm swiping left on women just for calling themselves 'authentic', liking clubbing and going to Burning Man.

When I do match with someone, we have awkward banter over messenger and then someone has to make the first move to make the friendship happen IRL. Most of the conversations are really banal so it's hard to say, 'Should we continue this conversation about nothing over dinner?' Plus there are women who simply don't reply to you, as if your opener of, 'Hey Jen, is that your dog in the photo?' isn't good enough for them.

The main barrier with my matches is that I'm too embarrassed to 'ask them out'. We've come so far: we're both on the app, we swiped right on each other, we're chatting on messenger, but we're both too tentative to put ourselves out there and suggest meeting up in real life.

It feels eerily familiar to my early days with Sam. Our messages were teasing and frequent, but as we are both shy, things could have been drawn out for months before we went on our first date.

Except, before we met, Sam had booked a one-way non-refundable ticket to go and live in Australia. Love, or maybe fear of losing potential love, makes us bold – I made a move. I invited him to my friend's birthday party, made it sound casual, he showed up drunk at 2 a.m., told me I was his favourite person in China, the next day I asked him out to dinner, he kissed me and we've been together ever since.

Not sure I can apply any of those lessons to this scenario.

Without any of that urgency, I don't know how to 'ask' the women out. Many women I've spoken with also struggle with this make-or-break moment, because they don't want to seem too forward or be rejected. But the entire point of the app is to meet up in person and expand your friendship group, not have five to six lacklustre back-and-forth exchanges before never messaging each other again. The premise fails completely if neither party makes a move.

Then, one day, over Instagram, I get a message from someone I've never met before. Her name is Venus. She is originally from Macau, but had studied in the US. She'd read one of my articles and recently moved to London and wanted to know if I wanted to have dinner. Remarkably – brazenly – she appeared to ask this with no qualms.

I feel so flattered. See, Ellen? Some people like disgusting Aries women like ME ME ME. People want to have dinner with me!

Venus and I meet for Malaysian food and I ask her about making friends in London.

'I was really lonely when I first moved here, but I found my *Sex and the City* crew on Bumble BFF,' Venus says.

'What? Really?' I ask, valiantly ignoring the *SATC* reference.

Apparently, Venus had a lengthy online conversation about fashion school with an Irish girl named Clarissa; they met for coffee, then brunch, and since then they've practically been inseparable.

'Clarissa introduced me to two other girls she met on Bumble BFF, and now we're all best friends. We hang out all the time.'

I nearly snap my chopstick in half. I want this! This is my dream!

But had she had any dud dates?

Venus said she had had one friend-date with someone who lived far away, and they haven't seen each other since (see? Distance equals doom), but Clarissa lived two train stops away from Venus.

'We just got back from a trip to Geneva together.'

I put down my chopsticks.

Now, I am tempted to say, 'You guys need a fifth in your *Sex and the City* crew . . . ?'

But Venus is twenty-five. I suspect she thinks I'm near death, the way all women in their twenties (previous self included) look at women in their thirties and beyond. I'd be 'old crone in the corner photo-bombing their group selfie and asking them to keep the noise down' to her Carrie, Samantha, Miranda and Charlotte. Also, I begin to sense that this dinner is more of a networking opportunity for her when she asks me for advice on filing taxes as a freelancer. Which is fine with me because she has given me something priceless.

Hope.

I go back to the apps with renewed enthusiasm, but with one key change. I adjust my settings to extend my age range. Seeing Venus reminded me that it's fun to connect with women who aren't my age. Venus and I liked each other, despite our age gap, and one of my closest former colleagues was ten years older than I am.

I adjust my app settings so that I can be matched with women fifteen years younger and older than I am. Immediately, a woman with long dark hair appears in my app. She's elegant. Forty-four years old. A novelist named Abigail. Who lives near by. I swipe right on her. *Ding!* We've matched.

She sends me a message. 'I've never done this before, do you want to get coffee? If it's bad, it'll make a funny story, at least.'

Good opener, Abigail.

I message her back, 'Yes! Let's do it!'

A few days later, I'm getting ready for my first friend-date from the app. I'm nervous. Would I be an attractive prospect?

In romance, potential suitors can pretend you have no chemistry or you weren't their 'type'. But because we can have as many friends as we want, being rejected as a friend is also brutal – the message loud and clear: 'I genuinely do not like to be around you.'

I wash my hair. And try not to be late.

I walk into the cafe and spot Abigail sitting in an armchair in the corner. I recognize her from her profile photo (another difference, I am told, from dating apps is that the photos tend to be accurate). She stands up and gives me a brief hug and then asks me what I want to drink. I order a flat white and settle into my chair, studying her surreptitiously.

Abigail brings the coffees over and we immediately start talking about writing – she's working on her second novel and deep into the edits. She's open about how difficult she finds writing the first draft. Her vulnerability sets the tone: she's honest and warm. She's doing Deep Self talk – this I can do.

She talks candidly about her recent divorce, mentioning that her ex-husband has a new girlfriend, so I take the plunge and ask her if she's started dating again.

This feels like a personal question to ask someone I've just met, but Abigail nods.

'Unsolicited dick pics are a very real thing,' she says.

'I'm very sorry to hear that,' I say.

'But the good thing is that I get to see some great bathroom tile designs,' she adds, laughing.

We talk about the relief of being on a friend-date, rather than sussing each other out to see if we want to sleep with each other.

'Isn't it great that you and I won't have sex with each other and then ghost each other?' she says.

It is.

Abigail is warm, but straightforward, and I like her immediately, which is amazing because on paper I wasn't sure we would have a lot in common. She's a forty-four-year-old single mom with a five-year-old kid. She has a Ph.D in archaeology and is the kind of woman who drops her kid off at school, goes running and then sits down to write epic novels. Will I ever be as great as this woman? I'm not sure, but I'm very happy to have met her.

I walk out of the cafe on a high. I met a stranger, had coffee and a great conversation. My first friend-date. A roaring success.

But I don't know how to proceed at this point. Do I contact Abigail again? Wait for her? This is when my friendship mentor, Rachel B, steps in.

'My biggest piece of advice is make the first move and also make the second move.'

I take out my phone and text Abigail: 'I hereby promise to never send you a dick pic.'

Abigail texts me back to promise me the same thing. She says she'd love to meet up again, but for the next few months she's very busy with book edits. We agree to get in touch in a month or so.

My date with Abigail had gone so well that I feel confident that by the end of this experiment I'll have about ten new best friends. We will go to Tenerife together and drink Bellinis on the beach.

My second friend-date is with Jade, who works for an arts charity. We arrange to see a comedy show near King's Cross on a sweltering hot day. She has red hair and gives off an artsy-vibe in a floral shirt. She buys us Aperol spritzes, which we drink while I sweat profusely through the entire comedy set. Halfway into the show, I notice that the woman sitting directly in front of me is wearing the exact same H&M dress as I am. And we've both sweated straight through it. I want to share this with Jade but feel too self-conscious.

After the show, Jade and I walk back to King's Cross together. And that's when I'm faced with a dilemma. What now? Do I tell her I had a nice time? Ask to see her again? Angle for a cheek kiss? Because we saw comedy together, we didn't really get to talk to each other, except for a quick conversation during the intermission, cooling off outside with our cocktails. I'd liked her a lot, in those fleeting fifteen minutes as we chatted about our jobs and the comedians, but now saying goodbye feels so very awkward. Jade initiates a hug and says we should do this again sometime. Lesson learned: don't meet up for a first friend-date and then sit in silence next to each other for two hours.

Date three is Zara. We meet outside the British Museum and we have a drink in the basement of a bookstore. She's fascinating – she grew up in France, but also has a hybrid Scottish accent and parents from Bahrain. But it feels less like a conversation and more like I'm watching a one-woman show on feminism, multi-culturalism and her boyfriend's racist family. I'm captivated by it, but I don't feel a connection. Would I listen to her podcast? Yes. Interview her for a profile? Yes. Become her new best friend? Not sure.

Then it's Lucy, an accountant, and while she's perfectly nice, we have nothing in common. I find myself looking for excuses to leave our coffee date early. Later, I grab dinner with an events planner who rants about her job for forty minutes; I quickly wolf down my pizza so I can bolt home as soon as possible.

I realize that with all of them, there's no spark.

Does there need to be a spark in friendship? I've always thought so: you want to have chemistry with someone when they're helping you move the dead body, otherwise it's just a very, very bad night for both of you.

And while loyalty and support are important to me in the long run, I want to laugh and have fun with new friends.

At this point, it's pretty obvious, though – I am ploughing through my friend-dates. I'm wining and dining women at the rate of a recently single John Mayer with a fresh haircut on a thirty-two-city road tour.

As I looked at my rows of message after message to different women, it dawns on me. I am the fuckboi of Bumble BFF: a Serial Dater. A fuckfriend.

But unlike a fuckboi, it's all because I am in search of that ineffable spark.

Not just a quick shag.

See, Abigail aside, each of these women was perfectly nice, but my feelings for them are tepid. And I can tell that the lukewarm-ness is mutual. Or maybe we just didn't push through the awkwardness barrier to get to the good parts.

Then something very dark dawns on me. Not one of my other friend-dates has asked to see *me* again, either. Who is the real fuckboi in this situation, hmm?

OK, I think it's still me.

But had I asked enough questions? Had I self-disclosed enough? Too much? I thought I could make friends easily if I was willing to try – now, I realize, I know nothing. What friends? Who can I trust? Unlikable people don't know they're unlikable, do they?

I have no choice but to persevere.

Everyone in London is so busy and tired from work, family, dating and sending/receiving dick pics. I'm beginning to feel nostalgic for small-town Texas. With literally nothing else going on, you can get twenty people to meet you in a car park to light a can of body spray on fire within ten minutes.

And how do other people date multiple people at once? How can you possibly stay motivated? Why would you *want* to? The admin is a nightmare. The small talk. The rote life-story swapping. There are so many Sarahs, Katies and Samanthas on the app that I can't keep up. I'm exhausted. There must be another way.

A few days later, I read a news article about a woman in New York named Natasha who had blindly sent hundreds of men on Tinder the same message: meet her for a first date in Union Square 'near the stage'. As dozens of men began mingling around the stage, looking for her, she appeared with a microphone and announced that she had asked them all there at the same time so she could save time and eliminate unsuitable matches.

In short, they were there to compete for her attention.

In a *Gladiator*-esque speech, she proceeded to ask the men who were in relationships to leave, for the men over five foot ten to stay and then said, 'I don't enjoy the name Jimmy – can the Jimmys please leave?'

A lot of men fled the scene as soon as they realized what was going on, but a good few remained and competed in sprinting and press-up competitions to try to win her time and affection.

Natasha is a genius. We don't have time to meet each person individually; better to gather them and eliminate the Jimmys as soon as possible. I needed to pull a Natasha and get my matches in one place so that we could all meet each other at the same time, find our potential friend soulmates in one night and move on with our busy lives having brunch and going to yoga.

I've been doing this all wrong. Only an introvert sets up one-on-one dates. An extrovert would bring them all together – happily! Right? I don't know but this is my haphazard guesswork at how they operate.

I compose a message that I can send to multiple people. This kind of debasement would normally take me weeks to muster, but I was changed. I was an extroverting, (fuck)-friend-dating machine.

'Hey I'm meeting some friends from this app for drinks at Simmons Bar in Clerkenwell at 6.30 p.m. next Wednesday! Would be great if you could join!'

And then I send it to thirty women. Like a boss. A care-free extrovert. My hesitance in being the one to ask someone out has been extinguished.

I wait with bated breath.

Then the declines roll in over the week: three have to work late, one has a netball tournament, two are busy with other plans, three are out of town and two have food poisoning. *Two* cases of food poisoning? Adults playing netball? This was farcical.

I lie down on the sofa.

Spontaneity is dead. Friend-dating is hard. Food hygiene in the UK is shot.

On the day of the meet-up, I show up early. A few other women say that they will try to make it, so I can't afford to be late for my own orchestrated mass friend-date.

I'm wearing jeans. A plaid shirt. Something that says, 'Hi, it's me, your casual new best friend.' I have rehearsed stories.

I feel friendly. I relax my face. *Look at me, I'm fun and easygoing and chill as fuck.*

And then I wait.

And wait.

I sip a cider.

And wait.

Easygoing Extrovert Me is growing slightly antsy. And becoming more Apprehensive Introvert Me with every passing glance from the idle bartender.

Only one person shows up. Amelia.

I suddenly feel like I've been catfishing her.

Do I tell her the truth? That I invited thirty women and twenty-nine didn't respond or bailed on me? That's she's literally the only person who said yes?

'Two other women were supposed to come, but they couldn't make it at the last minute!' I say.

Amelia digests this information with grace and dignity. Then she orders a large glass of red wine. She works in consulting and is wearing a business suit. I feel ridiculous in my oldest pair of jeans. Next to her blazer and chic ballet flats, I look like a teenager she is mentoring on how to get her first job.

I ask Amelia what brought her to the Bumble BFF app. 'I'm single and was looking for other single women to go to dating events with,' she says. 'That's why I came along to this group hangout.'

'Yeah, sorry about that . . .' I say.

'You're married, right? Well, if you meet other single women you like, could you put me in touch with them?' Amelia asks.

What, like, match-make you with friends who you'll like more than me?

Cool, cool.

'Sure,' I say.

After two glasses of red wine, Amelia begins to soften. She talks candidly about her love life. She's dated a 'lot of losers', but she wants to get married and have kids. She has the killer career, owns a flat and is from Essex so she has lots of friends in London. She tells me she admires me for being proactive and trying to meet more people.

'I have a very tight group of friends that I've had since I was a teenager,' Amelia says. 'And I'm really, really loyal to them. I pride myself on that. But I think we're outgrowing each other. When we hang out, it feels like I'm wearing clothes that don't fit any more.'

This is actually something I have started to hear from both men and women in their thirties. Lives and careers diverge at this age as babies are born, people move out of cities, jobs change. The friend you bonded with twenty years ago might not have much in common with you now.

Who hasn't reunited with someone from their past, only to realize the best parts of the conversation were when you two were reminiscing? You leave, disappointed and sad, knowing they feel the same way.

So much of this comes down to how much our circumstances change over the years. One friend back home is always urging me to get pregnant – I know she does this because she wants us to bond over motherhood, to make our very different lives similar again. And in New York, I recently met up with an old hallmate from university, Teddy. He cannot believe that I am married. It shocks him.

'Why?' I ask.

'Because you never dated anyone at university. Ever.'

Observing Teddy's perplexed face, I realized that he could only see who I used to be. To him, I was frozen in time, a nineteen-year-old in perpetual unrequited love on our snow-covered campus, clutching my books and wearing too much eyeliner. He didn't see me as someone who could change, or maybe he didn't want to accept that I had.

Which is hard to swallow, considering he aspired to be the campus seducer and I just found out he's been ordained a Buddhist monk. (Though, crucially, not in a branch of Buddhism that requires celibacy. Yes, I checked. Every woman – and man – in my graduating class checked.)

But hey. People change. On that day in New York, Teddy didn't see me as who I am now. Or at least, who I felt I had become. Being seen is something we crave out of friendship – that feeling of 'This person gets me more than I get myself.' When we lose that with old friends, the magic is gone.

On the bus home, I flop down, exhausted. Would I find new friends who really see me? Who understand me? I do not know. At the moment, I'm confused about how I only managed to get one woman to show up on the group date.

How did Natasha get hundreds of men to come to hers in New York? I google her and discover that she's an Instagram model with pillowy lips who was born to wear bikinis. Oh. That's how.

If I messaged thirty women, and only one showed up, odds are that for thirty to show up, I'd have to message nine hundred women. Which means I'd have to *match* with nine hundred women as well. Which means nine hundred 'How is your week going? Yeah, I'm happy it's the weekend, too' conversations.

Good God! I don't have time for this. I could become an Instagram poet in that time. Or do my backlog of taxes (though I wouldn't). I could start a catering business or train for and then drop out of a marathon.

I know that actual dating is *way* more brutal than this. I get that. But I'm married, so that challenge is off the table. Seeking genuine connections on friend-dates had made this my most personal challenge yet. And I wasn't doing very well at it.

On the bus, I swipe through the app absentmindedly. I stop on a friendly looking woman standing in front of a lake. One of her favourite artists is St. Vincent, someone I listened to on a near-constant loop last winter. And one of her emojis is a dumpling. Is this a sign?

No no no. The point isn't to go on a hundred friend-dates with a hundred women. It's to find a few that I really click with, who go on to become good friends.

At home, I tell Sam I'm done with friend-dating after my wine date with Amelia. I'm unlucky in friend-dating and that is that.

'How many friend-dates have you been on?' Sam asks.

'Six.' (There was also an unfortunate pub quiz friend meeting: I yelled a lot, we lost, and now *she* knows too much about how little *I* know about European history.)

'Just go on one more,' Sam says.

'Fine. I'll go with her,' I say, looking at the profile on my screen. It's the dumpling emoji girl.

'What's her name?' Sam asks. I glance down again.

'Lucky. Her name is Lucky,' I say.

'Lucky number seven!' he says. 'You've got to do it.'

I swipe right on her. Ding – we've matched.

Lucky and I arrange to meet for dumplings at Ping Pong and then see a comedy show at Soho Theatre. If I'm going on a friend-date that might bomb, I'm at least going to get some dumplings out of it.

Lucky gets the flu. Our date is cancelled.

Which reminds me to get the flu jab, thereby perhaps preventing me from contracting the flu, in which case, it is very lucky – for me. Not for our friendship.

And then it happens. Abigail, my very first friend-date, gets in touch and wants to hang out.

We decide to go swimming in the Hampstead Heath ponds. And that's how I end up getting a bikini wax. For Abigail. Because she's worth it.

A week later, both of us in black one-piece swimsuits, me with a freshly waxed bikini line, we stand on the pier. Abigail's never swum here before. Because I had been here before with Jessica, who had talked me through getting into the cold water for the first time, I give Abigail the same advice: don't jump in, as it might cause you to gasp for air and accidentally inhale water. Go slowly, and breathe slowly and steadily. But keep going.

Abigail gets in and begins to swim the entire length of the pond. I slowly follow after her and then float on my back.

Afterwards, we walk through the Heath and then she invites me into her house in Belsize Park to give me a book. A few months ago, this woman was a total stranger; now I am in her house, reading her book and discussing her writing.

I know I'll see Abigail again. In searching for that easy intimacy of youthful friendships, I'd discovered a more mature version. We aren't likely to stay up all night talking, swap clothes or spend every weekend together, because at this stage in our lives we are too busy. But in a big lonely city, knowing there's another person out there, even just one, that you can reach out to and say, 'Want to grab a bite?', and you know they'll show up, make you laugh and listen to you, feels like a precious gift.

Plus, Abigail has her shit together. Abigail would know how to get rid of a body.

Studies say that it takes six to eight meetings to feel like someone is our friend. When was the last time you saw someone new who you didn't work with six to eight times in a year? Unless you're dating, on a sports team together or flatmates, the answer is never.

By this definition, my best friend is the route 19 bus driver.

Other research says that, on average, it takes fifty hours of time with someone before you consider them a casual friend and ninety hours before you feel comfortable upgrading them to 'friend'.

Fifty hours? I'm not so sure. Add a little light trauma, and you can get there ten times as fast. At journalism school, I was paired with a classmate to work on a TV report. You can bet that a few hours of sobbing in the editing suite brought us together like nobody's business. Same goes for surviving turbulent plane rides, sadistic teachers and punishingly long jazz concerts. If you make it out alive, you are usually bonded for life.

Personally, I think meeting someone you really connect with twice, for a few hours, followed by extensive, emotional texting, is enough to feel like friends. And I think I'm on my way with Abigail.

Sometimes, new friends will ghost you. You never know what's going on in someone else's life – someone in their family could be sick, they could be going through something big that they need to focus all of their energy on, they could be recovering from heartbreak. We might never know.

As Rachel B, my mentor, says, 'You can't expect someone to behave like your friend before you're actually friends. I'm not saying people should be mean, but they don't owe you anything. So try not to be too hurt if they don't get in touch or reply.'

While friend-dates can be nerve-wracking, I'm once again shocked that strangers are a lot nicer and more normal than we expect them to be. No one outright rejected me when I 'asked them out'. I didn't 'meet a bunch of weirdos'. Not one. Nothing sordid. Zero dick pics. No vag shots.

And taking the first step might feel awkward, but literally nothing in life happens if someone doesn't make the first move. You lose nothing by offering a casual invite for coffee or a drink. Moving from the app to texting makes this much easier. If they say no, that's fine. At least you know.

And I know, too. I mean, I was pseudo-rejected by twenty-nine women in one night.

But I survived.

One night I message my childhood best friend, Jori, who is awake in Houston with her two kids. It's 3 a.m. in London.

'I don't know why this is so hard,' I say to her.

'That's because what you want is a shared history,' she replies.

She's right. I'd been judging these brand-new friends against the chemistry and warmth I had with my oldest, best friends. The ones who still saw old me but accepted the adult version of me. What I'd really been searching for was inside jokes and the closeness of a shared history which takes years to create.

Sometimes, though, friendship is like love. You can't plan for it. It finds you in unlikely places. Or in the most obvious place imaginable.

One evening, I get back from a run and am doubled over, recovering and panting in front of my building. The entrance opens and a woman pops out, taking out her rubbish.

'I'm not loitering,' I tell her when she gives me a funny look.

'Oh, I didn't think you were loitering,' she says. 'I thought you lived here.'

'Oh. I do. I do live here. On the third floor.'

We introduce ourselves. Her name is Hannah and she's from the Netherlands. As she turns to go back inside, I say,

'Hey! Do you want to swap numbers? Just in case . . . there's a fire or something?'

I can tell my year is already changing me. Talking to strangers has made me less shy and my experience on the friendship apps means that I'm fine making the first move, even though I still had to make it a bit weird with the whole fire thing. A few weeks later, Hannah and her husband have Sam and me over for dinner in their flat because we stored a package for them when they were on holiday. Hannah has hundreds of books and I leave her flat with an armful to borrow.

A few months later Hannah texts out of the blue, saying, 'Want to grab coffee with me right now?' And I do.

The elusive perfect friend-date: spontaneous, with good coffee, great conversation and no commute. We'd also had the spark, both having read several of the same books, both of us the same age, both of us struggling with similar things.

She'd been living downstairs the entire time. But if I hadn't gone through so many friend-dates and false starts, I know I wouldn't have asked for her number when we met. In fact, given how I normally treated my neighbours in London and how insular I was before this all began, I probably would have just pretended to be loitering.

Hannah and Abigail are beginnings. That's something. No girl squad, but a tiny little social life, just like A.N. Devers wanted. And I didn't have to become a rare book dealer. In a big, lonely city like London, for a shy introvert like me, it feels like a lot.

CROWD
CONTROL
or
networking

INT. BAR. NIGHT.

WOMAN stands at bar, clutching a drink in her hand. She turns to the MAN next to her, who makes eye contact. She gives him a tight-lipped smile.

MAN: Hi.
WOMAN: Hi.
MAN: So . . . do you know anyone here?
WOMAN: I know a guy who helps run this event. Robert?
MAN: (inaudible)
WOMAN: Sorry, what'd you say?
MAN: Oh, you're gay? You know, I thought so!
WOMAN: Huh?

MAN: You just said you're gay. So you're gay?
WOMAN: No – no, I didn't say that. I'm . . . I'm not gay.

Pause

MAN: So, what brings you to London?
WOMAN: It's a long story, but I married a British guy.
MAN: Oh. Oh really?
WOMAN: Um . . . yep. I did.
MAN: Wow. WOW.
(low whistle)
MAN (CONT'D): So you're one of those people.
WOMAN: What? What people?

Man's friend walks up.

MAN (to friend): This girl just told me she came to London because she married a rich guy!
WOMAN: What? Rich guy? NO! *British* guy! Not *rich*. He's British! BRITISH.

FADE TO BLACK

A variation on this sequence, ad infinitum, makes up the majority of my experience in networking situations. What I wanted to do after this conversation was say 'I left my oven on – BYE!' and immediately flee the scene.

I'd arrived at that event to try to make some professional connections. I'd tried my best. But sometimes, it all goes horribly wrong even when we are trying our best. So why bother at all?

Because even if we're smart and hardworking, a big factor in professional success is who you know. Research has shown that it is our outer circle of acquaintances, also known as 'weak ties', that bring about the most change in our lives. A 'strong tie' is our close friends and family, who are likely to have similar connections and knowledge to us. It is the weak ties, the people we are only loosely connected to, who are actually more influential on our lives. They bring new information, advice and perspectives: new job prospects, commissions, fresh inspiration or collaborators that we would otherwise have never discovered.

By nature, introverted and shy people tend to have smaller social circles. Which brings us to 'networking' and my clear need to have a go at being better at it. I'd talked to strangers. But what about entering an entire room full of them? Would these ties lead me to a bigger, fuller life?

Networking is all about meeting people and establishing relationships with new individuals with whom we can exchange new ideas or career opportunities. Well, that's the official definition. In reality, it feels more like *The Hunger Games* inside a crowded conference room: tepid Prosecco, name badges and awkward conversation with total strangers, but all animated by the sneaking undercurrent of, 'How can I use you to my advantage?'

Personally, I would rather volunteer as a tribute in a real-life Hunger Games. Instead of trading business cards, you could trade poisonous berries. Instead of small talk, you get to set killer wasps on your enemies. Both of which are far more exciting than a freelancer's happy hour soirée.

But I often sign up for networking events, because I want to believe this is going to be the evening that will change my life. This is the night I'll meet someone who will look into my eyes, see all of my wild, undernourished potential; take me under their wing, mentor me; and tell me I'm the new head of Netflix.

I also assure myself that by the time the event rolls around, I'll be someone else. Someone confident, social and gregarious. Able to pull off fishnet tights. Taller.

But then, when the day arrives, I'm a no-show. Skipping events is one of my top five hobbies, ranking just below watching videos of dogs jumping into piles of leaves.

Odds are, no matter who you are, you're just as abysmal as I am when it comes to sticking to plans. The United Kingdom is the 'cancellation nation' – a survey of 2,000 British people found that on average we each make 104 social arrangements a year but bail on half of them. (Only half? I'm impressed.)

But no more. After the rocky terrain of my friend-dating challenge where so many people cancelled (so much netball, so much food poisoning, so many migraines), I vowed to start showing up more. Last winter, my friend cancelled long-standing dinner plans because she was 'afraid of getting a cold'. She didn't even have the cold yet. Couldn't she have summoned the will to at least fabricate a real cold? How hard is it to send a simple sneeze emoji? The lack of effort was far more offensive than her last-minute cancelling.

I'm on holiday, I have to work late, my brother's in town, my netball team made it to the Olympics, I'm feeling plague-y, there's a Tube strike, *Bake Off* is on and it's Cake Week, my foot hurts, Mercury is in retrograde, my friend got tickets to see Beyoncé tonight and no she didn't invite me to go with her but it's making me very jealous. All code for: I just want to sit on my trusty sofa eating takeaway and I'm fine never meeting another person again and staying in my shit job for ever as long as right now, at this moment, I don't have to wear black tights and heels and get on the Tube and sit upright while stringing together cohesive sentences.

I've used all of these excuses and then some.

But I need to be the change I want to see in the world. This is clearly what Gandhi was talking about. I was going to network.

The problem is that the 10 per cent of times that I do actually attend the networking events I've signed up for, the same thing always happens: I reach the door, hear the din of conversation and stand there, coat in hand, stomach in throat. Then the door opens and reveals a full room with small groups of people already chatting in tight-knit circles, and I freeze. I don't know how to walk into the room and join a group. And if someone talks to me, inexplicably I either start rambling and over-sharing or become totally mute. Within fifteen minutes, I extricate myself, feeling hot and flustered, and head back home. Maybe now I could talk to strangers one-on-one on the street with no stakes, but in a high-pressure social atmosphere, consequences are bigger. One awkward misunderstanding or faux pas at an industry party could ruin your life for ever after you get the reputation as 'that strange woman who hovers'.

Most of my fear comes from feeling socially awkward, especially at an event where you are supposed to impress. Is there a way to learn to be more adept in these situations? After some exposing Google searches – 'how to be interesting', 'how to not be a loser in public' – and promptly clearing my search history in shame, I find what I didn't even know I was looking for: a charisma coach. Someone who holds the secret to effortless conversation and charm in professional settings. And is willing to share it with you for a fee. Who is this keeper of magical secrets?

The charisma coach is Richard Reid, a psychotherapist who coaches business leaders. He cites research that claims that magnetism is 50 per cent innate and 50 per cent learned. In fact, according to Richard, charisma is a set of behaviours that anyone can integrate into their personality.

We'll see about that.

I sit on the green therapy couch. Richard sits across from me, legs crossed. He's telling me why maintaining eye contact when shaking hands with someone new is one of the first ways to make a positive impression. I'm reeling from this because we just shook hands thirty seconds ago and I can't remember if I did this.

He assures me that I did. I settle back into the sofa, simultaneously pleased and prickled by a niggling doubt about whether he's lying to seem charismatic to me. Because it's working.

Richard maintains eye contact, his voice is steady, he smiles, he gesticulates, he has open body language. Charisma: 10/10. Would charisma again.

Richard tells me that so many of the things that come up in his charisma course overlap with his therapy practice: confidence, self-esteem, performance, body language, imposter syndrome. His course is popular with men – who are more likely to associate therapy with a stigma, and therefore would not go, but they are open to learning how to become more charming or successful at work.

I tell Richard that when I meet new people in a group setting, I become anxious. I'm fine one-on-one. But in groups of people, I panic. They seem to rotate around me but never touch me, like I am the sun, but instead of the sun, I am a social pariah. Richard nods, understandingly; a small encouraging smile and just the slightest furrow of his brow tells me that he empathizes, that it's tough, but there is a way through. God, he's good.

'The part of the brain that gauges situations is very, very primitive,' he says. 'It's what we call the reptilian brain. The human brain is pre-disposed to thinking about safety – we don't necessarily think about social situations as being explicitly dangerous, but the brain can perceive them in the same way that it would a physical threat.'

It comes back to me in a flash: the time I walked into a room full of hundreds of attractive women in heels and neat men in business suits for a generic meet-up I'd found online. I'd accidentally slammed the door very loudly on the way in and they all swivelled to stare at me in unison. At first I was confused: there was so much cologne in the air and so many well-groomed women in high heels that I felt like I had erroneously stumbled into a dating event. As I felt the endless pairs of eyes lingering on me, I felt a flush creep up my neck. I backed out slowly, like a hiker trying to placate a bear, and shut the door quietly behind me.

I push the thought out of my head.

'So it's just too many stimuli to take in at once?' I ask.

'Absolutely.'

Typically, introverts weigh decisions more carefully than extroverts. We're better at one-on-one situations because it's easier to judge how people are disposed towards us and what they might do next if there is only one person to process. Richard says that when we start interacting with ten people or more, it becomes nerve-wracking because there are too many things to monitor.

I tell Richard that when I enter a room full of strangers it feels impossible to make contact with people who are already in conversation.

I see Richard note my alert eyes and my position perched on the edge of the sofa.

'Go slow,' he says. 'Don't just throw your hand into a group and say, "Hi! I'm Jess" before they've even seen you. You don't want to alarm their reptilian brains.' I once saw a nature documentary where a cornered lizard squirted blood out of its eyes. Nope. I don't want that. Hard pass.

He tells me to make eye contact with people, smile and join on the end of the group. Nod at appropriate times. Then wait for a gap to join in and introduce myself. This feels like a manual for human behaviour 101, but I clearly need it.

My go-to move at these events is to grab a drink and then sit in the farthest, dimmest corner I can find, darkly admiring the fancy-free revellers from afar before transforming back into a bat and disappearing into the night. I try to describe this to Richard in a way that sounds sane.

'You're rehearsing being excluded from conversations without realizing it,' Richard says. He tells me I'm sticking to the periphery as a safety precaution, once again guided by my reptilian brain, who always wants an easy escape.

This makes sense. When I'm anxious, my mind goes blank as a slate and I actually become more reptilian: shifty and unable to control my own body temperature. It's the same feeling I get when I'm in the spotlight in front of a crowd.

Richard tells me to re-imagine the scenario as if I'm the host at the party and everybody there is my guest. He says this is a good way to shift my attention away from feeling self-conscious: offer people a drink, ask how they got there, ask if they know anyone else. Introduce them to other people. Make them take off their shoes and play bridge?

I nod. I don't say, 'I've never thrown a party in my life, Richard.' I like the idea of flouncing around like I own the place.

When I think about the concept of 'charisma' and those who seek it, I think of men spouting tawdry one-liners in an effort to be charming. Wannabe alpha males, who laugh loudly and slap their thighs. Intense eye contact. Chest hair.

Hair gel. Cheesy grins. Knowing winks. Tobacco pipes. Gold chains. Maybe I'm thinking of pirates.

Richard agrees that rehearsed behaviour is cringey and that charisma is all about the energy we bring to a situation. It's about assessing the room, asking the right questions and having the right responses. Matching the energy of the person we're talking to.

I look down at my legs on the green couch. I look at Richard. Screw it – this is the closest I'm ever going to get to free therapy.

'So . . . what would you say my energy is?' I ask.

Richard considers.

'The biggest thing you bring is warmth. And that's hard to manufacture. You come across as a very warm person. That's your biggest strength,' he says. Before I can react, he goes on:

'Your confidence is what you need to work on,' he says. 'You apologize too much.'

All right, Richard, it was just a question.

'You're hesitant with questions. You speak quickly.'

I said, all right!

I clear my throat and ask him how one can learn to be charismatic.

According to Richard, radiating charisma is actually easy and can be done in a couple of simple steps: ask an open-ended question (not something that can be answered with a 'yes' or a 'no'), listen to someone's answer and then show how much you care about their response by asking them a meaningful follow-up question: How did they feel about that? What was that like? What appealed to you about that?

And then, crucially, you validate their feelings:

> 'I work as a dog walker and hang out with dogs all day.'
> 'What's that like?'
> 'It's amazing, and I love it. Dogs are the best.'
> 'Yes, they are. That does seem amazing. I would love it, too! You are brilliant.'

That's it? That's all charisma is?

I think about the most charismatic man I know. He looks like Jude Law, he's a film producer and he . . . he does this to a tee. This is his signature move! You walk away from every encounter with him thinking, 'God, Ollie is such a good, kind, caring guy. And so handsome!' But all he really does is say, 'And how did you feel about that?' at exactly the right moment, echo your feelings back at you, pay you a compliment and end with a beguiling smile. That handsome little shit. That clever, sneaky, beautiful snake-man.

Just as I'm feeling slightly deceived by Ollie, Richard steps in again.

'Authenticity is also important,' he reminds me. 'You have to be genuinely interested in someone and in connecting with them or they'll sense insincerity.'

It's basic but necessary guidance. Most interactions at these events are Surface Self talk: what do you do, what are you working on – it rarely deviates into Deep Self talk: OK, but how often do you cry at the office? Do you get bullied at work? Do you ever think that maybe it's dog walkers who have everything figured out in life?

Richard tells me that most people are stuck in their work routines and they don't take the time to reflect on how they feel about things, or they think they don't have permission to talk about these things with other people. At networking events, people tend to be guarded or over-eager to please, but if you let them vent their feelings and show them some empathy and compassion, you can create a real connection. But you gotta move fast, because these encounters tend to be brief. It's essentially applying what I learned about talking to strangers, but to the max, revved up at top speed.

As I gather my things to go, I ask Richard if he's an introvert or an extrovert.

'I'm a massive introvert,' he says.

'What? No, you're not,' I say.

Richard looks startled.

'But you lead big conferences! You're active in the media and you have to be with people all day,' I add.

'I've learned to play up the extrovert side: it's a fact that extroverts have massive advantages, so I'm self-taught,' he says.

Ah, my master.

'Could you go to Glastonbury solo and make friends?' I ask Richard, as I put on my coat to go. I like to ask others how they would handle our ninth circle of hell.

'I could, yeah.'

'But would you *want* to go?' I ask him. Just to make sure we are on the same page.

'I can't think of anywhere I'd want to be less,' he says.

'Me too!' I say. 'Were you always this way?'

'Even when I was younger, I never, ever wanted to go.'

'I feel the same way. It gives me great pleasure *not* to be there,' I say vehemently.

He beams for the first time in the entire session.

'Me too,' he says.

In the lift on my way out, I think back over our final exchange and realize that I'd asked Richard a genuine question, had him admit his true feelings and then validated them with my own.

Now, who is the master?

Not me. I held the elusive secret to charisma in the clammy palm of my hand, but, as Richard had pointed out, I am lacking in confidence. In an effort to get geared up for more events, I start saying yes to more things. My friend Sarah (we were set up by a mutual friend who had moved away, but who knew I was looking for more friends) invites me to a book launch.

Shortly after I arrive, Sarah introduces me to her friend: Daisy Buchanan. She's the agony aunt for *Grazia*, and has written a book called *How to be a Grown-Up*. In her book, she talks about all the socializing she has done for her job. Plus, she's used to women coming up to her crying and asking for help. If anyone can help me get over myself and storm the London networking scene, it's her.

I want to know what she thinks would help someone gain confidence or be better at networking.

Daisy is game. She doles out advice for a living, and it shows: she's perceptive, thoughtful and nuanced. When I ask her about whether networking is really worth the pain for a shy introvert, she tells me, 'You absolutely never know when people are going to turn up in your life again. You have nothing to lose and everything to gain. You might gain friends and opportunity *and* an enjoyable evening.'

When it comes to the constant cancelling and de rigueur flakiness, Daisy explains that she has had panic attacks and cancelled on events because of anxiety in the past. 'Now I know the difference in myself when I'm anxious and it's making me ill,' she says, explaining that this is a perfectly valid reason to cancel. 'But if I'm just feeling a bit rundown and want to hide behind "self-care", then I know I should probably show up for my commitments.'

OK but what about if I really, really just want to stay home on my sofa?

'Sometimes the best thing for our mental health is Netflix and takeaway and sometimes, actually, it's so much healthier to leave the house, go outside, see people and experience something new.' The agony aunt has spoken.

Then she says conspiratorially, 'And any shy, introverted person should always go to a party with an exit strategy.'

I nod and take her final lesson to heart, feeling merrily bolstered as I excuse myself from the party because the Planet Organic next door is shutting soon and I need rice milk.

I tried a lot of networking events this year, and at each one I had the same three types of encounters. So will you.

You will meet one person who is very nice but with whom you have absolutely nothing in common. You exchange numbers you have no intention of using, and then they will say something like, 'I think we're supposed to circulate' and walk away. You'll think, 'OK, that's literally a line in *Bridget Jones*' and you'll be simultaneously relieved and slightly wounded by this cut from someone you don't know or particularly like. You will never ever see or think of them ever again.

You will meet one person who is interesting, and you bond over the awkwardness of the event. This person usually has impeccably applied lipstick, so you both respect and fear them. You ask about what they do and they ask you about what you do, and you are both genuinely engaged in the conversation. Then she says, 'I'm leaving the country for three months, but I'll be in touch when I get back.' There is a 50 per cent chance that she actually will. You follow each other on Twitter. (Or she emails you but your schedules are incompatible for the next few months. Either way, it will be three months until you can see each other again.) You will eventually grab coffee together. You might become best friends or Twitter friends who never see each other again. She may one day send a job opportunity your way.

You will meet one person, let down your guard now that you've been at the event for a few hours and had a few drinks. You're a tiny bit drunk (maybe on alcohol – or just high on how sociable you're being, my God, you're doing so well!), you ramble on for a bit. Maybe you confess things you don't really want to confess ('I used to be in love with my former boss!') and will definitely regret it in the morning. But before you know it, they sting you – something like, 'I love how you think about things in such a small-town way. It's charming,' and then you feel small and go get your coat and sit on the bus on the way home texting your best friend who lives abroad, asking, 'Do I think of everything in a small-town way???'

It's the jumping into conversations that is the hardest and most awkward part of the entire process. Think of it like plunging into a cold body of water (Daisy's analogy). After that first leap, eventually you'll warm up and the rest is usually relatively easy.

For one of my first outings after meeting Richard and Daisy, I show up at a happy hour event I found on Twitter for people who are interested in discussing films. I want to find out more about the industry, so decide this could be a great place to start.

As soon as I walk in, I recognize someone I've met before, a blond actor, who is deep in conversation with a dark-haired man. I resolve to say hello and remember Richard's advice: go slowly. With measured movements, keeping all my limbs in check, I make my way across the room, keeping the two of them in my eye line.

It's just like hunting, I think. Stay quiet, wait for the right moment; don't scare my prey.

Finally, I'm level with them. I hover in their blind spot just as the dark-haired man says, 'I'm from the North.' They stop talking when they realize I'm beside them.

'Hi!' I say. I smile. Like a normal human being.

'Hi,' the blond actor says.

Then he excuses himself to get another drink. I'm left standing with the dark-haired man (also why don't we call men 'brunette'? Something to ponder, though perhaps not the right ice-breaker at this moment).

'I'm Jess,' I say to him.

'I'm Paul,' he says. We look at each other and say nothing. The moment goes on for a beat too long. I'd read somewhere that it takes four seconds to create an awkward silence. We make it to eight.

ASK HIM A QUESTION, my reptilian brain commands.

'Where in the North are you from?' I ask.

'Just a small town in Lancashire,' he says, in a throwaway tone that implies, 'You wouldn't know it.'

I've been to The North. I can talk The North. I married into The North. (Who? Just some rich guy.)

'Oh? Where?' I say.

'Clitheroe,' he says.

'Oh! I've been to Clitheroe. I hunted for witches there,' I say.

'What?'

'You know how you guys killed all those witches up there? During the witch trials in 1612? I went to Pendle Hill to look for their ghosts on Halloween to write about it for a feature.'

Looking at Paul's face, I realize that sharing my passion for looking for the ghosts of dead witches at Halloween might not be the *right* fun tidbit to share about myself at networking events. I'd just been so excited to actually say something about Clitheroe. But had I gone too far? But then ...

'Pendle Hill? That's ... that's right next to my town!' Paul says.

'I know! I stayed in a haunted hotel in Clitheroe,' I say.

'Really?' he asks.

'Yes. How ... how do you feel about that?' I ask. I've been given a rulebook and I'm sticking to it.

'I think ... that's really weird that you went there but amazing!' Paul says.

'It is weird and it is amazing,' I say, validating his feelings and opinions. 'Do you believe in ghosts?' I ask.

Paul pauses, and then launches enthusiastically into a story about the time he saw the ghost of a twelve-year-old girl standing on a wall outside his house. I have so many legitimate questions that the conversation flows easily for the rest of the evening.

Fast-forward a few months: Paul and I are real friends now. I know!

Of all the people I've met while networking, Paul is my first proper success story, the one who stepped gratifyingly out of bounds of the circular three scenarios above. He's a travel writer and we're both freelancers, so we have a lot of common ground that isn't exclusively ghost-related. Now we read each other's work, talk on WhatsApp, and share travel and writing advice.

I now know that the only way for real personal connections to occur is to go out there, and do the best I can with Richard's charisma advice fresh in my mind (ask questions, give meaningful responses, reinforce emotions). The charisma charm offensive propels you through the awkward beginnings, allowing you to get to a real connection and reach the important questions: 'Do you know any ghosts? How old are they? Were they nice to you?'

Meeting Paul had been a bright spot in a sea of average networking events. See, try as I might, the thing I can't move past is that I have yet to actually enjoy a networking event. I might be getting there on the talking to strangers front but a whole bunch of them in a crowded, forced scenario is exhausting.

Was there a better way to network? Would I always actively hate this important part of professional life, even if I was getting slightly better at doing it?

Emma Gannon is a writer and podcaster who frequently features on lists called things like '30 Under 30'. She wrote the acclaimed book *The Multi-Hyphen Method*, hosts high-profile events and has met the Queen at Buckingham Palace. Her book emphasizes the importance of making personal, meaningful connections that can jumpstart your career. What's the secret to her networking success? Does she just jump from networking event to professional soirée and back again, and if so, why isn't she in a hole crying?

I email Emma and ask her what her game plan is in these situations. Her response changes my life:

'I honestly avoid these situations. I have never had any meaningful interaction at a stale networking event where people wear big name badges. A dinner or some casual drinks with a smallish group of new people, on the other hand, is absolutely amazing for "networking". The trick is to create an environment where you don't feel like you're doing it.'

I don't need to charisma the hell out of half of London. Emma just handed me a Get Out of Jail Free card.

I decide to only attend professional events that also seem fun. I figure out exactly what I'm looking for at these events: inspiration, knowledge, camaraderie, new friends, professional advice.

I stop signing up for big networking events and instead look for more interesting evenings. I come across one called 'Good Girls Eat Dinner' on Instagram, which is described as 'the most interesting dinner party you'll ever go to'. The evening involves mini-lectures by women in various creative industries served up alongside a three-course meal. I end up sitting next to a former magazine publisher and we bond over being introverts who will be bolting back to our quiet homes soon. She's now a life coach: she gives me her card and then introduces me to an editor she knows. It's clear to me that networking is actually about giving, not getting. Sharing what you know. We want to help other people who we feel a connection with. The dinner is a success, but best of all, it's so much more enjoyable than the normal shtick: mainly because we are sitting down and eating pizza.

Later that week, I attend a meet-up I'd seen on Facebook: several other writers are getting together for coffee and discussion at a cafe. It ends up only being me and two other women, but of course introverts love this: we actually get to know each other and exchange industry advice, while drinking coffee and eating scones.

After a month of exclusively attending events with either good food or excellent speakers, the plan seems to be working. I've been to small, intimate gatherings, evenings brimming with interesting strangers. I might even be enjoying it a little.

Somehow, there is only one mishap, at a charity event, where I tell a heavily pregnant woman who is desperate to get out of a hen do in Ibiza the following year that she ought to threaten to take her newborn and then she'll be swiftly uninvited.

'I AM going to take my newborn!' she exclaims, curling her hands protectively around her belly, as if I've just said I'm going to throw it into the sea.

'Oh, well that sounds brilliant!' I say, completing an exchange I will replay in my head every night in bed for a week.

I make a few rules before each event. Go with an intention. Talk to three people, with Richard's advice in mind, and aim to really bond or connect with one person. Psychologists also say that it takes time for shy people to warm up, so if you always leave after ten minutes, you're never giving yourself the chance to actually succeed. Stay for at least an hour.

Also, don't arrive late. This is very hard to do for an event that you're dragging yourself to, stopping at every distraction along the way, but when you show up in the middle of an event, the crowd feels impenetrable. Arriving five minutes early gives you a moment to ease your nerves and connect with people as they arrive.

The likelihood is that none of these evenings will change your life immediately. But the message from Richard, from Daisy and from Emma was, at heart, the same: it's a long game. It's a slow burn. Less of a hunt, actually, and more of a sprinkling of seeds in the soil.

So many friendships these days begin online, and Emma is a big advocate for bringing them over into real life at least once, to cement that bond. Which is why, a few months later, I'm eating homemade banana bread and sitting in front of a fireplace with Kate, a woman I'd met on Twitter. She'd tweeted that she had just recently moved to a new city and was having trouble making friends and did anyone else feel this way?

Someone else did. I replied, and now her two black kittens scurry around our feet while we drink tea in her living room. Is this making friends, networking with another writer or is this just the cosiest afternoon of my life? Does it matter?

Over the next few months, as I talk to more people, ask more questions and disclose more about myself, I notice that people start approaching me more. It's like I've changed on some molecular level: people walk into rooms and make a beeline for me. *Me*.

I think I might be charisma-ing.

It permeates all aspects of my life. While I'm working at a magazine office on a freelance shift, the editor next to me strikes up a conversation about what I'm working on. Then, I ask her a question about an article she edited about sperm donors and we start discussing it in depth (did you know that in the UK there was a sperm shortage and so we had to import vast amounts of sperm from Scandinavia? I did not!).

She and I spend a good twenty minutes talking about sperm (truly a magnificent topic), then dry shampoo, then book recommendations. We talk so much that we get distracted from our work. And it clicks. I've been on so many average friend-dates and had so many lacklustre networking chats that I now recognize chemistry when I see it. I take the leap of faith and ask for her number.

She invites me to her book club. This time, I don't have to walk into an unfamiliar flat full of strangers alone – I walk in with her, my new friend, who introduces me to everyone.

A small book club, at someone's house, eating homemade pie: this was where I want to be. It is somehow one of the most outgoing things I have ever done and also somehow feels kinda normal. Everyone here works in the same field, but we aren't talking about work. We are drinking wine and discussing the book over dinner. Casual. Intimate. This is what Emma had meant. And it all started with a single question: what was the deal with all this sperm from Denmark in the noughties?

As I type this, I'm actually supposed to be getting ready for a networking event this very evening. And I want to bail. So much. I want that sweet, sweet hit of cancelling on something that's good for me in the long run. I haven't grown out of this addiction: I'll always want that fix.

There are nights, especially in winter, when the sun has set at 3.45 p.m. and I know as soon as work is over I need to go straight home, have a bath, put on pyjamas, eat a bowl of pasta and watch *The Office* reruns. Or I want to bake an entire carrot cake with cream cheese frosting while blasting Ani DiFranco alone in my kitchen and then I need to eat as much of it as I want while drinking a cup of tea and reading a novel that has zero murders in it. (Though it is a stereotype that introverts like to sit at home and bake. An acquaintance tells me, 'Look, some introverts just want to watch a violent movie while eating salad.') There are nights when I'd pay good money to do this rather than go out. A cover charge for sitting at home. This will never change.

But somehow, through getting out of my comfort zone, meeting people and extroverting hard, I've grown to hate bailing on people. It stops relationships in their tracks. It prevents so many new beginnings from turning into something real. So if it isn't one of those anxiety-fraught nights when I'm genuinely on the verge, then I decide I'm not going to let myself bail. I'll put on my shoes and grab my coat and bag before I can even think to myself, 'Oooh, I have a frozen pizza . . .'

Emma thinks it's fine to say no to events, but that we should commit to the ones we've said yes to. 'I hate flakiness and I blame the Facebook "Maybe" button,' she tells me. 'It's not OK to say "maybe" and see if something better comes up. I believe in saying a solid "yes" or "no" because it's polite. Saying "no" is hard, but ultimately makes you a better person. For example, I've been invited to lots of parties (which is so nice!) but I am saying "no" to lots of them because I simply don't have time. It's not rude, it's being honest.'

Paul (has seen ghosts, from Clitheroe) tells me that when he feels too intimidated to walk into a room full of strangers, he tries to go with a friend or colleague and agree to split up for the first hour (this is an obviously great idea that I did not think to do once in my whole life before now). And I've learned that actually, you don't really have to schmooze. You can go to a Q&A or a guest lecture and then just chat with the people next to you for fifteen minutes at the end. Ask someone a few questions, listen to their answers, get their details if you want to meet them again. Following up with people I've genuinely connected with is key – otherwise, I might as well have stayed home with that pizza.

And obviously, always have an exit strategy.

THE WEDDING
IN GERMANY

a real-life interlude

Two days ago, Sam and I flew into Germany for a friend's summer wedding. Sam is the best man. The official wedding ceremony was held in a castle in the German countryside yesterday; today, the couple has booked a beerhouse for a second full day of wedding celebrations.

The groom wears lederhosen. The bride wears a *dirndl* dress (think classy German beer maid). She's standing on top of a table, addressing her guests. Confident, loud, funny.

At most weddings I attend, including this one, I don't know any of the other guests because I am Sam's plus one — obviously, Sam has more friends than I do. Surrounded by unfamiliar faces and enforced dancing, I spend a lot of the day finding excuses to pop outside, downing water so that I can escape to the bathroom and taking pretend phone calls in empty corridors. It's got nothing to do with the wedding or the people getting married, but after a few hours (usually in that agonizingly long break between the ceremony and the sit-down dinner), I simply run out of things to say. My energy is sapped.

The sad thing is, I love a wedding. Seeing people give themselves over to the sort of giddy public joy we rarely see in our day-to-day lives fills me with happiness.

But after my twentieth wedding, I began to secretly think that maybe weddings are a little . . . long. Like a socializing marathon I'll never have trained enough for.

Wouldn't it be fantastic if the celebrations came in at under two hours? Bride down the aisle, emotional vows, champagne toasts, salmon puffs, first dance, cut the cake, eat the cake, two fast Beyoncés, one slow Adele, one big Whitney, fin.

In Germany, though, after so much networking practice, I felt as ready as I'd ever be for the socializing marathon. I wondered if I would spend the day differently from the way I had at the last wedding I went to, where I wandered off alone and stared at the sea.

On the first day of celebrations, I was surprised to find myself in a very pleasant conversation with a Dutchman who told me about his job in the army. I ended up asking another guest about the best way to make friends in a new city (join an ultimate Frisbee team). I danced, a tiny bit, to Queen. I even debated the many merits of a cheese course with my tablemates late into the night.

Lots of people feel slightly apprehensive before big parties. I knew a girl at university who once, rightly, said to me: 'Just do what we *all* do before a big social event – buck up, spray dry shampoo in your hair and rapidly down two bottles of warm white wine upon arrival.'

Unfortunately, genetics stand immovably in my way. Because I am half-Chinese, I suffer from 'Asian glow', which bears zero resemblance to the pregnant-woman glow, although both involve excessive vomiting. My body cannot process alcohol properly – it leaves my skin red hot and my eyes bloodshot within an hour of drinking.

This also means I have an incredibly low alcohol tolerance. When I get drunk, I quickly either become the person sobbing quietly into the curtains or the one running laps around the dance floor playing a one-woman game of tag, *or* the one ripping her tights off and sleeping underneath the dessert table. And I don't get to pick which.

And so my one-glass-of-champagne reserves of charisma and social prowess are finite. We had gone to bed at 3 a.m. and reconvened at 9 a.m. for a group breakfast to start the next day of celebrating. There had been no chance to recharge; I had nothing left.

Now, sitting in the beerhouse on Day Two, channelling what little is left of my energy into pretending to like beer, I want to be there for our newlywed friends, for Sam . . . but I also really want to find a nice Alpine meadow to lie down in for a few hours and nap.

If I'm hand-on-heart honest, the only thing really keeping me going is that I find grown men wearing lederhosen one of the most simultaneously confounding and pleasing things in life, and they are everywhere today. I am exhausted, but I am also enchanted.

Then Anja, the bride, claps her hands together and climbs on top of the table. The guests around me pause, their enormous steins crash back to the tables – it's impossible to hold them halfway to their mouths for long.

My very favourite part of any wedding is the speeches. Yes, they have the potential to be atrocious, but more often than not I find them uniquely moving. I love it when people cry just talking about how much their partner, their friends and their family mean to them. I love to learn more about the bride and groom, and hear jokes and stories about them. But today I'm particularly in awe.

Anja is giving a speech at her own wedding, and it's something I would never have dared to do.

Sam and I got married in a barn in the Lake District. Our invite list was minimal (see: shintrovert), topping out at twenty guests for dinner. I knew I didn't want a huge wedding, and given that most of my friends and family lived on other continents, I didn't want to ask them to travel thousands of miles for lunch and a walk in the drizzle. (Also, if I'm completely honest with myself, a small part of me was afraid I'd invite them and they wouldn't come and then I'd be offended for ever. So I had a tiny wedding, thinking I'd outsmarted the whole system, and instead wound up offending whole swathes of people.)

My wedding was a good day, it's a very happy memory. But even then, I woke up the next morning feeling – above all else – relief. The pressure of coordinating a room full of drunk friends and family, emotions running high, all while trying to achieve peak hotness was over. Best day of my life? Perhaps.

But personally, I'd take eating leftovers in my tracksuit with my husband over the rigmarole of marrying him again.

In English weddings, traditionally, only men give toasts: the father of the bride, then the groom and finally the best man. Now I can't say I'm devoted to tradition as a rule, and I'm a feminist, dammit, but this was one rule I was happy to go along with.

While I couldn't have fathomed at the time how to juggle crippling nerves and public emotion, now, watching Anja speak – as she thanks her best friend and tells a story about her mother – I remember how I had felt at Union Chapel, so alive, so electric, and something begins to stir in me.

In the US, tradition dictates that the maid of honour usually gives a speech at the wedding rehearsal dinner. When I was twenty-five, I was the maid of honour at Jori's wedding back in Texas. There were twelve bridesmaids. Hundreds of guests. The rehearsal dinner was held on her family's ranch. I had to wear cowboy boots and a suede vest because the dress code was 'ranch formal', and perversely, I think this actually helped because I felt more like a barnyard entertainer than a vulnerable person crying in public, afraid she was losing her childhood best friend. I stood up, I spoke quietly, I cried loudly and I sat back down. Nerve-wracking moment, great memory.

The other time I was the maid of honour was in Chengdu, China, a few years ago. The original maid of honour was due to give birth at any moment and was stuck in Beijing – I'd been assigned as the back-up, plus the real maid of honour was also Chinese–American and named Jessica so it was an easy swap.

The wedding was held in a Chinese restaurant with a makeshift stage. Overall, the experience was not dissimilar from my TV reporting experience in that a make-up artist chased me around a room, hugely disappointed in both my eye make-up and how quickly I was sweating it off.

The Irish best man, Seamus, also had stage fright. We kept whipping each other up into a frenzy of hysteria about how we were going to die. How this would end us. Seamus coped by getting horrendously drunk and, next to him, I coped by shovelling food into my mouth, ignoring warnings about the ferociously hot, homegrown Chinese red chilli peppers. A concerned guest told me that they would wreak havoc on my intestines the next day. As if I was worried about my intestines. As if I was worried about tomorrow. I was addressing hundreds of people in an hour. Screw tomorrow, pass the spicy beef.

Just before my speech, the wedding planner grabbed me to tell me that I was also in charge of the tea ceremony. As maid of honour, I needed to serve tea to the bride's parents, then to the groom's parents, onstage in front of everyone. I had to do all of this while kneeling to show respect; if I presented the tea cups in the wrong order, the wedding planner implied that there was a fifty-fifty chance my Chinese ancestors would smite me. Then I had to say in Mandarin to each elder, 'Please drink the tea.' I was so petrified of screwing it up that when the time rolled around for my speech, I spoke for about twenty-seven seconds.

Did I stress about publicly speaking at both these weddings? So much. But it felt different because I was doing it for my friends. I would never shirk from something my friends had asked of me. Especially not on such an important day. Of course I'd do it for them. For me, though? God no.

At my own wedding, I was relieved to take the backseat. I was already so worried about my British in-laws meeting my parents for the first time, about walking down the aisle in a long, form-fitting dress, about wearing heels, about my mascara running, about stuttering on my vows, about everyone getting along, about the photographer showing up on time. I was so anxious that I didn't have the capacity to factor in a speech on top of all of that.

But I wish that I'd been as brave as Anja. She may be wearing a *dirndl* but she is smiling and happy and sloshing beer from her glass. I am struck by how saying things out loud, declaring them to people, makes them seem more real. How these once-in-a-lifetime occasions come and then they go. How I do not want to regret not doing the thing – whatever the thing may be – any more.

When I get to my hotel room after the wedding, I sleep for eleven hours straight, but not because of the after effects of a wild, boozy night. I just needed time for my brain to recover from all the emotion and different stimuli and new people it had encountered that weekend. It wasn't the wedding's fault – it was a great wedding, one of Sam's favourites ever. It was my fault. And it kind of always would be. I'm anti-social anywhere after Hour Three, which is when I turn into dust.

Grumpy dust. And I'm finally accepting that I can't train myself out of that, no matter how many networking events I go to.

I will never win Most Popular Wedding Guest. I'll most likely be remembered for hanging out near the bathroom dithering with my phone.

When Sam and I are back in London, we have dinner with his friends Mikko and Cassie. A few years ago, we'd also been to their wedding (I'd stared at the lawn furniture instead of the sea). I ask if they are introverts or extroverts because it's my new favourite question, especially for couples.

Before they answer, I hazard a guess that Mikko, who is Finnish, is an introvert.

'Way to stereotype me and my countrymen,' he says.

'Right, but are you?' I ask him.

'I could happily be alone on an island for a week,' he nods. 'That would be bliss.'

'Whereas I'd kill myself,' Cassie, who is English, interjects. 'I wouldn't last a day.'

'You wouldn't last five minutes,' Mikko says.

Looking at them, I realize that I have only been to one other wedding where the bride spoke. Theirs. Cassie had stood up and given a brilliant, funny, heartwarming speech – probably the best speech of the night. Cassie must be a natural, I think. She is one of the most extroverted people I have ever met: she loves festivals and I bet she's made friends on the Tube.

But that night she confesses that she never gives presentations at work and used to stutter so badly at school that she had never really spoken publicly before her wedding day. This is astounding.

'Were you nervous?' I ask her.

'Well, I was just telling people that I love them. I didn't say anything groundbreaking or interesting. I just waffled away about all these people that I love. That's all it was.'

'Just the thought of showing emotion to a group of people makes my hands start to clam up,' I say. 'You didn't feel that?'

She pauses, considering, and then shakes her head.

'If you're lucky enough to have people who love you and who you love, then how wonderful is it that you get to tell them?' she says. 'I just really wanted to tell them how much they all meant to me.'

Well, when she put it that way, I felt like a selfish arsehole.

Researcher and public speaker Brené Brown says that connection is why we're here. That humans are neurobiologically built for it – but the only way we'll ever make connections is to allow ourselves to be seen, really seen.

Apparently, we're not designed to watch TV, sit at our desks and stare at our phones. We're wired for connection with others – and the quickest way to connect with another human is by showing vulnerability. But when I imagine doing that in public, well ...

Dry mouth. Short breaths. Vomit. Showing vulnerability in front of an audience is scary as hell to me. Though I don't think I'm alone in this.

In Viv Groskop's book, *How to Own the Room*, she writes, 'Some women don't need so much help with public speaking as with the self-doubt and self-loathing that hold them back from getting involved in it.'

If I had given a speech at my wedding, it would have been horrible. I would have lost it, taken one look at my mother and sobbed. Ugly-crying caught on camera for eternity. I would have blubbered. Stuttered. Told a joke that didn't land. Offended my grandmother. Shown off a less than ideal upper-arm angle. Guffawed in an embarrassing way that would haunt me for ever.

It would have been awful.

It might have been amazing.

The chance to publicly tell my parents how exceptionally moved I was about all they had done for me and to thank them for accepting Sam into the family so seamlessly. How grateful I was to my then-eighty-five-year-old grandparents for flying from Los Angeles to London and then enduring a hellish ten-hour drive in a van in the hammering rain to the Lake District. To my brothers for wrangling my grandparents into that van. To my in-laws for being so kind. To my maid of honour Jori for walking down the aisle moments after she had accidentally rammed her face into a cabinet, giving herself an immediate black eye, which also selflessly made her look a tiny bit worse for when she stood next to me. And for so much more, of course.

Every time I think about these things, I feel a twinge of sadness. There's a not-insignificant part of me that's sad that chance is gone for ever now. I'd told them these things one-on-one, right? Or maybe I hadn't and they didn't know.

If I had my time again, I would panic, feel nauseous and then go into the tiny hotel loo and take those deep breaths the way Alice taught me, until I was steady enough on my feet to go out there, tap a glass with a spoon and take centre-stage.

I hadn't known Alice then, but how different I feel now. Now I know how saying words out loud can give weight to a moment and show that I take my words and story seriously. That I could be scared, but I could still do it anyway.

Frankly, it was wonderful to watch Anja give a speech at her own wedding – not least because the men deserved to hear how pretty they looked in their lederhosen.

FREE-FALLING

or

improvisation

'Imagine you're in *Indiana Jones and the Temple of Doom*,' the man says. 'One by one, I want each of you to walk into the centre of the "temple" and "die" an imaginary death, until you create a pile of bodies. How you die is up to you. And remember, you're dead, so stay in character after you do this.'

I look around at everyone else. They're grinning and jumping around, excited for this first exercise. I hate these joyful bastards.

The instructor starts humming the film's theme tune. He gestures for the rest of the class to join in the humming.

'Dun dun dun duh, dun dun duhhhh . . .'

This might be the end of me. I'm allergic to all of these things: earnest enthusiasm, elaborate performance and spontaneous action in front of strangers.

I shuffle back so as to avoid going first. The first man enters the 'temple'. He elaborately mimes ducking to avoid a low-swinging pendulum, then stumbles, trips and falls back on to a sword that goes straight through him. A girl follows in behind him, miming getting shot with a succession of arrows from an invisible assailant, and collapses near the man.

Another person enters and swiftly dies. And another. Another. It's getting closer and closer to my turn.

'Dun dun dun DA, dun da dun dun dA . . .'

I am in my own personal Temple of Doom. It's my turn. My feet move fast because I'm nervous, but I'm so flustered that, while dodging the bodies, I end up tripping and falling palms first on the ground. My right hand skids across the floor so fast that I get carpet burn on my palm. I land so squarely on top of a fifty-year-old Canadian man that he and I are now married in the eyes of God.

He kicks me off, clearly failing to commit to his death, and I bite back a yelp.

I lie on the ground, strangers' feet in my hair, my nose buried in the ground, my hand stinging and starting to bleed. The humming of the theme tune carries on.

No. I can't do this.

'What's the best way to meet more people?'

I posted this question on Facebook, vowing that I would do whatever people suggested. You know. Crowd-sourcing. Hive mind. Tribe. The masses. My community would give me brilliant ideas that would change my life.

Then some arsehole in the tribe replied with, 'Improv comedy.'

Is there a phrase that carries a greater sense of dread than 'improv comedy'? That is guaranteed to make people scream in horror when you mention it at parties? Only 'Gwyneth's jade egg' or 'cash only' can compete.

When I ask my go-to extroverts what they think about doing improv, one says, 'That is my worst nightmare.' Another one, a stand-up comedian, says, 'I would never!' and puts her hand over her chest, like she is a swooning Southern belle I've greatly offended. Great, so this was something that makes extroverts uneasy, and I'm barely halfway through my year. And it's not just that they don't want to perform it. They don't even want to go and watch it.

I think this may be because improv people are theatre kids off their leashes. And boy, are they evangelical. Improv. Marmite. Primark. Those chewy tapioca balls in bubble tea. They divide the nation: you either really love it or you really, really hate it.

So what exactly is it? 'Improvisation' is live theatre where the plot, characters and dialogue are made up spontaneously by the actors onstage.

It's basically what children do when left to themselves: they 'play'. It's generally considered: adorable when you're five in your back garden; encouraged at summer camp; tolerated at university; and a terrible career choice that invites pity and judgement if you're over twenty-five.

To me, improv is free-form dying. Like jumping off a cliff, but you can't look down because oh, that's right, no one told you what's going to happen next and you don't want to see the hellpit you're going to land in. My mind always blanks when I'm put on the spot – in improv, there is nowhere but 'the spot'.

This isn't only about performance. It's about spontaneity. Making it up as you go along. Surrounded by other people. You can't plan for what's going to happen next, you have to react, but you're not sure how and you often have no control over who you're interacting with and what nonsense they're going to throw at you.

You know. Like real life. Which is why it's so bloody scary to me. No matter how much we plan, life is a set of unpredictable curveballs, one after the other. I'd love to get better at rolling with them.

What's interesting to me is why do so many other people cower at the idea of doing improv or watching it? 'My worst nightmare' my extroverted friend had told me. Live, made-up theatre: this is really people's worst nightmare? This is what is keeping people up at night?

See, everyone says they hate the idea of participating in improv because you have to make it up as you go, you can't plan ahead, you can freeze under pressure or you can be caught looking stupid – and everything that happens is all your fault.

It's true. All of these things can and do happen in improv. Plus, given the improvised nature of the performance, watching it can also be anxiety-inducing. It can go terribly wrong, and audiences don't want to cringe on behalf of the performers or sit through bad comedy for an hour.

But I think people really can't stand it for another reason. And it's this: while watching a regional comedy troupe acting out an Uber journey through Nudist Narnia, they observe the performers' joyous, earnest expressions. The audience sees how genuinely happy and safe they feel in their whimsy.

And they think the same thing I do:

Your vigour for life appals me.

Nearly everything in adulthood is goal-oriented: increase productivity, function on less sleep, make more money, run faster, cycle further. Fifteen-minute meals. Seven-minute workouts. Even meditating is less 'path to enlightenment' and more 'how meditating can help you smash your work day'!

That's because as soon as you enter the real world, play-time is over. Kaput. Done. There are no more outlets for sheer whimsy. We're just expected to be finished with it. For ever. Or be satisfied in getting scraps of it from Twitter memes, Beyoncé dance classes and pets' Halloween costumes (introvert whimsy).

Which explains, in part, why the music festivals I avoid are so wildly popular: it's the only socially acceptable time for grown men and women to wear tails, frolic in capes and cover themselves in glitter and face paint like it's a seven-year-old's birthday party (extrovert whimsy).

After my marathon networking schedule, I'm feeling this lack of play more than ever. Why does everything have to have an end goal? Why do I have to talk to Susan and try to impress her? Why is she always trying to get me to crowd-fund her start-up? Why can't we just have fun?

Years ago, I attended a one-off weekend improv course when I first arrived in London. I'd just moved here, and I was in that sweet spot between two worlds where I was trying to shake off who I was in my previous life while still utterly beguiled by the prospects of who I might become in this new life. The course was free and I didn't know anyone in London who I could accidentally run into – it was my chance to be brave. I'd never have this chance again. But that was the day I was confronted with the Temple of Doom: I left halfway through and never returned. I was too self-conscious, too cynical, too closed-off. My hand wound eventually healed, but my embarrassment did not.

But here it is again. Improv. Back in my life.

After the Facebook suggestion lands on my screen like a tiny undetonated digital bomb, I do some research and am surprised to find out that most courses in London for this month are already sold-out. But then again, improv is one of the only ways for grown-arse city-dwellers to have pure unfettered playtime and not be arrested or committed.

I sign up for an eight-week course. Eight separate occasions of structured but spontaneous play with total strangers.

I also write a will.

I'm late for my first class because I've stood in front of the entrance debating the merits of going to Nando's instead. I arrive in the classroom, a black basement with no windows, just as the instructor takes the floor.

Liam's demeanour is alert, but gentle. Like he's been specially trained to soothe spooked horses, which is the best way to describe the vibe of the people in the room. Fourteen other beginners and me, sitting in one long row facing him.

'Improv is not about being funny. It's not about being clever. Or quick,' he says.

I'm confused. Wasn't improv all of these things?

'It's really about being open and in the moment. And going with whatever your scene partner offers you,' he continues.

He doesn't waste time: he gathers us around in a standing circle where he leads us in our first warm-up game: passing around invisible balls. We pretend to pass around a red ball to each other. Then, we are throwing fire balls, then bowling balls, then bouncy balls.

All imaginary.

I really don't want to lose you here. Please don't storm off, queasy and disgusted. Because this activity, in real life, is actually fine. I'm as surprised as anyone.

Everyone in my class is enthusiastic in the fake-ball-throwing game, but not 'drama student inhaling a bag of Maltesers during the interval at *Hamilton*' enthusiastic. It's more 'normal adult who is self-consciously playing a silly game that they have paid to participate in'. Plus, it is a game with balls without all the fraught anxiety around accurately catching and throwing them.

After five minutes, my fringe starts sticking to my forehead from all the exertion of playing these intense imaginary sports. I wish I'd worn trainers – I didn't anticipate improv would be so physically demanding.

Reading my mind, Liam asks us to sit. And he introduces the concept of 'Yes and . . .', the foundation stone of all improv. Whatever your partner in a scene says, you have to go along with it (yes) and then add something to the story (and . . .). Here's an example of how this might work:

Character 1: 'Hey Julie, I love these homemade sausage rolls that you've brought into work!'

Character 2: 'Well, I wanted to make your favourite food seeing as it's your last day here.'

Character 1: 'It was just time, you know? What with the rabid bee infestation in my office . . .'

Character 2: 'We all thought you handled the bees really well.'

Liam divides us into groups of four. One by one, in our groups, each of us is supposed to contribute a few phrases at a time, building off what was previously said, to create a story. The game is called 'Remember when?'

I'm initially overcome with shyness, as I always am in these situations, but I'm emboldened by knowing everyone else is a beginner, too. None of them know each other either. Plus, no one seems judgemental or disapproving.

A bearded, blond, man-bunned guy named Clover designates himself the leader of my group, which is fine with me. The two others in my group are a tall guy and a woman with blue hair.

'Do you remember when we bought some milk?' Clover turns towards me.

'Oh! Oh yeah! I drank it and . . . got an allergic reaction because . . .' I turn to my left.

'You drank it directly from the cow,' Blue Hair Girl says, looking back at me.

'I did, I did, yeah . . .' I say, turning to the tall guy.

'And the doctor told you that you wouldn't live . . .' he says.

'If you drank it again . . .' Blue Hair Girl says.

'So you drank it again . . .' Tall Guy says.

'And you died,' Clover says, looking at me.

'Right,' I say.

Ten minutes into my second-ever improv class and they've already killed me off.

'There are no mistakes in improv,' Liam says from the back of the classroom. This feels very much like a blatant lie, to coerce us, like 'Bikini waxes don't hurt if you keep getting them!' or 'This is the last round of press-ups.'

My group and I try again:

'Do you remember that time that we all swapped shoes?' Clover asks.

'And we all wore high heels?' Tall Guy says.

'. . . But then I got gangrene?' I say.

Throughout the exercise, I could not stop giving myself diseases, allergic reactions or hypothermia. In the American version of *The Office*, Michael Scott (Steve Carrell) takes evening improv classes, and he hijacks every scene by yelling, 'I've got a gun!' It turns out that my own version of 'I've got a gun!' is 'I've got malaria!'

We try again.

'Do you remember that time we bought that jar of pickles?' Clover begins.

'And it was the last jar in town,' Tall Guy says.

They turn to me.

'And . . . we buried it and swore we'd never tell anyone about it!' I blurt.

'But then we wanted a roast dinner . . .' Blue Hair Girl says.

'And we wanted those pickles . . .' Tall Guy says.

'No, no, no. We kept it buried for twenty years, remember?' I say.

Why are they screwing up the story? I discover quickly that the biggest improv obstacle for me – aside from the life-threatening illnesses – is that I always come to the scene with a fully formed story in my mind and stubbornly refuse to deviate from it. In this instance, I wanted the story to be about secrets, broken loyalties and the apocalypse – where the pickle jar would save us. I wanted unrequited love between Clover and the Tall Guy. I wanted there to be a kiss in the rain. I did not want this to be about a roast dinner. Pickles don't even belong in a roast dinner. How could I work with these people?

Generally speaking, I am less of a 'Yes, and . . .' person and more of an 'OK, but . . .' person. I knew performing would be scary, but going against my *every* basic instinct is a mind-fuck that I had not anticipated. And it is making this place outside my comfort zone even more uncomfortable than I'd feared it would be.

So much of my feeling safe in life was predicated on planning ahead. Typically introverts like to be prepared, and I'm no exception. I anticipate all the likely negative outcomes in a scenario and then come up with a potential solution, no matter how outlandish. I like knowing what to expect, even for the simplest of things. I read reviews before starting a TV show, do extensive research to find out the best dish to order at a new restaurant and check exactly how long a cab ride should be. In exercise classes, I am the person asking, 'So how much longer on the bike?'

I like to have a sense of what's going to happen next – and improv consistently pulls the rug out from under me.

Liam calls me out on this. 'You can't plan ahead. You have to build on what your partners are giving you. If you're sitting there thinking "wizard, wizard, wizard", I guarantee that by the time it gets to you that won't make any sense.'

I try to get out of my head and listen to my partners, but I can't help trying to plan ahead anyway, and Clover keeps throwing me under the bus with his own story ideas. In one scene, Clover wants us to be zombies and I want us to be pioneers. We somehow end up on dead pioneers, and neither of us is thrilled.

In the final exercise that day, Liam puts us into pairs. We have to create and act out short scenes based on locations Liam is shouting at us. As we're all 'playing' at once, mercifully no one is watching us.

In my first scene, a man and I talk about the virtues of a stapler at 'a city office' and we are both so bad and so boring that I'm grateful everyone else is too busy to hear us.

For the second scene, I am paired with a woman named Maria.

'Garden centre!' Liam shouts from the back of the room. Garden centre? What happens at a garden centre?

I don't know what to say and neither does Maria, who is looking back at me blankly.

'Look at these shrubs!' she yells, pointing ahead of us, at what is actually a beanbag chair.

I look at the imaginary shrubs.

'Very green!' I finally say, loudly. What we lack in content, we make up for in volume.

I'm not even sure what a shrub is. Is it a bush? A small tree?

I have never been to a garden centre in my life.

'What do you think this shrub is doing?' the woman asks me.

I freeze.

'I think there's something wrong with this shrub,' the woman adds, her eyes pleading at me to join in.

Spontaneous. Free-flowing. Yes, and . . . ?

'Ma'am, this shrub is PREGNANT!' I shout.

Now it seems I have two levels of play – fatal diseases and birthing a baby shrub from an imaginary shrub vagina.

And in that moment, I realize that there is something scarier than theatre kids unleashed – and that is *me* unleashed.

What is hiding in my brain? What embarrassing garbage is lurking, just ready to pop out, finally unfettered from all the usual filters of normal life?

After safely delivering the shrub's baby (7 pounds, 6 ounces, the mother is doing fine, thank you for asking), class is finally over and I stumble out the door, spent.

*

In the next class, Liam bellows, 'You're two scientists! Go!' from across the room. I'm paired with Clover, again.

He slips on his pretend lab goggles and mimes holding something small in the palm of his hand and panicking.

'AHHH!' he says.

'AHHH!' I say, accepting his suggestion. Clover keeps gesturing towards his hand.

'What is it? What have we discovered?' I ask, letting him lead.

'Well, I DON'T KNOW, I can't see it!' he says, gesturing wildly to something invisible in his hand. Clover is the most enthusiastic improv-er in the class.

'Oh . . .' I say.

'But *you* can! Describe it to me!'

I stare at the space in his hand.

'It's . . . white. Small. Squishy. It's . . . it's . . . it's alive!'

Clover starts panicking at this revelation. His hand shrinks up. He starts hopping up and down and I, in turn, panic. Around us, other groups shout in their own mad scientist scenes.

'It's shrinking! You're hurting it! You need to soothe it!' I yell at Clover.

'OK, OK! How?' he asks.

'You need to sing it musical theatre to feel better!' I shout.

Clover stares at me, processing this.

'Musical theatre will cure it?' he asks.

'Yes!'

Clover launches into some wildly impressive jazz hands as he sings 'New York, New York'. I join in, both of us directing our warbling at his hand as we kick our legs in unison. Aaaand . . . scene!

It is safe to say, I don't recognize myself at all in this.

I'm normally so caged, so rehearsed, so hesitant to speak in real life, that often I just rely on conditional responses, especially at the office. Work sometimes feels like an endless sequence of saying, 'Good. Busy!' to coworkers' obligatory 'How are you?'s.

But here, stripped of lines, direction, rehearsed scenarios, Me Unleashed has spoken again. And I am getting a thrill from it. It is making me laugh and it feels like my brain is shifting. It is refreshing to break out of the boring, rote version of ourselves that can take over when we're at the office.

Naturally, there are limits.

In class three, Liam asks me to demonstrate a new game with him in front of my classmates. In the scene, his character eggs me on to perform ballet. I do not want to perform ballet in this scene, with everyone in the class watching. After some waffling, I ruthlessly have my character break their leg on a tractor so I am now confined to the floor, which is better than having to dance in front of my classmates.

Liam never asks me to demonstrate again.

Am I good at improv? No. I'm OK at best, but I freeze all the time, waiting for my brain to give me something to work with. 'Freezing' is literally the same thing as the 'blanking' that happens to me when I'm onstage. But here, people find freezing funny, because you have a partner who can control the situation if things go south. In fact, mistakes are sometimes the best part. It is usually interesting because we have no idea where it is going.

And even though freezing can be hilarious, I struggle to escape my own persona.

'All right, and now you're in the Amazon!' Liam shouts, starting a new scene.

'Let's go for a walk through the jungle,' Clover says. I look around at the fake jungle.

'Could you kill that spider for me?' I ask him. 'That really big one. And walk ahead of me so that you walk through spider webs first? Do you think this place has ticks with Lyme disease?'

Later, Clover and I are leaving at the same time and end up walking to the station together.

'What character were you playing in the last half of class?' he asks me.

'What do you mean?'

'You know, that kooky character you're always playing. It's hilarious.'

I say nothing at first as I realize:

I WAS PLAYING ME. THE CHARACTER WAS REAL ME.

There is no way I'm admitting that all those weird thoughts were actually mine. Instead, I say the pithy, brilliant fallback nugget we all utter when someone has found us out, and we have no alibi:

'Yeah, good one.'

Even though every class is intense, full of people I don't know well and moving quickly, I start to have fun. Each class cracks open my shell a little more, and I become less scared and more animated. Crucially, this doesn't mean I get better at improv or develop any capacity for creating organic, realistic interactions. In one scene, at the farmer's market, I shout, 'WHO IS SHE????' as I point my finger at an invisible mistress selling parsley when I'm meant to be haggling for goods.

It turns out that I actually like the fast pace of the class. Because we're always jumping from scene to scene, or imaginary world to imaginary world, I feel free from the endless, agonizing loop of being myself. I don't have to be her: shintrovert, anxious, shy.

For a few hours, I am unburdened from my real life because it's impossible to worry about making rent, your passive-aggressive boss or your private life. I don't talk about my job or health or worries or parents or money. No commutes, deadlines, or diets. I am far too busy playing a drunk scientist in a canoe off the coast of Papua New Guinea.

In one scene, in one of my final classes, I am playing a lawyer prosecuting a woman, Eniko, for being on Tinder too much. I am pacing my 'courtroom' in front of the rest of the class. In this exercise, we pluck random lines out of a hat to insert into key moments.

'And isn't it true that every time a Tinder date meets you, he says . . .' I begin.

I stick my hand in my pocket.

'TAXI!' I read off the paper.

Eniko and I both burst out laughing. So do our class-mates.

And the feeling comes over me suddenly, sharply.

Oh no.

My vigour for life appals me.

I'm sure it comes as an enormous surprise to you and it certainly came as an enormous surprise to me but . . . I love improv. And not just a little bit. I am a complete convert. I've become 'one of them'.

Don't get me wrong. I don't bound out the door to my flat singing show tunes and skipping into class announcing, 'JESSY PAN PAN IS HERE FOR THE IMPROV PARTY!' before banging a gong.

But I want to.

Sometimes I still struggled getting myself to class because the idea of being 'on' for three hours with fourteen other people always made me feel tired before I'd even arrived. But after every single night with that group, I left feeling giddy. I wanted to shout it from the rooftops, to nudge sad-looking strangers on the Tube and whisper, 'You should try improv!'

Psychologists say that improv classes can help alleviate social anxiety and stress – the exercises encourage you to think quickly on your feet, speak in front of others and become less obsessed with perfectionism. There's even an 'Improv for Anxiety' class at the famous Second City comedy club in Chicago.

It makes so much sense to me because spending a few hours a week in a safe space made the entire world seem kinder and more manageable. Mistakes were so easily forgiven – no one ever seemed to get annoyed or mad when I froze. As long as I stopped giving myself gonorrhea to try and move every scene forward, no one seemed to mind.

Improv is one of those things that is so fun to be a part of but excruciating to observe if you aren't involved. Like extreme PDA on the bus or conversations about astrology.

Every Wednesday, for three hours, we were just making shit up. That's all we were doing. As a team.

Before my course, I never worried about the lack of play in my life. Now I don't want to live in a world without it.

Looking back on that Temple of Doom pile up, it seems so clear to me now that it was just the wrong exercise for me. Too physical. Too showy. No space for collaboration or fun. Plus, everyone in that first classroom had been larger than life, jumping and shouting and making every scene physical with wrestling matches or competitive dancing. I will always shirk when there are several loud, competing personalities in a room, even in improv.

Because personally, I'd much rather be playing a scene with one other person where we are arguing about Scrabble while locked in Reese Witherspoon's guest bathroom. That is the kind of space I thrive in.

One evening, on my way home, I accidentally bump into a woman with blue hair on the Tube.

It's Laura, from my improv class. We look at each other in recognition, followed quickly by mild horror.

We're not in our safe space any more.

'Hi,' she says quietly.

'Hi,' I say, matching her volume. Like the guys in *Fight Club* with black eyes and broken jaws, seeing another improver outside of that space is awkward. We don't actually know each other and we share a dirty secret.

Silence. She looks around the carriage.

'This is my boyfriend,' she finally says, pointing to a tall blond man next to her.

Don't ask. Don't ask. Don't ask.

'How do you two know each other?' he asks.

The bearded man squashed between us looks up, interested.

'We . . . we met at improv,' Laura says.

I bite my lip. I see the other commuters silently digest this information.

'Oh, so be funny together,' he says.

'That's not how it works,' Laura replies.

My theory is that improv is so avoided because it's a rarity to see unbridled joy in our adult lives. We keep our emotions in check, and it's collectively agreed that explicit displays of strong feeling are uncomfortable for everyone. It's safer for us to remain low-key and miserable.

After a few years in London, I had become cynical and worn down, but this course had awoken something that adulthood had quashed: I love playing, even when I'm not that good at it.

In my final classes, I ended up laughing so hard that I cried. Either from watching my classmates or from particularly gifted people in my scene. Sometimes, I would be full-on shaking with laughter, as tears streamed down my face. The catharsis was like a high. A reset button after you've been stressed and bottled up. I hadn't even known these people a few weeks ago, and now I was lying on the floor weeping next to them – and loving it so much.

I am an introvert, and the delight I experienced in improv confounds me. I'd forgotten that 'playing' was actually wonderful. I'd also forgotten that I could be decent at it. I had experienced moments of exhilaration during some of my other extroverting attempts, but here was something I felt wholeheartedly sure I wanted to be a part of my life.

Before now, being in the spotlight, drawing attention to myself in any fashion, had always filled my body with adrenaline and paralysing fear – at *The Moth*, my body was so tense and rigid onstage. That adrenaline behaved so differently when I was playing out unrehearsed scenes in a safe, friendly space with people I liked. The fear had transformed into excitement: I became dynamic, looser, freer. Happier.

Which means I have to reckon with the most hideous thought I've ever had.

I may be a secret theatre kid.

I might actually be a joyful bastard.

EVEREST

or

stand-up comedy

'People told me I was funny my entire life,' successful comedians always say in magazine interviews. 'Friends kept telling me, "You should be a comedian!"'

My brother Adam is considered the funny one in my family, and a fun, long-standing Christmas tradition as teenagers was visiting my Chinese aunt in California, who would survey my two brothers and me and announce, 'Adam is *also* the best-looking!' before patting our cheeks and walking off, leaving devastation in her wake.

So yes, no one had ever said to me: 'Hey you, in the corner, hiding, you should get onstage and take this mic. Yeah, you with the fringe! Eating macaroni! Stop crying! Get up there and show us what you've got because I can tell you're gonna be a star!'

When I tell other people I'm going to try stand-up comedy, they always touch my arm, furrow their brow and say, 'You are so brave,' followed by, 'That is my worst nightmare,' just in case I was considering making them do it, too.

It's my worst nightmare, too. But because it was the biggest feat I could imagine pulling off, it also felt like one of the most important. It combines pretty much all of my shintrovert fears into one gruesome event. And it feels like the ultimate chance to see if I am or am not always going to be that person afraid and waiting in the shadows.

Many comedians identify as introverts, which makes sense: they're incredibly observant, and have chosen a career where they are often alone (even when they are performing to sold-out arenas, it's still only them onstage).

For this task, I'd have to wrangle with my intense shyness, which is defined as a generalized fear of judgement from others. According to recent research, 40–60 per cent of the population identifies as shy, and public speaking is the number-one fear in America. It's amazing the human population has managed to spawn at all; our species truly has alcohol and cold winters to thank for helping us procreate.

I take comfort in finding another comedian who is shy. Comedian Rhod Gilbert decided to address his own debilitating shyness in a BBC documentary. He thinks that comedy can be a cure for shyness, in what he calls 'comedic behavioural therapy'. He recruited three shy people to test out his theory, to miraculous results: despite performing stand-up comedy, they did not spontaneously combust in a fit of sparks and humiliation.

There's a lot I've learnt this year: I know how to assist the birth of an imaginary shrub and strike up conversations on the street and platonically date multiple women, but making people erupt with laughter feels like an impossible feat of wizardry.

Unlike performing at *The Moth* at Union Chapel, this isn't just pure public speaking. Comedians interact with their audiences, sometimes even inviting them into the conversation. And while I've started talking to strangers and have walked into several networking events alone this year, this is a giant leap into the murky deep end of my pool of social anxiety. Comedians are also expected to be quick on their feet: I'd have to become looser, and less rigid, and embrace the spontaneity I'd unearthed in improv. While onstage. I'd have to harness all of my extrovert lessons at once.

Stand in the spotlight. Interact with the masses. Make them laugh. Be quick on my feet. Don't crumble to dust.

In a year of facing my fears, stand-up comedy was my Everest.

And everyone knows that you don't climb Everest alone unless you want to die. You need to buy the right clothes, and you need to tell your entire family that you love them and that you might never see them again. And you need a Sherpa.

And so I had to find my Sherpa guide.

I mention this challenge to Paul (remember, the real life friend from Clitheroe that I met during my networking ventures?). He tells me that his girlfriend had taken a stand-up comedy class for beginners in King's Cross. He said it had transformed her confidence. It had made her feel invincible. And she'd had a lot of fun doing it.

Fun? I'd almost rather do nearly anything than perform stand-up comedy. Which is why I know I have to try. Because this could not be further from my comfort zone – I owe it to myself, and to other introverts (and honestly, all other sane people who fear doing this), to go to the battle lines and report back. Because I'd rather do stand-up comedy than wonder 'What if?' for the rest of my life. I'd rather do stand-up comedy than be insecure for ever. I'd rather do stand-up comedy than look back and wish that I had been braver. I couldn't go back in time and give a speech at my wedding, but I could attempt to do this. And after watching *Into Thin Air: Death on Everest* the other night, I'd certainly rather do stand-up comedy than actually climb Everest.

At 3 a.m. one night, in a fit of the resolute confidence that comes to me in the early hours, I sign up for a seven-week comedy course. Then, like a drunk shopper bingeing on Amazon orders, I fall asleep and wake up the next morning with no memory of my recklessness.

While brushing my teeth the next morning, it comes back to me, and I am filled with regret. This woman staring back at me in the mirror, toothbrush in hand, has betrayed me. But it's too late. The money is already gone. So is my resolute confidence.

On the first day of class, I have a spare hour after work before it's due to start. And so I go home, climb into bed, lie down in a dark room and assume the foetal position. This is my version of rallying. For some people, it's punching the air or yelling at themselves in the mirror or doing lunges. For me, it is yelling into my pillow, 'But I don't want to go! I don't want to! I don't want to!' I saw my youngest nephew do this once and found it surprisingly effective.

I punch the pillow one more time.

Come on. I couldn't give up now, facing my biggest fear after coming so far.

What's the worst that could possibly happen? (Answer: spontaneously combusting in a fit of sparks and humiliation.)

My Sherpa guide to comedy Everest turns out to be a forty-two-year-old stand-up comedian named Kate Smurthwaite, who leads the comedy course for beginners in the King's Cross neighbourhood. She is tall and imposing.

'Go and get your own chairs from below the stairs! I'm too old to do that for you,' she tells each of us as we enter the classroom for the first time.

Fourteen of us eventually file in and sit in a circle, upright on our plastic chairs. There's a hyper energy in the air. Looking at the others one by one, I realize that, save for one or two quiet souls, I'm sitting with a group that is mostly made up of extroverts. I've finally found them! Here they all are! (Just kidding, they've always been easy to find, they are so loud.)

We go around the circle and introduce ourselves. The group is made up of eight women and six men ranging in age from early twenties to mid-forties.

Kate doesn't waste any time. We go straight into our first writing exercise: making a list of ten things that we hate. The logic is that the best material comes from things we feel passionate about. My mind blanks as I try to think of things I hate. 'Techno music?' I write. 'People who talk in movie theatres?' I can't think under this pressure at all. 'Group activities,' I add.

We are each to share one thing from our list; the person to our left has to tell us why that thing is actually brilliant. The aim is to get creative juices flowing, reverse our thinking, and get used to performing in front of each other.

'Before you declare what you hate, stand up and introduce yourself and then say, "I am a hater!"' Kate instructs us.

A girl in her late twenties with long, dark hair stands up. 'My name is Vivian, and I am a hater!'

Kate leads the class in lots of encouraging whoops and shouts.

'And I hate . . . grown-ups on scooters!' Vivian declares. I nod in staunch agreement. The blond man from Essex on her left turns to her.

'Oh no, see, that's the best thing ever! These days people grow up too quickly, so it's so great that these people are just reliving their childhood,' he says, assuredly.

A well-dressed posh woman in heels reveals that she hates tights because they're so expensive, hard to put on and they always ladder. The man to her right, a good-looking guy in his late thirties named Noel, tells her, 'But tights are chic and warm! That's *two* great things right away. Double tick!'

What a dumb, handsome idiot Noel is.

As each person declares their hate, Kate leads us in cheering in solidarity. Yes! Boo to men who ride scooters! Fuck tights! Down with software updates! Damn those people who don't let people off the Tube before muscling their way on! Death to auto-tune!

The best thing about this exercise is that everyone in class really goes for it. No one hesitates or is too cool. There doesn't seem to be one dickish character in the bunch. Everyone claps in support of their shared hatreds.

As I study my new classmates, I realize this could double as group therapy. It's clear that everyone here must have *some* hole in their life: professional, social, or romantic. No one really seems to be here to actually become a comedian professionally – they are here to try on a different part of their personality, to meet new people, to escape the safe, boring clutches of normal life. We have each looked at our status quo and decided: something needs to change.

Kate explains that the course consists of five classes, one rehearsal and then a showcase where we each perform five minutes of material at a comedy pub in Leicester Square in front of a real audience.

Then she says, 'Let's talk about nerves for a minute.'

My hands immediately go hot. I've had so much fun hating on Justin Bieber with the class that I've forgotten what we are actually here for – to learn how to perform stand-up comedy. To perform in front of a crowd.

In six weeks, I'm going to be onstage. My heart rate picks up just thinking about it.

'The most powerful thing you can do to overcome nerves is make friends with the people in this room.'

We study each other, uncertainly.

'During these six weeks, we will all carry each other through this. If you feel nervous, tell people about it. Go to the pub with each other. Have coffee before class. Grab a drink after class. Go to comedy gigs together. Share material with each other,' she says.

Before I know it, class is over and everyone is gathering up their things and heading for the door. I'm confused. She just told us to all be friends and yet . . . everyone's bolting separately. Where are all of my new best friends going?

'Does anyone want to . . . write down their email and phone numbers in my notebook?' I hear myself calling out, waving my notebook in the air.

Vulnerability has been the hardest part of this year. I am, once again, acting on psychologist Nick's adage – nobody waves, but everyone waves back.

My classmates all turn to me. 'Yes!' they say, in excited unison, as they rush over towards me.

One small mass email, one giant leap for introverts.

By our second class, we have lost two good men. We never hear from them again.

But the twelve others do show up (and will continue to do so over the course). Even after improv I still can't get over this. How rare is it to get twelve strangers in London to show up at 7 p.m. on a Tuesday evening seven times in a row?

In class, we play lots of games. Kate assigns us worksheets to fill in as a way to structure our five-minute sets, but I don't fill mine out. I'm still pretending I don't have to do this performance, the same avoidance that made me not rehearse my Moth story.

One of the biggest hurdles when it comes to performing comedy is that, to me, it is fundamentally a person standing onstage declaring to the audience, 'I am funny, am I not? Hahahaha!' I find that entire concept deeply embarrassing. But nobody else in my class seems to feel this way.

I'd once read that embarrassment is a healthy emotion because it signals to others that we care about the social code. When we trip in public or realize we are waving to someone not waving at us, our blushing is an apology for breaking the code. It's sad to find out that deep inside of you is . . . a desire to commit to societal norms.

Clearly I feel that my telling jokes onstage is a direct violation of the social code and will possibly lead to total anarchy.

'Do you think 50 per cent of comedy is just performance: a funny voice or like a silly, apt expression?' I ask Sam after class one night while we're watching a Jack Whitehall comedy special.

'Yes. Would you do a funny voice?' he asks. I get embarrassed when I slip into baby-talk when I'm petting a dog. Even when it's only me and the dog in the room. So, no, I'm not doing a funny voice.

I'd rather just tell my stories onstage in a normal tone of voice. No dramatic pauses, no funny expressions.

'That way if I fail and no one laughs, then it's OK because I didn't humiliate myself by really putting myself out there and performing it earnestly,' I say to Sam.

'That makes no sense! You're far more likely to fail if you don't perform,' Sam says. 'You're just setting yourself up for failure.'

Yes, but to me the failure is much more embarrassing if you try.

'All right, guys, it's time for the talent show!' Kate shouts, clapping her hands together. *What?* I look around, confused, as the rest of the class begins moving their chairs to the back of the room. I'd missed the previous class and, thus, had also missed our homework assignment: prepare for the talent contest.

Kate does not care that I have nothing prepared.

'I don't care whether your talent is impressive or whether you're just dicking about. But no matter what, I want you to sell it to me like it's amazing. You know what I mean?' she says.

She stands up and uses her stage voice to bellow, 'Ladies and gentleman! You're gonna want to tell your grandchildren about the things you're about to witness today! Clock the date so that you can say that you saw the world's greatest on this very day!'

I'm going up third. I inhale sharply.

'Ladies and gentlemen, welcome to our top talent competition! Please welcome the first contestant of the evening – Vivian!' Kate shouts. I know that Vivian, having also missed the previous class, hasn't prepared to perform either. Will she make an excuse? She seems a little shy, like me, but as soon as Kate says her name, she's off like a rocket to the front of the room.

'Thank you, good evening! Today I'm going to show you something incredible! I'm gonna recite the alphabet but . . . I will recite it in the medium of sign. That's right! British sign language! At *lightning* fast speed. You will *never* see British sign language at this speed!'

Vivian pauses dramatically. She closes her eyes and takes a deep breath. And then suddenly she starts moving her hands in rapid succession for five seconds.

'Done!' she exclaims before making an elaborate bow.

I am in awe. She managed to make something up on the spot.

But now it's one person closer to my turn. Anthony, who writes an infamous blog about the gay scene in London and is arguably the most naturally funny person in our group, leaps up. As he's performing his talent, a dance called the Dutty Wine (I don't know what this is, but it looks very hard), with his neck and legs circling in two different directions, I sit on my hands, panicking. What is my talent? I can't sing. I can't juggle. I can't do the splits. I have nothing.

Anthony's hips are winding down and now he's on the floor gyrating. I stare at his arse, willing it to give me some ideas. I can't say 'Pick me later!' or 'Pass!' It's not an option. Anthony takes his seat. *Decide to do it and just do it.*

'Please welcome Jess P, contestant number three!' Kate calls out. *I have nothing. Just start talking. Something will come.* I walk up and stand in front of the class. I look at their expectant faces. *Sell it. You don't know what 'it' is yet, but sell it anyway. You did improv. Something will come to you.*

'My talent is . . . really important. It is very . . . valuable. Today, yes, this very day . . . I will be able to . . .'

Shit. Shit. Shit.

'Look at you . . .' I stare at them. 'And psychically tell you . . .'

Come on, brain. What have you got?

'Your favourite Matt Damon movie! Here we go!'

I run over to the closest person and lock eyes with an Indian woman named Sohini.

'*BOURNE IDENTITY*!' I shout in her face. She cowers. I rapidly move on to the next person.

It's Noel, the handsome idiot who is an Aston Villa fan who drinks beer. '*Ocean's Eleven*!' I scamper over and stare into the dark eyes of Alexandros, a well-travelled, groomed man from Greece with enviably slender ankles. '*The Talented Mr Ripley*!'

I keep moving, faster and faster. I stare into our teacher's eyes.

'*Good Will Hunting*!' I shout in her face.

'Yes!' she says, stunned.

'*Rounders*!' I say, triumphant to have remembered it, to a girl named Allison. 'I've never seen it,' says Allison.

Commit hard.

'You'll love it!' I say.

I rapidly run through the rest of my class audience staring into their eyes. '*The Martian*! *The Bourne Supremacy*! *The Departed*! *The Bourne Ultimatum*! *Saving Private Ryan*!' I run over to my final classmate. Have I named every single Matt Damon movie? Are there any left?

'*We Bought a Zoo*!' I yell triumphantly, my hands in the air. My classmates look doubtful at this final title. Look, it *is* a movie. No, you're right, no one has ever seen it. Look it up!

And then I take a bow and take my seat, spent. The group looks stunned, either from my psychic ability or from my shouting in their faces. I'm rather stunned myself. I'm not shaking, I don't feel too weird or vulnerable, and I don't quite understand why.

The talent show continues. A guy named Tom juggles. Another guy does a press-up with a glass of water on his head. Then, one of the quietest people in the entire group, Allison, is up. She takes a deep breath. Pauses. And then she opens her mouth. She belts out the most soul-shaking rendition of Boyz II Men's 'I'll Make Love To You'. By the end of it, the rest of us are swaying in our seats and slow clapping to the beat.

I'm shocked, not just by how good she is, but how much she has gone for it. Of everyone in the class, Allison is the most shy. She always breaks eye contact and tries to make her body smaller with her posture, as if she can curl herself into a ball and disappear. But tonight she'd transformed into a sensitive nineties R&B crooner for a few brief moments.

At the end of class, Kate says, 'I hope after this exercise that you notice that everyone loves it when you say things like, "This is going to be amazing. Omigod, you guys, prepare for this!" We love to watch someone give it 100 per cent, even if they're bad. What we can't bear to watch is someone give it 10 per cent,' Kate says. 'Then we're thinking, *Why should I watch you?*'

Don't you hate it when your husband's right?

'When we watch *Britain's Got Talent*,' Kate goes on, 'what we love the best are the people who are really shit. Right? We love that. When they're great, it's good too, but what's great about them being shit is *not* that they're shit, but that they're trying really hard and *then* they're shit,' Kate says emphatically. '*That's* what so great about it. Someone being shit at being shit is just shit. But someone trying really hard and then being shit is *amazing*,' she says.

I write down in my notebook, '*Someone being shit at being shit is just shit.*'

I don't want to be shit. And I certainly don't want to be shit at being shit.

Our comedy showcase is two weeks away and I haven't actually written any material. Every time I'd tried, I'd been seized with terror and immediately gave up.

Instead, for the past month, I had kept a list in my phone of funny thoughts I had. I added to it a few times a day, anything that raised an internal titter, but I could never bear to read over them again. I'd been holding out hope that they would be brilliant, and I'd just string them together with some transitions and be golden. Most of them occur to me as I'm falling asleep. I'd reach for my phone, waking up Sam in the process, and type into a Notes app, and then I'd go to sleep, hoping the comedy gods would do their work.

I finally consult the list and wonder if a demented elf has snuck in during the night and put this together. None of it makes sense. 'Kale cigarette' I have written. Is this how I discover I have multiple personalities? 'Darcy emojis' I have underneath it. Oh . . . had I imagined Mr Darcy had his own . . . emoji set? Very niche, but I would be interested in that product.

I also have written, 'I am the only adult I know who takes naps. Is this self-care?' and beneath that, 'In your act, sing "A Whole New World" from *Aladdin* when I got my UK passport and went through the fast-track immigration queue. Could add choreography?'

I also have a long, rambling description of a dream where I stole two black Labradors and a cherry pie, both from the Queen, with the note 'best dream ever'.

End of list.

This is bad. Very bad. Not even a funny voice could save this routine.

I confess my lack of decent comedy material to Lily, Vivian and Toni, three women from class whom I now meet every week for drinks (I asked them after we'd first met and we've been doing this ever since). We're all panicking about the showcase and arrange to meet up on Sunday at a pub for a writing workshop (on the weekend! Like real friends!) with a few others from class.

Toni, a twenty-two-year-old actress, and I arrive at the pub at the same time. She orders a beer and I grab a cider. We sit across from each other in a booth, and Toni asks me what my comedy routine is about.

'I think I might do a bit about where I'm from – Amarillo, Texas. Do you know the song "(Is This The Way To) Amarillo"?'

'No,' Toni says.

'No?' I ask.

'Literally never heard of it.'

'Oh, OK. Never mind then.'

I'm back to nothing.

Lily and Vivian arrive and we decide to go around the table to share our material. Except none of us want to go first. We clutch our notebooks to our chests.

'I don't want to . . . this isn't a joke . . . this isn't anything,' I mutter, looking down.

'Yeah, I don't have anything good either,' Lily says. The group falls silent.

Vivian finally breaks the imposter syndrome apology routine that we're all bandying around. She normally has a gentle demeanor, but right now she is yelling at me, 'JUST SAY IT. JUST READ IT. IT'S FINE. Read what you have. Right now.'

I nod, more scared of her than of sharing my material.

'Well, I want to talk about being from Texas. Maybe something about guns . . . how if they don't like my act, I'll . . . kill them? Shit. That's not it. That's not edgy, it's terrible . . .' I say, trailing off.

The girls are looking at me blankly. Kind but pitying. I go on with a bit about how I recently visited Lancaster, the Paris of the north-west.

'Oh. You guys aren't laughing,' I say.

'But we're smiling,' Lily says. 'We like what you're saying, but . . .'

'But the point of comedy is to make people laugh . . .' I say.

'Just push it further,' Lily says. 'What part of Texas are you from?'

'Amarillo,' I say.

'Wait. Wait, wait, wait – you're from Amarillo?'

'Yeah.'

'You HAVE to talk about that song!'

'But Toni didn't know it.'

'Toni is Australian!'

I turn to Toni. 'What??'

Toni smiles and nods, while sipping her beer. I'm terrible at recognizing accents, but I should have known that Toni was far too loud and smiley to be British. And apparently, this song is only famous in the UK.

'You should break down that song and what it really means as a person from Amarillo,' Lily says.

I make a few notes on my paper and look through the rest of my jokes.

'And I want to talk about English football matches. Because where I'm from, people yell nice things and there they yell things like, "Get on with it, you bunch of useless twats!" What do you think about applying this to real life? Like, say you're cheering on your boss at the London marathon and instead of your sign saying, "You got this, Linda", you write something like "Come on, you stupid loser!"'

'Yes!' they exclaim.

'Or how about, "Come on, Linda, you slow, lazy bitch!"' Lily suggests.

Perfect.

I head home with some semblance of what I might write about. I feel safe with these women. We are all scared out of our minds and our WhatsApp group has descended into a chaos of workshopping punch lines and encouraging notes. We're fast friends on this treacherous journey because we have to be to survive.

Later that week, I stay up late trying to write my material, but I keep second-guessing myself. I think it's time to admit that I may need professional help. Again. I once saw Rob Delaney running in my neighbourhood, but it didn't seem like I could assume we were friends based on that. Sara Pascoe says no but sends her best wishes. I try to attend a Rhod Gilbert gig and accost him afterwards, but he's sold out until the end of time. And at a book signing, I muster the courage to ask Robert Webb if he is an introvert or an extrovert and he waves me away, saying, 'Oh, I don't know!'

I keep looking. When I share some of my material about being half-Chinese with Lily, she says that I should see this guy named Phil Wang.

I go home and watch a clip of him on *Live at The Apollo* and instantly like him: he's goofy, he's witty and he talks about race in an accessible, funny way.

'Could you be my mentor?' I ask his clip.

I contact him on Twitter and he says he can briefly meet for coffee that week. He's just got back from tour and is about to go on holiday.

*

'Do you workshop your comedy with other writers?' I ask Phil, immediately trying to get my questions in fast. We are sitting on a small boat on a canal near Paddington Station.

'No, because I've done that before and when they never find a particular joke funny, then I lose faith in the joke,' he says.

'Do you think if your friends don't like the joke, then it isn't funny, or do you think they just didn't get it?'

'I think they don't get it in the context of a comedy club or within the rest of the set. So now I don't do it any more. I trust my own taste.'

I constantly doubt my own taste, but I know that I need to start believing in it if I am going to be able to do this.

'What do you do to prep before a gig?' My questions are rapid-fire, as are Phil's answers.

'I meditate for fifteen minutes every day with an app, and I try to meditate for five minutes before. And I try to do power poses. Which help a lot.'

'Like what?'

'Like trying to make yourself bigger.' He puts out his arms like he's trying to intimidate a bear. I can't imagine doing that. That feels ridiculous.

I ask him about bombing onstage.

'There are things wrong with certain rooms, but if you bomb, it's probably your fault. What separates the real comedians is that the real comedians are the ones who can bounce back after bombing,' he says.

We walk together back to Paddington Station, and I tell Phil a little bit about the year I've had trying to extrovert.

'I hate hanging out in big groups of people,' he says. 'How are you supposed to know whose turn it is to talk?'

It's something I worry about, too.

We briefly hug as we separate at Paddington Station, headed in opposite directions.

I'd talked to a professional, taken a class and now it was time to start writing. Showtime was creeping up, and the terror loomed large.

I finally hunker down one night and write my set. I include a bit about the Tony Christie song and explain how his beloved 'Sweet' Marie is from Amarillo and how she went to my high school and how she was less sweet and more of a subtle racist. Then I try to make a few notes about what it was like to be Chinese in small-town Texas, including a particularly haunting experience about learning the phrase 'yellow fever' when I was twelve. By the time it's 4 a.m., I have a full five minutes.

Does it work? I have no idea. But it's what I have.

When I think of performing it, I feel sick. I wish public speaking was a dragon you only had to slay once, but it just keeps coming back. I'd performed at *The Moth*, I'd survived, and yet I was still fearful. But *The Moth* had shown me I could do this. I was capable. Why was this still so hard for me? And weren't there bigger things to worry about?

A few months earlier, sitting with my father in the ICU in LA, I'd had the most intense weeks of my life – so why didn't this feel easy in comparison? Most people who go through emotional upheaval and survive end up saying things like, 'But now I can do anything!'

Not me. Earlier this year, I'd seen my father pull through life-threatening surgery and I was *still* being a neurotic shit about this?

Apparently so. I'm learning this is how life works: we nearly die, and ten minutes later we're throwing fits about getting a speeding ticket on our way back from the hospital.

At our final class, Kate gives some advice about performing.

'Look, guys, if you see your friends before your show, don't fucking cry. OK? No one wants to see that,' she says.

I glance at the floor. I'm barely not crying now, Kate.

'You can have one drink before you go on, but that's it. You have to be smarter than the audience.' That's how Kate has always talked about the audience: we are going to war and they are the enemy. We have to control them. And if they defy us, we must subdue them.

Kate stands up in front us and starts clapping her hands together in a slow beat. 'Come on guys, put your hands together!' she says.

My classmates and I join in.

Kate stops clapping, but gestures at us to keep going.

'Once you're onstage, you have the power. You can tell the audience to do something, practically anything, and if you say it with confidence . . . they'll just do it. They won't question why.' She looks at us pointedly, as our clapping slowly ceases.

As we are leaving our final class, Toni glances at me and comes across to put a hand on my shoulder.

'Hey,' she says. 'Remember – this is fun!' She studies my face. 'Or at least it's supposed to be fun.'

This honestly had not occurred to me.

I practise my material on Sam, a lot. I know now that the true test of a strong relationship is yelling into your partner's face, 'I DON'T THINK YOU UNDERSTAND WHAT A JOKE IS!' and them yelling back, 'I KNOW WHAT JOKES ARE, I'M JUST NOT HEARING ANY!' and managing to stay together.

He has a lot of feedback on my delivery.

'You need to commit harder. You say some jokes like you're scared of the joke.'

'I am scared of the joke,' I say.

'You need to commit so hard. You need the audience to believe you.'

'But I don't really believe in this joke,' I say.

'Then don't say the ones that you don't believe in. And you need to act it out more. If you can't do that, then don't do it.'

I cut any jokes I feel iffy about. I practise and record myself, making sure I hit five minutes.

I cannot fall asleep.

It's showcase day, and I have exactly half an hour to lie in bed screaming into my pillow and then I have to get ready and head to the Comedy Pub in Leicester Square.

After the screaming is done, I get in the shower and realize I've invited no one to come see me except for Sam because I don't want to humiliate myself in front of people I actually know. I text Lily and Vivian; it turns out they are bringing lots of friends. I frantically text all of my new friends at the last minute, but none of them can come. This is 100 per cent my fault for inviting them less than twenty-four hours in advance, but it stings nonetheless. Though maybe a secret part of me hadn't wanted to have that added pressure of my new friends in the audience.

While I'm drying my hair and my tears, I text Sam's friend Shaun. He's done stand-up comedy before and I know he'll enjoy it a lot whether I die onstage or succeed. He replies in seconds, telling me he's game. I have come to love spontaneous people.

I get lost on the way and finally arrive at the Comedy Pub, sweaty and dishevelled, an hour before show time. I fly up the three flights of stairs to find Kate talking with the rest of my class onstage.

Kate goes through the order list. Vivian volunteers to go first. And then there's silence. Kate studies the rest of us.

'I need the people who brought a lot of friends to perform last so that their friends stay the entire time. Who has no friends? I want you to go in the first half.'

I put my hand up.

'Great, Jess will go second,' Kate says.

Great. No Mates Jess has the second slot!

The next hour goes by fast. I stand in the toilets and do a quick set of the breathing lessons that Alice taught me. I do a little sniffy mother-in-law just for good measure. I make my body big, like I'm attacking a bear, as Phil had recommended. I feel ridiculous but also agile and loose and powerful. Huh.

I put my hair half-up and then go into a stall and silently say the entire comedy routine to the wall. It's imprinted in my brain.

For a moment, I look at myself and realize what I'm about to do. I feel frozen in terror. I'd read somewhere that you can gain perspective by imagining yourself talking to yourself on your own deathbed. You're supposed to imagine what Deathbed You would say to Present You in this moment. For me, Deathbed Jess always looks suspiciously like my Chinese grandmother and when I lean closer to her as she beckons me, she always whispers, 'Go . . . to . . . medical school.'

But now I really try to picture my own frail hands. Am I eighty-five? I look eighty-five. My hair is grey and curly. I should have someone dye my hair for me when I'm in my eighties. Maybe my unborn children. Did I ever get rich? I can't tell. I see my small hips. Deathbed me has the perfect physique for hipster dungarees – finally! Good to know. Eighty-five-year-old me is sleeping. But. Still. I really try to visualize lying there, near death. That woman doesn't know why I care at all about what these people think of me when I have four working limbs. I lean over to her. She says, 'You go up there and you tell that crude joke about Asian fetish and yellow fever. YOU DO IT FOR ME.'

Somehow, I'm ready.

On the way back to the room, I pass some of my classmates, who are involved in a small kerfuffle on the stairs.

They're surrounding Tim, the blond guy from Essex. Tim has just announced that he's decided not to go on after all.

'I'm not ready,' he says to us, holding his beer. 'I'll do it some other time.'

We try to coax him to go onstage to just tell one joke. Perhaps the true story about how he lost his virginity (the girl had kept yelling, 'Pump! Pump!' which he thought meant go faster and faster, when she was really asking for her asthma inhaler) but Tim wouldn't budge.

I have been Tim so many times in my life. I was always Tim before this year started. Going so far and then refusing to actually go through with it.

Tonight, I'm not giving myself the option to quit.

Suddenly, people from outside start pouring in. It's only friends and family, but soon the place is packed. I count roughly sixty people.

My classmates and I are instructed to sit together in the back corner. Vivian asks me if she should put on the red lipstick she brought.

'Always,' I say. War paint.

She shows me her hand. It's trembling. She passes me her handwritten notes. 'Yell these at me if I forget my jokes,' she says.

The lights dim. Anthony is frantically applying 'confidence oil' to everyone's wrists. I offer mine and he rolls it on. It smells like lemons.

The room is buzzing, everyone is seated and I see Kate heading towards the stage. The lights are going down. Oh God, this is really happening.

Kate tells a few jokes and lets the audience know that we are all beginners.

'I want you to treat this like a one-year-old's birthday party. If you see anything remotely competent, you clap and cheer,' she says.

And then she introduces Vivian to the stage. I'm nervous for her, but when I see that she's found her flow, I start to feel scared for myself. I know my time is coming. Am I starting to lose my voice? Is that a tickle I feel coming on at the back of my throat?

I can hear Vivian wrapping up her act. My heart is racing but I feel ready. I have practised. I believe in the jokes. I know that I have to speak slowly and deliver the lines the right way to get a laugh. If they can't understand me, then they aren't going to get the jokes and then I'll have no hope. And I must commit to delivery. Commit hard. Try.

'Please welcome to the stage the fantastic Jess Pan!' Kate calls out.

And I'm up.

I don't remember walking to the stage, but I know I must have. I do remember fidgeting with the mic, trying to get it out of the stand and moving it to the side for what feels like ages. My brain screaming: *Get the mic out. Get the mic out.*

OK. Mic is out. Now talk to the audience. You're onstage! Act like it! Sixty people are staring at you. Say hi to them. Act like they are a good friend you've just seen at a party.

'Hello,' I say.

'HELLO!' they shout back. I can hear my classmates all the way from the back. 'How are you guys doing?' I ask.

Ambiguous din is the only response. *Keep going.*

'So, I'm from Texas . . . I'm from this place called . . . Amarillo.'

My classmates whoop in response.

And this is the moment, I have the power and I am going to get a room of sixty people to sing '(Is This The Way To) Amarillo' with me. I'm going to do it. Yes, I am. I am going to sing in public.

I'm about to start the song when I see a man in the audience waving his arm at me. 'I'VE BEEN THERE!' he yells and then points to himself.

Omigod. My first heckler. I haven't been onstage for thirty seconds yet.

'Me too!' I yell back. 'I've been there, too! *Because I was born there.*' Zing!

Now shush, heckler! Just let me settle into the routine. This horse is likely to bolt. Settle in. Settle in. Wait, now I'm supposed to be singing.

'Guys, should we just sing a bit of the song? Yeah?' I ask, trying to sound casual and natural. As if I've ever led a sing-along in my entire life or even participated in one. But the audience doesn't know that! They just know what they see: a short Asian woman dressed like Sharon Horgan, telling them to sing this Tony Christie song.

'Yes!' they yell back, obligingly. Just like Kate had said they would.

And then I have to do it. I have to commit. Which means singing. I start alone. A nightmare in every way possible.

'Is this the way to Amarillo . . .' I start to croon tentatively, partially in hell, partially blacking out.

Mercifully, the audience takes over.

'Every night I've been hugging my pillow . . . !' they sing along with me.

'OK, that's enough,' I say to the audience, firmly. I make the 'cut off' gesture under my throat. They obediently stop singing. Here we go now. Now it's all me.

Onstage, under the lights, it's like an out-of-body experience: I settle into the routine. It flows, perfectly formed, as if separate from me.

I feel hyper-aware of my body, I can feel the tips of my fingers gripped tightly around the microphone, and yet it's like I'm not there. I look at the audience and see nothing, as if I'm in my own universe. My voice is strong, but not too fast. The anxiety is there, but it's not spinning out of control.

As soon as my act is over, I fumble with the mic and tell my legs, 'Don't you dare fall off the stage now,' and I look up and Kate is there to take the mic from me and then I'm scurrying back to my seat, to sit next to the rest of my classmates. I hear clapping. I hear cheers. I feel my soul being returned to my body.

I sit safely in the darkness. I can feel my classmates patting my back and whispering 'well done' and my face is hot, which means it is also bright red. But I did it. I said everything. I hadn't rushed. I hadn't faked being sick.

When I performed at Union Chapel, in that darkness, I'd felt something shift within me. But this, making people laugh out loud at my dumb jokes – this is making my whole body tingle. I can't help but put my hand over my mouth in disbelief – I'd just summited motherfucking Everest! My cheeks are still burning, but not in an ashamed way. More of a 'Can you believe we pulled that off?' red glow.

Still buzzing, I sit in the audience, watching my classmates also take the stage for the first time, and nail it. We'd helped each other get through this, and everyone is so on tonight. Soon, I forget myself because I am laughing so hard as Anthony dances onstage as part of his routine. But when the lights come up, I look around and feel dazed.

Honestly, I didn't know if I was going to get through my set. But somehow, I had made the crowd laugh. A man comes up to me, points and says, 'YOU. You made me laugh,' and then he laughs again and walks away. What?

I realize that I do not recognize myself from who I was a few months ago. I'm a little unnerved, but elated because now I know: things that seem impossible can suddenly become possible. A big part of this year was the desire to be brave enough to do something that felt so contradictory to the kind of person I thought I was.

Sam hugs me tightly and says, 'You were so good.'

Shaun pats me on the back and says, 'That was better than coke.' I'm bowled over by this astonishingly high praise from someone who works in advertising.

My classmates and I stay out, celebrating.

That night, a star is born.

That star is Anthony.

Seriously, though, that guy was amazing.

When I finally get home that night, I remember that I had Sam record me on his phone. I don't want to watch. I don't want to. But I do.

I half close my eyes and then hit play while shovelling ramen into my mouth. Jesus Christ, I am singing in public. I am moving my hands in a way I do not remember. I am swaying side to side, like I'm on a boat, riding these waves out, desperately trying to find my sea legs. I didn't even know I was doing it.

I . . . I look like I'm having fun. And I sound . . . confident. It doesn't feel like it's really me onstage. Afterwards, Lily had said, 'You seemed so comfortable. Where did that confidence come from?'

I'd always imagined that tonight, right before I got onstage, if I did enough prep and work and rehearsal and bear postures, I'd be filled with the supreme confidence to perform my routine perfectly. But self-confidence doesn't find us: we have to push ourselves to do something hard, live through it and then confidence will eventually follow. I'd faked confidence, and by doing so, created it. It really did feel like a feat of wizardry.

TALKING
TO MEN
a real-life interlude

One night, Sam and I are at a group dinner with some of his old friends and their partners. The men and women end up self-segregating. Sam and I are sitting in the middle of the table, at the cut-off point. I turn my head to my right to face the women and he turns to the left to talk to the other men.

In less than ten minutes, the women have plunged straight into Deep Talk. Two women, who just met this evening, discover that both of their mothers have Parkinson's disease.

I say 'discover' but the word I really mean is 'share'. They decide to open up to each other. When Laura tells us about what a difficult time she is having watching her mother suffer from the disease, the woman next to her confides that she is experiencing the exact same thing with her mother. I can see the relief on Laura's face. *Someone understands me. A total stranger understands this particular awful pain more than most of my close friends.*

It changes the temperature of the evening. Everyone on the right side of the table becomes more open, more honest, more willing to share and listen.

Later, when Sam and I are taking the Tube back home, I ask him for an update on his friends whom I hadn't found a chance to talk to. He tells me that two of his friends had switched jobs, and so his end of the table only talked about work.

'I wish I'd been in your conversation,' he says.

In almost every interaction I have, I find myself thinking back to that one particular lesson from my very first challenge in the classroom when Mark told me that we needed to engage in Deep Talk to form real connections with other people. I've been trying to practise going deeper in conversations, sidling straight on past the easy stuff and asking the questions that really open up space for something more meaningful.

The dinner with Sam and his friends hadn't felt atypical to me because, well, let's make no bones about it: over the course of the year, I'd simply found that it was easy to get into Deep Talk with other women. Maybe it was because we usually had more in common, maybe it was because we're generally encouraged to talk more openly about our feelings – I don't know why, but it just seemed like every time I took that leap into the uncomfortable unknown, women would leap right in after me.

By contrast, when I tried the same tactic with men, they would, more often than not, shut me out. One of Sam's friends I've known a long time is going through a break-up. He seemed different when we met up recently. Slightly wounded. I tried, gently, to ask what went wrong, and he blocked my efforts by getting up to grab another drink. I tried again. He blocked me again, this time pulling out his phone. Another male friend simply ignored my questions, feigning momentary deafness, and changed the conversation. I'm no expert on social conditioning, toxic masculinity or gender studies, but it was striking how differently these conversations tended to go with men.

I can't help but think back to my encounter with Chris, my vulnerability tennis partner who I met all those months ago in the School of Life classroom. How he was lonely and had trouble making friends, how he wanted new ones and how it felt like he was only able to admit this to me because I was a total stranger. He couldn't tell his wife that he felt this way.

I don't think Chris is an outlier. Research suggests that men are significantly lonelier than women. That one third of men feel lonely regularly. When I discover that one in eight men report that they have no one to discuss serious topics with, my encounters make a lot more sense.

A few days after that dinner, I catch up with my new friend Paul over coffee. He is telling me about a time when he cycled from the Netherlands to Spain – a many-months-long endeavour that he completed solo. I try to imagine myself in this scenario.

'Were you lonely?' I ask.

Paul pauses, taken aback by the question.

And this is the problem with Deep Talk. Not only do you have to be a bit vulnerable *and* a bit ballsy to ask the questions in the first place, but you're also asking whoever you're speaking with to be the same: open up, take your hand and embrace the depths.

Paul furrows his brow. After a beat, he nods.

'Yeah, I was,' he says.

'What did you do to combat it?'

'I wrote in my journal a lot,' he tells me. 'I went for walks. But I was still really lonely.'

He tells me that he's good at talking to new people, but that in most of the places where he stopped along the way people were pretty guarded.

When I play back this conversation in my head, I wonder how differently pre-sauna Jess would have handled it. Given that I didn't know Paul well, I would have probably asked about logistics, or how many miles he covered per day, or what kind of bike he rode. Maybe, at best, I'd have launched into a story about a bike seat I'd used in Beijing that was such a literal arse ache that I could barely walk for two weeks, followed by a monologue about the realities of life with thigh chafing.

I am so impressed by how open Paul is with me. He could have lied and told me, nah, he doesn't get lonely, that he relished the time alone on the road, he was a lone wolf, a cowboy striking out into the sunset with nothing but his trusty metallic steed.

One of the most vital parts of Deep Talk is that it has to be a two-way process – both parties have to be willing to share, to disclose, to be vulnerable. If you initiate it with someone but don't give back, you're likely just harassing innocent people to share extremely personal information.

I realize I probably shouldn't go around asking men about their loneliness and not share my own experience of it. Since we're all in this together, I'll tell you, too.

There was a time in my life when I was so lonely that my only friend was a deaf cat named Louis, except I was very allergic to him, and also neither of us particularly liked each other. Louis belonged to my flatmate in Beijing, who was rarely around, so it was usually just Louis and me. I could be home for three hours, but because he hadn't heard me, I would regularly turn a corner and he'd jump three feet into the air in shock – which in turn would set me on edge.

After work, I'd come home, eat dinner alone and then go to bed. Louis would spend his nights tunelessly howling outside my bedroom door at 2 a.m., but he'd vanish every time I peered through my doorway to investigate why. It was like cohabitating with a Victorian ghost.

Looking back from a safe distance on those long days spent alone, I can just about frame it as a funny anecdote, but the reality was far more painful. I recently found my journal from that time and I had written, 'I'm so lonely that I actually think about dying.'

Not so funny.

I wasn't suicidal. I've never self-harmed. I was still going to work, eating food, getting through the day. There are a lot of people who have felt far worse. But still, I was inside my own head all day, every day, and I went days without feeling like a single interaction made me feel seen or understood. There were moments when I felt this darkness, this stillness from being so totally alone, descend. It was a feeling that I didn't know how to shake; when it seized me, I wanted it to go away so much that when I imagined drifting off to sleep and never waking up again just to escape it, I felt calm.

I remember it happening most often when I'd wake up on a Saturday morning, the full weekend stretching out ahead of me, no plans, no one to see, no one waiting for me. Loneliness seemed to hit me hardest when I felt aimless, not gripped by any initiative or purpose. It also struck hard because I lived abroad, away from close friends or family.

These days, a weekend with no plans is my dream scenario. There are weekends in London that I set aside for this very purpose and they bring me great joy. But life is different when it is fundamentally lonely.

During that spell in Beijing, I made an effort to make friends at work. I asked people to dinner. I moved to a new flat, waved (an arm's-length) goodbye to Louis and found a new roommate, a gregarious Irishman, who ushered me into his friendship group. I had to work hard to dispel it, and on some days it felt like an uphill battle that I might not win, but eventually it worked. The loneliness abated.

It's taken me a long time to really believe, to *know*, that loneliness is circumstantial. We move to a new city. We start a new job. We travel alone. Our families move away. We don't know how to connect with loved ones any more. We lose touch with friends. It is not a damning indictment of how lovable we are.

Introvert or extrovert, shy or outgoing – loneliness can catch you, no matter who you are. And it's common. It's been described as an epidemic, and a minister for loneliness has been appointed in the UK after a study revealed 9 million people in Britain often or always feel lonely. It's not just the obvious candidates – the elderly, people living in remote locations – who struggle either. Today's 16–24-year-olds report feeling lonelier than those of any previous generation. Between social media, email, and meal and grocery delivery apps, we can outsource most in-person encounters to our phones, and the reliance on this technology increases with each passing year. Everyone experiences loneliness at some point in their life. But even though the issue is heavily covered in the media, it still feels like stepping on to treacherous ground to bring it up face to face.

After my dinner and coffee with Paul, I notice that loneliness naturally comes up a lot in conversation with others when I explain the impetus for starting my year of extroverting: sitting alone on my sofa, my best friends scattered around the world, and wondering what the hell was wrong with me. Once I explained this honestly, men I knew slowly began to open up to me.

One man, a new friend's husband Tom, tells me that he felt loneliest when he moved to Geneva to start a Ph.D programme. He'd been warned by a friend of his, who had recently moved to Paris for work: you will get so lonely that you will end up at a bar alone, sitting by yourself, looking to make friends. Tom had laughed – that was ridiculous. He'd never do that.

He lasted a week before he broke. His friend was right. He was 'going so crazy' that he went to a bar just to be around other people. He ended up talking to some guys there, and the following day he was playing football with them. He says that he kept going, going to events alone, talking to people, actively trying to make friends until he finally did. Sometimes it failed spectacularly, but eventually some friendships stuck.

Tom tells me he's an introvert and we discuss the misconception that introverts don't get lonely.

'Of course we can,' he says. 'Human contact is important. You can Skype or FaceTime, but at some point you want real contact.'

Introverts crave a particular kind of connection, so while extroverts might get a buzz from a busy city where they have small surface reactions with people, introverts tend to feel lonely in crowds, even if they are interacting with a few people. (In other words, we're difficult to please.)

One of Sam's friends, Pablo, tells me that he felt loneliest when he was travelling alone, staying in a hostel. He'd be reading on his bed while everyone else around him seemed to effortlessly become best friends with each other.

At improv, I become friendly with one of my classmates, Edward, who's an outgoing guy in his twenties. So obviously, on our walk back to King's Cross station, I ask him about the last time he felt lonely. Edward becomes quiet, shrugs and then tells me he'll think about it. Later that night he sends me a message saying that he feels incredibly lonely living in London right now. He's just moved back to the UK after spending five years abroad and he feels lost, and out of touch with his old friends. He tells me he actually feels lonely pretty much every moment he isn't doing improv.

'Improv does way too much heavy lifting,' he writes. 'It's the only time I don't feel . . . empty.' I feel my heart breaking reading those words. I had never suspected he felt this way.

There's this feeling that we should be self-sufficient, islands on our own, but secretly, introvert or extrovert, we all crave finding 'our people' and physically hanging out with each other. Sometimes in small doses, sure, but we still crave intimacy. Why can't someone gather all of us up with a big net and put us in a cosy pub with a fireplace and feed us nice snacks? Why must talking about loneliness and breaking out of it be so hard?

When I ask Edward what he and his work friends talk about, he tells me, 'Football.'

'Just football?' I ask.

'Yep,' he says.

'But when you go out to the pub together – is it still only football?'

Edward nods.

When I first moved to England, I fell slowly but surely in love with football. It was everywhere. Without even trying, my brain began to soak up knowledge about English teams: big fixtures, facts about players, controversial managers, relegation battles. I watched my first penalty shoot-out during the World Cup 2014 (Brazil vs Chile): men cried, I cried, Neymar cried, I was done for. I loved it.

I quickly realized that with football I had a source of endless small talk. As a freelance editor, I work in many different offices, full of people that I don't know. I often sleep badly the night before embarking on a new gig. It's that apprehension everyone has felt the night before starting a new job (except I have it every few months).

But with football, I can join in pretty easily. When I walk into a new office and a group gathers around the kettle talking about the FA Cup, I have something to say. For someone like me, it is like a gift from on high. Safe, ever-present and easy.

Football is the perfect vehicle for extroverting. For light conversations. For meeting new people. For breaking the ice. For silent cab rides and client drinks.

Football opened up a door for me – an easy way to quickly connect with a massive demographic (the majority of which are men – male supporters outnumber women two to one in the UK). But often once I've walked through that door, I find out that I am locked in a small room. I like talking about football for . . . forty-seven minutes. Maximum. Maybe an hour if it's during the World Cup. Then, I'm done. But once I've initiated it, I can't escape football chat. It is like trying to escape an enchanted maze – all dead ends and giant European goalkeepers blocking my way out. Turn right, and I'm trapped talking about transfer windows. Turn left, and we're talking about the Euros. Now I'm stuck in a loop about V.A.R. and CAN ANYONE HEAR ME IN HERE?

It leads me to a thought that I'm not even sure I'm legally allowed to have in a European country without the threat of deportation. Do . . . do we talk about football too much? Does this ultra-connector, this social leveller, this thing that brings together so many people, actually prevent us from real human connection?

It comes up with Benji, a comedian friend I'd met via my comedy classmates.

'People tell me I'm always asking hard questions,' Benji says. 'My friends are always calling me "heavy". Like, "Why do you have to be so heavy? We're not in therapy, mate."' Though this last bit is probably because Benji is a psychiatrist by day.

At the same time, other friends are relieved that Benji is willing to venture on to more difficult topics. He tells me about a friend of his whose wife is struggling to conceive – no one in their friendship group is asking him how IVF is going or about the effect it's having on his relationship with his partner. Another friend's cousin committed suicide but none of his other friends will broach the subject.

'Sometimes my friends can't get past talking about "the match last night",' he says.

Benji understands why his friends act this way and push aside his questions, even though it drives him mad. Football is a defence, but it's also fun to talk about – it's enjoyable and light. And also maybe people would rather talk about Messi than think about, say, their crumbling marriage. (It's probably also why pub quizzes are so popular – a social activity where there's very little time or pressure to talk about our personal lives.)

Football has been a conversational lifesaver for me so many times, but I wonder if I've enabled a monster. Because I don't just want passable chitchat, I want to break through the barriers, I want to *know* you.

Terrifying, I know.

*

Over coffee, a new friend I've matched with on Bumble, Annie, is telling me about a guy she's been dating for about two months. She says Sunil is kind, he's funny, he has a good job, he's handsome and they have a great sex life. She says all this with a wistful look in her eyes.

'So what's the problem?'

'I don't know if this is important, but . . . it's all banter,' Annie says.

'What do you mean?' I ask.

'We never have any . . . "deep chat". He talks about movies or what's going on at work, but we never have any meaningful conversations,' Annie says.

I think back to the American woman, wearing pearls, back in the classroom at the beginning of my year. She struggled to ask me a single deep question.

'Well,' I say. 'Have you tried asking him any deep questions?'

'Not really,' Annie says. 'It feels so awkward. And I don't want him to think I'm too serious.'

Maybe Sunil was hoping she would. Maybe he was saying the same things to his friends: she's sexy, smart, kind but the talk is all shallow.

When Annie first tells me this story, I feel myself jump immediately to frustration. How could she not ask him the questions she really wanted to know the answers to? And how could he not have asked her anything either?

But then I remember how hard this really is. When Sam and I had been dating for about six months, I struggled with this, too. I was bursting with all the questions I wanted to ask him, but it felt too exposing because it showed what I had been thinking about and how serious I was about him. I wanted to know about his relationship history. I wanted to know about his most recent ex-girlfriend. Did he end things or did she? Did they say 'I love you' to each other? Did he still pine for her? Did he want kids? Did he ever want to get married someday? (To, I don't know, an Asian–American woman with a low centre of gravity?)

When Sam and I were living in Australia, one winter weekend we rented a cottage in the countryside. We toured local wineries by day and at sunset we wrapped ourselves up in blankets on the porch overlooking the valley below, tucking into our bounty of wine and local cheese. I can't remember who initiated it (OK, fine, probably me), but we decided that during this magic hour while day turned to night we could ask each other anything.

This moment in our relationship changed everything. I got to ask all my questions and so did Sam. We also had to answer them. I think for both of us it's the night we tipped over from infatuation to falling in love. Even now, the phrase 'wine and cheese hour' is shorthand for this safe space, when we need to sit down and reconnect. This is so bougie and painful to admit, especially because I don't even like wine and this is now far more likely to be 'coffee and Jaffa cake hour'. (Vodka and Pringles works, too.)

I tell Annie about how powerful that openness and mutual vulnerability felt.

The researcher Arthur Aron claimed he knew how to make two strangers fall in love. He created a list of thirty-six intimate questions and argued that if you and a potential partner ask (and answer) these questions, then stare into each other's eyes for four minutes, the chances of the two of you falling in love would increase. The thinking behind it is that these questions accelerate your connection. Could this really work?

I send Annie the article with the list of questions. 'Try this,' I say, as if I'm a doctor sending her a prescription. The questions are hard to ask: What is your most treasured memory? What is your most terrible memory? They're even harder to answer: If you were to die this evening with no opportunity to communicate with anyone, what would you most regret not having told someone? Why haven't you told them yet?

Sam and I are eating dinner at our local ramen restaurant, but tonight I'm lingering over my noodles longer than usual. He's telling me about his friend who has just moved to Japan and seems to be struggling to make friends.

'How do you know? What did he say?' I ask Sam.

'He hasn't said anything specific. But he's spending all his time at work and the fact he hasn't got any stories about the nightlife and the expat scene is significant for someone like him. He's not used to being alone,' Sam says. 'He just seems a bit down.'

I think back to my previous conversations with men, some successful, others never going anywhere.

'I wish he could just tell you. I wish more men could admit these things,' I say.

A few minutes later, the door to the restaurant opens and a man enters. He sits down at the table next to us, alone, and sets down a book. I glance over to read the title. It's *Daring Greatly: How the Courage to Be Vulnerable Transforms the Way We Live, Love, Parent, and Lead* by Brené Brown.

Omigod.

I know this sounds too good to be true, but it is. I swear on all that is holy, including Neymar's right foot. The universe was listening to me.

Brené Brown is the researcher and professor who had inspired me to find a reliable, trusting friend – a friend who would 'move the body' with you. She also espouses the power of vulnerability in her now famous TED Talk, the one that had made me rethink giving a speech at my own wedding. And now, here is this man, alone, reading her book.

Of all the ramen joints in north London, he walked into mine.

I look at Sam meaningfully, nodding towards the guy and his book. Sam shakes his head firmly: no. I nod vigorously: yes. Sam shakes his head. I take a deep breath.

Cometh the hour, cometh the woman.

'Is that a good book?' I say, leaning over our table, towards the man.

He looks up. Then I see the expression on his face. I have disturbed this man, this man who just wanted eat his delicious ramen in peace at 8 p.m. on a Saturday and quietly read about the power of vulnerability.

'I don't know. I've just started it,' he says. He purposefully opens the book and starts reading. Door shut. Curtains closed. *Bugger off.*

Oh God, I am 'that person'. A chatty nightmare who terrorizes innocent people going about their daily lives. And because I'm obsessed with Deep Talk, I am also in danger of becoming the person who ruins every fun moment with a protest of, 'But what about the children?' The party guest that friends describe afterwards as 'that lady who frankly scares us'.

The man is already reading the book on vulnerability and loneliness. I shouldn't bother him. He's on his way. He's good.

Sometimes, it's good to ask Deep Questions and sometimes it's better just to be quiet. To live and let live. My old mode of being, which I had forgotten was sometimes so sweet. Especially to the strangers around me.

Our bill comes and we pay. We put on our coats, and Sam and I walk into the cool night. I take one look back through the window to steal a glance at the man – he's still intently reading the book.

We amble home, bellies full of hot, salty noodle soup, our hearts bursting, and back just in time to catch *Match of the Day.*

LA-LA LAND

or

travelling solo

I board the Stansted Express at 6 a.m. on a Tuesday morning. It's still dark outside, and I can't remember the last time I was up before the sun.

I sit down on the train and rip open the envelope that arrived in the mail last week. There's a handwritten note inside.

> Hi Jessica,
> Embrace what you don't know.
> Have fun,
> Sarah

I don't know Sarah. All I know is that she's the one who chose where I'm flying to today. I'm leaving the country; I'll end up somewhere in Europe. Only Sarah knows the rest.

One note in the envelope told me to arrive at the airport by 6.30 a.m., where I will board my flight to the unknown.

It's the closest a layman will ever get to receiving a note that says, 'Your mission, should you choose to accept it . . .' and I am desperately hoping my mission isn't too painful.

At exactly 6.30 a.m., my destination will be unlocked. All I have to do is scratch off the code in the second, sealed note in the envelope. I will type it into my phone and then all will be revealed. On the train to Stansted, I look out of the window and watch the sun slowly starting to rise across London as I wait for the clock to tick down. Would I land in a new city like Bologna, eat giant plates of pasta and ride an orange Vespa? Would I drink strong coffee and walk by the sea in Stockholm? Explore the back streets of Madrid?

6.28 a.m. In these final two minutes, the possibilities are still endless. I could end up anywhere. Doing anything. Having the time of my life.

I'm in search of something more than a new place, though. I'm in search of a feeling and a state of being: that magical time when you can't possibly predict what's going to happen next or who you are going to meet or where they are going to take you. In this state, everything flows, every surprise is a delight, and new people guide you to special adventures. My neighbour Hannah (future best friend?) told me that she calls the thing I'm looking for la-la land. Sometimes you can fall into la-la land (not the musical) on your doorstep, but it's easier to access this feeling of infinite possibility when you are in a foreign land.

6.29 a.m. When in life do we have the time and room and space for this kind of surprise and adventure? Hardly ever. For holidays, we stay in positively reviewed hotels, eat at restaurants with excellent TripAdvisor ratings, go to the places with the most Instagram tags. There are standardized versions of every holiday spot – we leave home looking for a new adventure and return having enjoyed a near-identical holiday to everyone else we know, complete with the same photos of us jumping into the sea from the same spot.

There is no mystery. There is no enigma. There is rarely la-la land. By not knowing where I am headed, and relying on the kindness and insights of strangers instead of using social media or guidebooks during my stay, I'm hoping to find it.

With just sixty seconds to go before my destination is unlocked, I think: I could be watching a Scandinavian indie band in Oslo in a few hours. Drinking red wine on a terrace in Bordeaux with a winemaker named Gerard. Wandering the canals in Amsterdam with a wooden pipe in my mouth.

6.30 a.m. It's time. I find a 20p coin in my pocket and scratch off the code on the paper. I key it into my phone. The numbers begin flashing:

5, 4, 3, 2, 1 . . .

I hold my breath, until finally, finally my secret destination is revealed:

Budapest, Hungary.

Oh.

Whenever I travel, I tend to over-plan. A part of introversion for some people is being too much inside your own head, being overly cautious and not opening yourself up to other people. Which means less spontaneous adventure and more agonizingly detailed activity spreadsheets, with plenty of scheduled breaks.

So I decided to take a trip to the literal unknown. With no guidebooks, no internet tips, no Instagram searches. I will take the advice of people I meet along the way and be open to adventure in a brand-new foreign land.

Which is why the big reveal feels so anti-climactic. Because I've been to Budapest before. My parents went on a cruise along the Danube and when they disembarked there I met up with them.

Here's what I remember about Budapest:

1) Gorgeous views of the city from a castle
2) A museum called the House of Terror full of Nazi and Soviet nightmares
3) Frowny locals
4) Goulash

That was seven years ago. Budapest had been fine, but I hadn't really loved it. I can't quite remember why, but I wasn't sure I'd ever return – and now I was on my way back. The company that booked me on this trip is called Srprs.me. Like, 'Surprise Me!' Well, it definitely was a surprise – not least because I would never book a holiday flight that required me to be at Stansted at 6.30 a.m.

When you book your holiday on the Srprs.me site, you can pick up to three cities to veto. I chose Munich, because I'd just been there for the wedding; Barcelona, because I'd read that they're currently protesting against over-tourism;

and Marseilles, because a woman I had met at a networking event a few weeks ago told me ominously that she had been drugged there and then said, 'It's fine . . . FINE. But *never* go to Marseilles.' Like a reverse fairy godmother, she gave me advice while clutching a glass of Prosecco and staring away with a haunted look in her eyes. I took her very seriously.

I paid £220, and the site assured me that they would take care of accommodation and the flight. A week before the departure date, they sent me the weather report so I had some semblance of what to pack. All I had to do was prepare for 'amazement and ceaseless adventure'.

Done, Srprs.me. You're on.

My parents were convinced that Srprs.me was really just a for-profit kidnapping operation in which idiots (me) fork out money and essentially fund our own abduction. Like the Liam Neeson movie *Taken*, except I willingly board the plane, my belongings neatly packed, and later disembark and run into the arms of my kidnappers yelling, 'I'm herreee! What's for lunch?'

So. Budapest. Hungary.

What do I do at the airport? I can't buy a travel guide. That's breaking the rules.

I make a beeline for the DutyFree perfume aisle and spray Chanel 'Chance' on my wrists to symbolically invite spontaneity and luck into my adventure. I slather Crème de la Mer all over my face, because that shit is expensive. It is not integral to adventure, but I'd rather fly by the seat of my pants with youthful skin. Then I rub Kiehl's lotion on my hands because aeroplanes are very drying. OK, NOW I'm ready.

Budapest. Yes, and . . . ?

My hotel room is sparse, but clean and decent-sized. Large windows. A mini-fridge. I unpack. I'd packed a fancy, floor-length dress because I'd imagined going to the Italian opera in Rome. A white bikini in case I was on the beach in San Sebastian or diving into the Aegean Sea. I put my things down and pack my bag for the day: some Hungarian cash, a black swimsuit (quick Danube dip?), my bottle of water. Ready.

I go to the door to unlock it. And struggle. I try to turn the key but it won't budge. I'm locked in. I can't get out. I try to wiggle the key again, frantically. It's stuck. I've locked myself in. I start sweating and feel a strangled yelp rise in my throat.

I'VE BEEN TAKEN. I HAVE KIDNAPPED MYSELF.

I run over to the room phone and press zero.

'Help. I'm locked in my room!' I shout breathlessly.

'Are you inside of the room or outside of the room?' the man on the end of the line asks, long-sufferingly.

'The inside.' How else would I be calling you?

He doesn't even try to stifle his heavy sigh.

'I'll send the maid to let you out,' he says.

A few minutes later, a confused maid does let me out. She tries to show me how to use the key and I mime to her (thank you, improv) that I understand how to use the key but that it's a very sticky lock.

She steps outside in a demonstrative flourish to lock me back in the room and test what I have learned. Once again I am stuck.

When I'm released the second time, I immediately pack up to switch rooms.

Take two. Backpack on, passport tucked away, I pull my hair into a ponytail and tighten my shoelaces.

If I'm going to succeed at this, I will have to pretend I am Jason Bourne, thrust into a city with a mission. Except Jason wasn't really into making friends. He was a trained assassin. Running for his life. Maybe this isn't the best metaphor but it's helpful in the moment.

I suddenly feel very free. Where to? I could go anywhere.

I check my phone and see a message from Charles, my travel mentor.

Charles was Sam's tour guide on a two-week trip across America about fifteen years ago and they'd stayed friends ever since.

He has led multiple group tours across America, ranging from wholesome families to drunken bachelor parties and buses full of Australians, and not one of them has died, despite many trying their very best to with idiotic, booze-fuelled antics, like stealing people's guns in New Orleans.

He has been to all fifty states in the US and trekked his way around Southeast Asia, South America, India and Australia.

But that's not why I chose Charles as my mentor. I was much more interested in his secret ability. See, Charles is one of those people who stumbles into la-la land nearly every place he goes. He's the first to admit how lucky he is. He actually says things like, 'It doesn't really rain on me.' He wanders into bad situations and emerges wealthier, with fifteen new best friends. He forgets his passport and still makes his flight, then gets upgraded. He's that guy.

It's hard to listen to Charles for too long without hating him. Which is made extra hard because he's extremely friendly and likable. He even looks like Ben Fogle. It almost goes without saying that he is an outgoing extrovert. We could not be more naturally different.

But when over dinner in London I tell Charles about my mission, to go out and meet strangers and have a good time and make friends without using my phone or guidebooks, he looks concerned.

'That would have worked ten years ago,' he says. 'But everything has changed now. In my old tour groups, the group would bond and become good friends. Now, we'll all go to a bar and they're on their phones looking at people on dating apps instead.'

I had been afraid of this.

'It's much harder to meet people now. Before I could easily do it in a hostel or bar.'

'Were you good at it?'

'I was excellent at it,' Charles says.

He's just stating a fact: Charles is a people magnet. The funnest guy in the room. You want to be in Charles' orbit.

'So you'd just walk into a bar by yourself in a foreign country and meet people?'

'Absolutely.'

'Aren't you afraid of them murdering you?'

Charles is on his second glass of wine. He looks at me.

'Fuck no.'

'Never?' I ask.

'I have zero of that in me. You have . . . all of it,' he says, gesturing at me.

I'm silent, thinking about this.

'Jess, I can't remember *ever* thinking somebody's a murderer.'

That's because you're a man, I think, darkly.

'I think that ten times a day,' I say.

'Well, that's probably why you're bad at meeting people,' he says. 'You can't think like that and expect to make friends.'

'What if I fail at meeting a single person? Or having one adventure?' I ask.

'There *is* no fail,' Charles says. 'Do it or don't do it.' My Yoda has spoken.

And so I book my trip, my mind whirring with tough scenarios I might get myself into when travelling alone. Who holds your bag when you pee? What if you don't see the sign for the right train station? If your wallet is stolen, who will spot you? What if you become ill? What if? What if? What if?

Charles's message says this:

YOU GOT THIS! Embrace the unknown, choose your response and make your own weather. :)

By 'choose your response', I think Charles means that we can decide to alter a less-than-ideal situation into a good one just by changing our outlook. Something I'm not a natural at. And I honestly don't know how he expects me to make my own weather.

I survey the streets of Budapest. I am at a total loss. Yes, I need to embrace the unknown, but I also don't want to wander straight into the sprawling suburbs or fall straight into the bottom of a well. I turn back around and ask the guy at the hotel desk, Gabor (no relation to Zsa Zsa, he tells me), which direction I should go in and he points directly ahead outside the front door.

'Everything is that way,' he says.

It's a sunny, blue sky day. I walk and see a sign for the opera house. The opera! I could go to the opera after all! I don't need Italian opera, I have Hungarian opera!

But as I approach the building I see that there is scaffolding wrapped all the way around the façade; it's partially closed. At a booth outside the entrance, a man tells me that there are no performances, but I can still take a tour.

I wander into the opera house entrance and look at the ceiling's gold mouldings and fresco paintings and chandeliers while I wait in the queue to buy a ticket. The ticket booth man greets me.

'Hello! How can I help you? Two tickets?'

I turn around and there is an Asian man in his forties behind me.

'Oh, we're not together,' I say.

Yet.

I pay for my ticket, and after the Asian man purchases his, I turn to him.

'Where are you from? Are you travelling alone, too?' I ask him, this man who is my future best friend.

'I'm from Borneo,' he says. A woman and a girl appear by his side. 'And this is my family.'

The woman looks at me accusingly.

Great. I've hit on a Malaysian man in front of his wife. First stranger down.

Looking around at the growing crowd of tourists assembling for the group tour in their various caps and bumbags, I have a little moment.

I haven't eaten today, it's 3 p.m. and I don't want to be here.

I want to see an opera but I don't want to do this tour.

Who am I trying to impress? I answer to no one but myself. I choose my response and toss my ticket into the bin.

After flagging down two strangers who seem baffled by my question of, 'So where should I eat?', I head to an information booth and ask the Hungarian guy in his twenties manning the booth, 'So, rather than where you tell tourists to go, where would YOU go eat lunch right now?' and he pulls out a map and points me towards an area called Október 6. I make my way in that direction and stop at the first restaurant, with red and white tablecloths and little jars of paprika on each table. After a very salty meal of wet pork and red peppers over soggy chips in an empty restaurant, I walk through the city, looking up at the imposing Neo-Renaissance and baroque buildings.

Alone in my head I suddenly remember what psychologist Nick said: 'Nobody waves, but everyone waves back.' I start to smile at people as they pass. No one smiles back.

Confused, I start googling Hungary stats (technically not cheating – I'm not looking for travel tips, I'm merely studying up on the locals). I land on an international ranking system comparing 65 country attributes among 80 nations. On the 'Fun' scale of 1–10, Hungarians rate a 1.6. Italians score a 9.1. (Brits get a 4.2.) So maybe it's not just me. I catch myself in the reflection of a store, scowling. Personally, I'm an even 0 right now.

The buildings are beautiful, but everything feels inaccessible to me: big, imposing or empty. Normally, I'd go to a museum or gallery, but that's not really a great way to meet new friends, and 'meeting people' feels, to me, like an integral part of finding la-la land. My eyes are glazing over. It's not even 7 p.m., but I can't keep them open after not sleeping last night. I decide to walk back to my hotel and re-group.

I end up falling asleep and wake up twelve hours later. 7.30 a.m.

I can't tell Charles that I spent my first day in Budapest asleep. I pack my day bag to try and redeem this holiday. And myself.

After I get a tip to head to a bathhouse from a barista, I head towards the Danube and cross over the bridge, wind whipping in my hair. When I reach the Gellert Baths, I immediately fall in love with the Art Nouveau building, with its tiled arcade and painted dome ceilings.

In the locker room, I change into my black one-piece and flip-flops (flip-flops are always necessary, no matter the destination). I shove my clothes in the locker and look around.

I literally have *no idea* what I'm doing. I'm going to go take a bath . . . with other people? Isn't that . . . swimming?

Essentially, I am going swimming in Hungary. Also, I keep calling it Hungaria in my mind because I used to have a roommate from Bulgaria.

I follow some other bathers up some stairs outside, where I find a gorgeous blue pool with colourful mosaic tiles. Trees surround the grounds – orange and yellow leaves because it's late summer.

This place is stunningly beautiful. I gingerly climb into the water. It's warm, but not hot. Like I'm sinking into the womb. There are only a handful of other people in the pool. I shake my head in surprise – I've found an unexpected oasis and I suddenly feel incredibly happy, elated at the surprise of ending up here.

I ease my body in and then do breaststroke across the length of the pool. I flip over on to my back and take in the regal surroundings. Floating there, I close my eyes and take a deep breath. The air is warm with a slight bite to it. I open my eyes, looking at the blue sky and the orange leaves on the trees.

OK, I really like this. Despite hating the idea of travelling alone without a plan, I'm now in a foreign country, having fun by myself. Somehow, I have ended up floating in a giant bathtub staring up at a Hungarian sky. Honestly, it feels liberating. Sure, I had been slightly miserable yesterday and I'd dragged my feet through Budapest. But apparently I didn't need to be tied to spreadsheets or five-year plans or itineraries. I could find a sliver of adventure by myself in unknown places.

After swimming, I wander around exploring the grounds and see a queue of men entering a wooden doorway. Ah, yes, the sauna. My old friend. It's crisp outside, and so I bound over to warm up. As I enter the sauna, the darkness is discombobulating.

It's always awkward to walk into a room full of strangers – but it's stranger still when you're wearing a swimsuit and all the strangers are chubby topless Hungarian men in their fifties who give you a hard stare as you walk in.

Still, I've been in worse rooms.

I spread my towel out and sit, the heat engulfing me. As I settle back against the wooden slats, it comes to me in flashes: the spa receptionist, me dressed in black sweats, roasting the water out of my body for the weight loss contest. I look around me, at the Hungarian men. I try not to think about how I could easily beat all of them in a fitness and weight loss competition.

Instead I focus on how far I've come. I'm not scared and depressed like the last time I was in a sauna, I'm in a moment of unexpected idyll in a very unlikely place. Who'd have thought that would ever happen?

Eventually I grow hungry. After changing back into my clothes, I go in search of food. I'm craving a delicious slice of cake.

I cross the Danube again and wander around for what feels like hours. With no destination, it feels impossible to pick a place to stop. Finally, I reach a large square and spot a place called the Café Gerbeaud. It's grand, in the way so many things in Budapest are. There is a window display full of colourful cakes and shiny eclairs.

The room has high, arched ceilings with a pea-green trim and floor-to-ceiling window alcoves. Faux marble floors and chandeliers. I take a seat in a corner by a window, facing the room. And it hits me: I've been here before. With my parents. We had asked their concierge where to find the best cake and he had told us to come here. I'm sitting next to the very table we sat at seven years earlier. About to order the best cake.

When it arrives, the Gerbeaud cake is a rectangular slice of dark, shiny chocolate over shortcrust pastry with almond-apricot jam and layers of chocolate.

It looks gorgeous. Almost too good to eat.

Almost.

I take a bite.

It's dry. Extremely dry. The whole thing tastes like a desiccated Fig Newton with bitter chocolate on it. Last time I was here, this cake was delicious. What had happened?

My low blood sugar is making me disproportionately furious.

This is CAKE. How can cake be bad? How do you fuck up cake, Hungary???

In *The Great British Bake Off*, sometimes Paul Hollywood will bite into an exquisite masterpiece, make a face and say, 'You need to work on your flavours.' And I always say, 'Oh come on, Paul! She made a beautiful cake in the allotted time! I'm sure it tastes FINE!'

Now I know that he was right because fuck this shiny, pretty, parched cake.

My idyll shatters.

I drink my coffee and push my cake aside with a mixture of shame and contempt.

Jason Bourne doesn't cry over bad cake! Jason Bourne doesn't cry. (Although he should. Because toxic masculinity.)

The truth is, regardless of my afternoon at the baths and the sense of adventure that brought me here, I haven't connected with anyone since I arrived and I feel painfully alone.

It's a strange paradox. I want desperately to be hanging out with people but the idea of talking to strangers makes my stomach hurt. A lot of my shyness that I thought I had banished has returned in this unfamiliar city. Had my comfort zone only been able to expand when it was home in London? Was I not really changed?

I hear a voice and glance to my right.

In the corner next to me is a bearded man with curly, dark hair and a big frame. He asks the waitress for his bill in English, but he has an accent. This is my chance to strike.

Plus, I need intel.

'Hi,' I say to the curly-haired man. 'What did you order?'

He picks up the menu and points to a picture of a fancy vanilla éclair.

'Was it good?' I ask.

'Yes!' he says.

'Where are you from?'

'Greece,' he tells me. 'Are you here for work?' he asks. I guess my vibe doesn't scream 'local'.

'No, I'm . . . I'm just visiting for fun,' I say. It's the truth. Ish. 'What are you in town for?'

'I'm a manager at the World Wrestling Championships this week,' he tells me.

Bingo! I would go to a wrestling match! This is what the universe wanted me to do.

But then the man tells me that the matches don't begin until after I fly home, and before I can follow up with an earnest interrogation about his career choices, he gets up and leaves.

'Take care!' he calls, as he disappears out the door.

Undeterred, I order the éclair he'd recommended. It arrives looking immaculate, but I'd been fooled before. I dig my spoon into it and take a bite: coffee-flavoured whipped cream, fondant topping, bourbon vanilla. It's delicious. The Greek man may only have been in my life for a fleeting moment, but he has saved the afternoon and my need for cake. I consider us bonded for ever.

No one else in the cafe is alone. I'm usually fine eating on my own in public back home, but back home there was none of this crushing loneliness that had just sprouted up, the cumulative effect of two days of not connecting with anyone. That's because time passes differently when you're trying to kill it. In London, I could easily spend a few days alone, enjoying this solitude, but here, in a foreign city, slightly overwhelmed by everything, and with nothing to really do, my mind is going all over the place.

I'd gone around London asking men how they felt about loneliness, feeling like if we could just talk about it, it would break its spell and disappear for ever. And now here I am in Eastern Europe – and loneliness has hunted me down again. Just like the other times when it has descended upon me, I feel aimless and lost.

I haven't brought any books to read on this holiday, which is a first for me. That's because I'm not supposed to be reading – I'm supposed to be meeting fantastic new friends at every corner, exciting people who order tequila shots and take me to secret gardens or steal boats. Where are these people? Why haven't I found them yet?

Suddenly, with all this time on my hands and all this time alone in my head, I find myself missing my parents, wishing I saw them more, missing Sam, who would make this weekend fun, missing my friends who live scattered across the world and doubting all of my recent life decisions. Like a surprise solo-trip to Budapest.

Even though solitude is important to me, I like it on my own terms. And right now, I'd really like it if Sam or my parents or Rachel or a surprise friend-date walked through that door.

Then I remember – I know someone from Budapest! Eniko, who I'd met in my improv class back in London. Before I can stop myself, I text her, asking her for tips. I tell myself this is fine and definitely not cheating: she's a local, I met her at an improv class while extroverting my heart out. It. Does. Not. Count.

She texts me back, 'You should definitely eat at Zeller Bistro.'

Reinvigorated with this insider advice, I finish my éclair and make my way across the city towards Zeller, which twinkles with lights in the distance. Just try to talk to someone tonight, I tell myself. Just one person. You've been doing this for months now. You know it usually goes fine. You even have the data to back this up. You've interviewed social psychologists. You took a *class* in this. You're highly trained now.

You can do this.

When I arrive, I note that the restaurant is incredibly romantic: decorative plants and leaves hanging from the ceiling, warm lamps, candles on the table.

I take a seat at my table for one and a waiter tells me the specials. I'm contemplating the truffle soup when I hear someone say, 'I'll have the truffle soup.' I look to my right and see a woman who looks a lot like me, also eating alone. She then orders the beef carpaccio and I realize she has an American accent.

I look at the candles and the plants. A couple at the table next to me are holding hands and looking into each other's eyes. A big group across the room is laughing, loudly. They pause and then break out into a new roar.

I brace myself for what I'm about to do.

'So, where are you from?' I shout across to the woman at the table next to me.

I have become my mother. It has happened. I've been pushed to the brink of loneliness, and I have caved. The woman starts and then glances over at me.

'Chicago,' she says.

'Are you travelling alone?' I ask.

'Yep,' she says. She picks up a piece of bread. I look around the restaurant, at the groups, at the romantic couples. I can sit here and stare at my phone while sitting by her, staring at her phone. Or I can choose to be open.

'Want to have dinner with me?' I ask, gesturing to my table.

'Oh . . . OK,' she says. I realize, given our proximity, I have put her in a position where saying no would have been the more excruciating choice. The next thirty seconds are agonizingly awkward as she moves her shopping bags, her plate, her drink and her purse over to my table. The Hungarian waiters watch on.

She takes the seat across from me.

'I'm Jess,' I say, standing up and offering my hand.

'I'm Wendy,' she says, taking my hand.

'And I'm Mark,' a waiter interjects near us. 'And I'm Lukas!' another one says. They shake hands with each other, laugh and then high-five.

Cool.

Wendy, my dinner mate (new best friend?) is visiting Budapest, then Vienna and then Bavaria alone. She prefers travelling solo because in the past she's been saddled with travel partners who don't want to explore or eat the local food. I tried to see it through her eyes – that solo travel is rare and precious and gave her enormous freedom to do whatever she wanted.

I also want to ask, 'But don't you get struck by devastating loneliness that drives you to do things like cry at a cake?' But

I've just met Wendy, this is our first date and I'm also busy shoving the free bread the waiter has brought into my mouth. Then I devour my ribs and potatoes, my first decent meal since I've arrived.

Wendy just applied to medical school, and I feel suspiciously like my dad sent her to me as an example. My wily doppelganger, who has researched everything in Budapest to a tee.

The waiter brings the bill over and then says, 'You made a new friend! I've never seen that happen here.'

He doesn't know what bad cake and a lonely day can do to a person.

Eniko had also recommended a pub, so I invite Wendy to come with me. We chat as we wander the streets of the old town and gradually I feel that sense of aimlessness that has plagued me all day beginning to slip away. In Wendy's company I feel grounded somehow, here in this time and place. Less rootless. Like I exist.

The bar feels more like ten bars in one with multiple rooms spread over two floors. Each room has different kinds of music – Europop, jazz, Oasis.

Szimpla Kert is a 'ruin pub' so it's actually very old, but it doesn't feel that way. Wendy insists on us ordering *palinka*, a traditional Hungarian spirit (a friend who orders shots!). The bartender hands us clear-coloured shots of alcohol. I down mine, and feel the heat of the alcohol spring instantaneously to my cheeks. I shudder and order a cider instead. Screw tradition.

Wendy and I wander and settle in a room where a woman is playing 'Memories' from *Cats* on the piano. We sit in half of a broken bathtub and face a group of Europeans (it's unclear where they're from exactly, but they are blond and their confidence is high and the men all have long hair) smoking shisha out of hookahs. The old ruin walls behind them are adorned with the terrifying and the crazy: a decapitated baby doll, real old school portraits of anonymous twelve-year-olds, pewter plates, child toilet seats, paintings of grey cats, Slinkys. It all somehow feels totally normal.

In the bathtub, Wendy talks about her job as a lab technician in Chicago. I listen to her, feeling a vague affection for her, this woman who has shocked me out of my loneliness and accompanied me to this must-visit bar.

Wendy tells me that for breakfast she ate at the New York Palace Café, but she fears that might be too lacklustre for me. 'Because you live in London so you must eat in palaces all the time,' she says.

Sure, let's go with that.

I tell her that she has to go to the Gellert Baths, where I'd had my unexpected moment of bliss in the blue, outdoor pool. Where I'd floated under the trees, in a rare state of Zen. It feels nice to swap travel tips with someone I've met randomly on the road.

On the way to the loo, I accidentally walk into the men's room, flee, then run smack into a British stag do. While bolting from them, I am absorbed into a crowd that is pushing me into a room with a Europop song sung by a precocious girly voice.

When I finally get back to the bathtub, Wendy says she's ready to go home. I wonder if I should actually be staying out, trying to meet new people for this undertaking, but my phone is on 8 per cent battery life and I have no idea how to get back to my hotel without it.

Ten p.m. in the liveliest bar in Budapest. Isn't this the ideal time to have an adventure? Yes, but it's also the ideal time to get murdered. Despite Charles' advice, I still feel this way. Even after everything I've done this year, I still don't feel comfortable approaching strangers in bars at night alone.

On the way out, Wendy and I pass a food market, and I stop to buy *langos*, a traditional Hungarian snack. It's essentially deep-fried bread dough covered in a hefty serving of sour cream and smothered in grated white cheese. It is bigger than my face.

I eat it because I feel like I have to. This is *langos*! This is tradition! Wendy approves!

Soon after, Wendy and I bid farewell to each other. I wish her luck on her next travel leg to Vienna, and she tells me she will follow me on Instagram. Perhaps Wendy is not my future new best friend, but she's definitely a welcome ally in a foreign land.

As I make my way back to my hotel, alone on the dark and empty streets, I'm extra alert. Passing grand unfamiliar buildings, I get a happy buzzy feeling as I wander through this city I didn't know I'd be visiting again.

For about ten minutes, I feel transported back to when I used to walk home when I was living in Beijing. It was a magical time because so much of my life was still unknown. Everything in Beijing had seemed so exciting: the charming tiny alleys, the street vendors, the cyclists.

It's difficult to maintain that sense of wonder in the city where you are settled. Sure, every now and then you glance up and notice the astonishing beauty of the trees you scuttle past every day on the way to the supermarket, or feel a glow of pleasure as you settle in a beloved cafe down the road from your flat, but most of the time we're too caught up in our daily lives to really notice. Travelling abroad reboots that setting in our brains.

Right now, I'm in Budapest, and I am finally looking up.

Six hours later, I'm in my hotel puking up fried bread.

It is there, on the bathroom floor in Budapest, that I finally admit to myself that I am not having the time of my life here.

Though some of it is my fault, Budapest is also a little tough. She is a beautiful, cold mistress. She's imposing, mysterious, unsmiling. She doesn't know what salad is. She is obsessed with bathing. She scares me, a little.

I have failed to connect with her. To seduce her. To make her laugh. To fall in love with her.

These days, we talk a lot about authenticity, especially in relation to travel. To really dive deep into a place, you need to meet locals. But I'd found that I couldn't just walk into a pub and chat with a bunch of Hungarian men. I can't crash a lecture hall. And while the waiters I met were perfectly friendly, they definitely didn't want to be coerced into an intimate friendship at the local baths (or maybe they did, I don't know, but I probably shouldn't investigate this too thoroughly).

In the sitcom *The Good Place* (spoiler alert, if you haven't got to the end of series one, skip the next paragraph immediately), the characters, who have died, are told they are in The Good Place (heaven), when they are *actually* in The Bad Place (hell). Eleanor, the main character, always figures out she's been duped, usually from one big, glaring clue, like having to endure three hours of spoken word jazz from her 'soulmate'. At each moment of discovery, Eleanor stands up and declares, 'Oh, THIS is The Bad Place' in shock.

'Choose your response,' Charles had said. So far I've been letting my knee-jerk response to the destination and my pre-conceptions overwhelm any new possibilities. I'd arrived in Budapest unfairly biased towards it already being The Bad Place from my previous time here: OK food; not super friendly; dark, bloody history.

The next morning, I walk out of my hotel and go right instead of left. Today, Budapest will be The Good Place. I will make it so.

I buy a coffee in a cute cafe. A handsome Hungarian man serves me. I smile at him and he smiles back.

Yes, that tiny gesture is so big that the day already feels different. I ask him where I should go, and he writes down the address for the Szechenyi Spa Baths.

It's about a forty-minute walk away and I wander through the quiet streets, savouring the different energy in these residential areas.

When I reach the bathhouse, I take in the enormous, majestic, yellow building. There are several outdoor baths in a large courtyard and dozens more inside. God, they really do love their baths here.

I wander around the pools before heading for a quick massage. A Hungarian woman de-cricks my neck, which hasn't been the same since my flight, and restores it to normal. I sit in a very, very hot steam room that smells like eucalyptus. It all feels good. There are people, so technically I'm extroverting, though it's mostly couples.

I swim in the outdoor pool, then hit the dry sauna before I venture into the underground natural mineral baths.

They are warm and dark and smell like egg farts. I try to embrace it.

What did you learn, Jess?

That sometimes you just have to embrace the unknown and smell the thermal farts.

I dive back into the outdoor pool to rinse the smell off.

My hair wet, I get dressed and wander the streets again until it is time to grab a taxi and head to the airport.

Jess, what did you do in Budapest?

Washed myself fifteen times, walked fifty miles to nowhere and barfed up fried dough. You?

I had swum in multiple baths and met new people, but I had eluded la-la land. Or la-la land had eluded me. Maybe you can't find it when you are looking for it. Maybe that is a key feature of the place. I had tried to book a ticket there, and that's the only sure-fire way never to arrive.

In the departure lounge, my flight turns red on the board. It's delayed. By several hours.

NO. No no no.

I'm going to miss the last train home. I'm going to have to take an Uber or a taxi. I'm going to arrive into London at 3 a.m.

I scour the airport for potential North-East Londoners, my shyness eradicated by exhaustion and thriftiness. I need to find someone to share a ride home with. After a couple of false starts, I happen upon Jaime, a Chilean man. He tells me he's staying with friends in London and points to an address a three-minute walk away from my flat. I yelp in joy.

It is a Hungarian miracle.

Jaime gets up and comes back with a beer and takes the seat next to me.

He tells me that he works with Hungarian locals who have told him all the good, secret bars and restaurants that tourists don't know about. And a live music festival in small venues all over the city.

'OK, well, it's a little too late for that, Jaime,' I say, eating a Mars Bar. 'Your knowledge is no use to me now.' Any shyness I have ever felt has completely evaporated: frankly, I am over it. It's midnight and I still reek of chlorine from the baths (I did not shower after the bathhouse, thank you for not judging me at this fragile time).

Desperation can bond people, but you can't engineer it. Luckily, desperation has found me.

Finally our gate is announced and we make our way towards it. I lose my passport four times in my own bag in the boarding queue because I'm so tired. I bid Jaime goodbye until London as I settle into my seat on the plane.

I want a do-over. I want to book a trip to a destination unknown again and specify that I want them to pick somewhere delicious and ultra-friendly. But there are no do-overs in life. This is a lesson I'm still learning as an adult. This trip happened. These days were real. This is life. Stop acting like it's a rehearsal. Stop railing against goulash. I don't get a second chance.

When we land back in London, we disembark and the cold London fog envelops me as I struggle to put my coat on. My bag strap comes undone, and I glance up to see that Jaime is waiting for me at the door. He lopes across and picks up my bag for me while I wrestle my way into my coat.

There's a theory that to survive in the workplace you need a 'Work Wife' or a 'Work Husband', someone platonic that you can count on to get you through the day. I think there's a strong case to be made that each of us also needs a Ryanair Spouse. Just a friendly individual who waits for you at the door, holds your coat when your shoelaces have come undone and tells you that your passport is in your back pocket, where you just put it thirty seconds ago. Someone you can angry-cry with when delays are announced. They could assign them when you buy your ticket.

Jaime and I get into an Uber, and we're both delirious with sleepiness. He starts naming places that he would rather have had a surprise trip to than Budapest (Madrid, Vienna, Buenos Aires) and I remind him that if I hadn't landed in Budapest, he'd currently be on a National Express bus, alone.

As we make our way down the North Circular, he says I should think of the trip as the choice of taking the red pill or the blue pill in *The Matrix*. The blue pill is security, happiness and confined comfort. The red pill is Wonderland, freedom and uncertainty. Which pill do I want to take in life?

I look out the window at London in the darkness.

'Sleeping pill,' I say.

The driver drops Jaime off at his friend's house and a few minutes later I'm in my flat, making myself cheese on toast at 4 a.m. It's delicious.

People rave about Budapest. Mostly new couples, who hold hands while marvelling at the Gothic and Neo-classical architecture, eat one good bowl of goulash, drink a decent cup of hot chocolate, take the river cruise down the Danube at night and then have sex on 800 thread count sheets. But really, location is irrelevant: with that amount of oxytocin coursing through their bloodstream, they would have fallen in love with Coventry.

I didn't have the adventure of my dreams in Hungary. Clearly, worse things can happen at sea (which is the main reason I didn't take that night cruise), but also, I likely had zero drops of oxytocin in my system.

Every place I've ever loved, like Beijing or Melbourne, I've known intimately. I've seen travel and adventure through the eyes of my most extroverted friends for so many years that I've stopped thinking about what really matters to me, what I *actually* enjoyed about visiting new places. I like slow travel. I like exploring an entire city or village for a week and then picking my favourite spots and walks to do again so that they feel like mine. I like recognizing local characters, like the old man in Beijing who took his birds to the park or the guy in Sydney who walked his goats. In Budapest I wasn't swept away by the marvel of just being in a foreign city because I knew my time there was so limited – I didn't have several days to bond with locals or get a real feel for the culture. I knew that I'd only skim the surface as a weekend tourist.

Though I didn't have the time of my life, I did arrive back in London feeling confident that I could take care of myself if I had to. That I could occasionally be spontaneous. That I could make a friend when I was feeling lonely as hell. And that la-la land, while out of reach this time, was still a possibility for me.

A recent study says one in two travellers thinks the best thing about travelling is getting out of their comfort zones. I left one too many comfort zones for this particular trip to be fun for my personality type – maybe I could do a surprise destination if I could take someone with me, or enjoy a mysterious destination if I could buy a travel guide when I arrived. Maybe I could get by solo without any guidance if I could choose the destination.

I hear Madrid is nice. The opera is currently open and Spanish locals are rated the friendliest in the world. And apparently they do really good dessert.

SCOTCH
COURAGE

or
stand-up comedy,
round II

It's nearly midnight, and as I walk into the pub the first thing I notice is that it's nearly empty, save for a couple sitting in the front near the stage. Surely, the only thing worse than performing comedy is performing comedy to thirty empty chairs. Nothing has prepared me for this version of hell.

The couple stands up and gathers their coats.

I'm on them in a flash.

'Guys, guys, guys. Where are you going?' I ask them. I sound like a bro, trying to get hot women to stay at a party.

'We just saw a really terrible open mic set,' the girl says, apologetically. The guy nods, sadly. They are about twenty-five and adorable.

'So . . . ?' I ask them.

'It was unbearable,' the guy says, in a soft Scottish accent.

'They made me eat a banana,' the girl says.

'What?' This is alarming. 'Who did this to you? Where are they? Are you OK?' I ask, looking around the room, suddenly Sherlock.

'I don't know, he pulled it out of his magic hat and dared me to eat it,' she says. Right.

'My show is going to be good! And I'm not going to make you eat a banana. I promise you.'

They look me up and down. I glance around the empty pub and the empty chairs and tables.

'This is my second gig! Please stay. I need you,' I say, my voice getting higher and higher. I hear a cough and look to my right.

Lily is standing a few metres away, looking alarmed. I am scaring people, including my own friends. I turn away from her. There's no time for her disapproval. Her *manners*. Her sense of civilization.

I ask the couple their names and they reluctantly tell me: Adam and Jenny.

'Jenny, I promise you that you'll laugh. Adam – I really need you here.'

Adam looks at Jenny. Jenny shrugs. They put their coats back down and take their seats again.

So the transformation is complete. I used to be afraid of talking to strangers and now look at me: I'm bullying them.

See, I'd wanted to try stand-up comedy again because my initial success had confused me. Who was that person onstage? Was it a fluke? Could I actually get good at this? And, most troubling of all, do I like the spotlight?

My second comedy gig is at the Edinburgh Fringe Festival. I don't know why I thought my very next gig should be at the biggest and most prestigious comedy festival in the world. I'd done the equivalent of winning my first game of tennis against my dad and then asking for a spot at Wimbledon.

I might not be ready for this.

But Kate hosts an open mic night at midnight every day at the Fringe and she had agreed to let Lily, Vivian and me each have a five-minute slot.

We were all giddy on the train up. The three of us arrived at our Airbnb and we practised our routines in front of each other using hairbrushes. We had run around the city eating grilled cheese sandwiches with haggis, drinking hot chocolate and watching some of the most talented comedians in the world.

Vivian had performed the night before, brilliantly, to a crowd of twenty-five. Lily had nailed a performance to a group of forty. And now I am about to perform to Adam and Jenny.

It's 11.45 p.m. Fifteen minutes before the show. I make a beeline to the toilets to talk to myself. I am like Clark Kent, except all I do is yell at myself in the mirror and emerge the exact same person.

In the end, there are eight people. Adam, Jenny, two members of crew, a couple in their forties from Sheffield and two drunk Scottish girls who seem lost. Plus, Vivian and Lily, who sit in the front row. There are about thirty empty seats.

I'd felt so confident after my first gig. Doubly so after watching that video and realizing that a good chunk of my inner turmoil wasn't visible to the human eye. The MC calls my name and I make my way on to the stage, past poor Jenny and Adam clapping politely. *OK. I am ready for this.*

'Hello,' I say. 'How is everybody doing?'

Lily and Vivian reply 'GOOD!' in obligatory loyal-friend unison.

I swallow. I am so scared I can barely move. I don't dare move my feet. Or my hands. I'm afraid that if I move the earth will cave in from beneath me. Finally, I say my first joke, about being from Amarillo.

And – nothing. There is no laughter. I hear nothing. I had even delivered the line with that tone that always makes me cringe from other comedians, that self-satisfied tone of, 'Isn't that so funny?' – and, sensing my neediness, no one had laughed.

Keep going, keep going. I say another line. Silence. Actually, imagine that sound, in movies, of a glass being set on the counter, of a solitary cough in the darkness.

That was what I heard.

No laughter.

I'm about to do my bit about being an American in the UK. I try not to lose momentum and bust out some of the enthusiasm that Kate had told us was so vital. *Go big. Get them back on your side.*

'So I'm not from here,' I say. 'But I love it here! I LOVE England!'

If I could impart one piece of advice (and just one! One tiny one!) it would be that when you are performing comedy in Scotland, do not earnestly proclaim your devotion to England.

The Scots do not love England.

'BOOO!' the drunk Scottish girls yell from the front row. 'BOOO!' yells the bartender in the back.

I stare up at the bright lights, see glimpses of dead eyes not laughing, the Scots booing me. Just take me now, God. I cannot go on. I have violated the social code and now I must die.

'I can't believe Jenny and Adam had to see me that way,' I cry out to Lily, on the Royal Mile. 'I promised them that I would be good!'

Lily is frog-marching me somewhere I can down a vodka as quickly as possible.

'Those Scottish girls in the front row were drunk,' Vivian says. 'I swear I saw one of them nearly fall down when she came out of the toilets. And then her friend went straight in. They were on drugs. Lots of them. So many drugs.'

I don't say anything. I'm still reeling.

'And that couple from Sheffield? I really don't think that guy spoke English. Did you see how he didn't speak when the MC asked him questions?'

As soon as we arrive, Lily starts introducing me to people. Lily is an extrovert with a capital E: she chats effortlessly with cab drivers, couples in the queue for comedy shows and other performers. Men and women alike adore her. At one point, Vivian exclaims, 'I can't take it! Lily talks to too many strangers! If you're never going to see someone again, why bother?'

Well, for one, convivial Lily is offered more free food than anyone I have ever met. It would be irritating if she didn't share it, but she always does.

Somehow, that night when I died on that stage would go on to become one of my favourite nights of the year. At around 4 a.m., Vivian, Lily and I walk the thirty minutes back to our flat along the windy, hilly Edinburgh streets, singing tunelessly, but merrily.

I haven't experienced this precise, intense sense of giddy closeness and warmth in new friendships since university. After more than a decade without it, I thought those halcyon days were over. It makes me wonder: is this la-la land? We'd met fun strangers, we'd laughed a lot, we'd wandered all over the city and into different pubs and bars, and we were in a beautiful city we didn't know.

Either way, if you're going to bomb your stand-up routine, it helps to have people like Lily and Vivian, who introduce you to people as, 'This is my friend. She's a comedian and she loves England,' without any further explanation, making you realize how ridiculous life can become very quickly.

When Vivian and Lily climb into my bed holding cups of tea the next morning, I feel overcome with emotion, and not just because they have woken me up after only three hours of sleep. I had told Chris, the stranger who I'd played vulnerability tennis with all those months ago, that I was scared a moment like this would never happen again.

'All of my closest friends have moved away or we've grown apart and I'm afraid I'm never going to have a new close friend that I can tell anything to and it makes me sad,' I had said. What I had also meant was, 'What if I never have the cosy, closeness of a friend casually climbing into my bed with a cup of tea, gossiping about last night?' I didn't even know Vivian and Lily four months ago, which feels unbelievable to me.

The adventure is all over too soon. I head back to London earlier than the others. On the train, alone for the first time in a few days, I put on my headphones and gaze out at the Scottish coastline, the rugged cliffs and wide-open beaches looking positively Mediterranean in the bright sunlight.

Without the distraction of the festival and without Lily and Vivian, I am suddenly upset at how badly I had performed. All of the confidence that had appeared after my first gig was now gone, evaporated into the sea air. After I had performed at *The Moth*, I had felt invincible. Since that big moment, so much had happened: I'd made friends with strangers, I'd swum with potential new best friends, I'd fallen deeply in love with my weekly improv class. But I'd also slipped into a grey mood in Budapest that I couldn't shake and this week I had come crashing down from the giddy heights of my first-ever comedy gig. Why can't confidence and optimism come with a lifetime guarantee?

I need my comedy mentor, even a reluctant one.

I pull out my phone and text Phil what happened. He replies immediately.

'Fringe audiences can be tough. Especially if you say you love England,' Phil texts me. 'That was never going to be an easy gig. Don't take it too hard, Jess. You've got a late night fringe gig out of the way and you're still alive.'

Right. He was right. Exactly.

'God speed, Jess. All the best for your next gig.'

Yeah, OK. Dream on, Phil.

INTROVERT INTO
THE WOODS
a real-life interlude

Leaves crunch under my feet. I'm walking through a forest.
Alone. At dawn. My hair is dirty, I'm hungry, I'm dehydrated
and I don't know where I am.

I knew it. I began this experiment fearful that the year
would end with me in the woods communing with wolves
and eating weeds.

I pick my feet up to move through the thick leaves, looking up at the green canopy of trees above me. The sky is
just beginning to lighten. I'm trying not to think about
ticks and mosquitoes. Then I hear a rustle that hasn't come
from me.

I freeze. There aren't supposed to be other people for
miles. That's what the man had said. The rustle also stops
abruptly. I rub my eyes and squint through the forest.
Another crunch of leaves.

'Hello?' I whisper softly, terrified.

Did you hear the one about the introvert who tried to extrovert for a year and ended up murdered in a forest?

Willow is a blonde twenty-five-year-old with a micro fringe and a septum piercing. She grew up in south-east London: a former wild child who is polyamorous, a libertarian, a wearer of orange lipstick. The one who meets strangers on stopovers in New York and ends up in jazz bars with them at 4 a.m.

We met while working at an advertising agency a few years ago. She sat behind me, facing the opposite way. Her signature move was swivelling her chair around and nosing her way into all of my work conversations, which was annoying because a) what a Leo and b) she always seemed to know so much about everything despite being eight years younger than me.

Willow talks to everyone, is up for anything and says yes to everything, including running a half-marathon with zero training on a day when it was so hot that it melted off her orange toenail polish. She's confident that everything is always going to turn out OK and that people are going to be there for her – and that, miraculously, always seems to be the case, whether it was when she hitchhiked from London to Brussels and slept on strangers' sofas along the way or travelled through India alone, getting her name tattooed in Hindi on the bottom of her foot by a stranger she'd met who happened to own a tattoo gun. Willow is mystifying to me.

Willow now lives in Stockholm, but we arrange to catch up over coffee when she's in town visiting her family. When

I tell her about my year – the comedy, the talking to strangers, the travelling alone – her response is disturbingly familiar. 'Omigod,' she says, 'but you hate all of those things.'

'I know,' I nod. Willow doesn't fully understand why I hate these things. In the last three months alone, Willow has said yes to: raves, tequila shots on a Monday, couch-surfing in Copenhagen and rescue cats. We are completely different – and she was partially one of the reasons I was inspired to start this year of extroverting.

Once we've established that I have essentially agreed to do things I would usually run away from at speed, Willow suggests that I come camping with her and her friends.

Despite her casual tone, I suspect a catch.

'What friends?'

'Just some women I met recently. One of them has a giant bell tent set up in a forest. We're driving down from London to escape the city and to . . . have a journey together.'

'A journey?'

'Magic mushrooms,' Willow says. 'In a forest. At sunset. It's going to be spiritual.'

Hmm.

'Aren't you afraid they could be the kind of mushroom that kills you?' I ask.

Willow explains that one of the women, Evie, is married to a mycologist who forages for native magic mushrooms. What about Lyme disease? The ticks are dead now, Willow says. What about getting there? Her dad's car. Willow has an answer for every concern I throw at her.

'I think it'll be good for you,' Willow says. She uses psychedelics for fun, but she also writes about their medicinal use. Willow tells me how psychedelics are being used to treat people with depression and post-traumatic stress, and to promote creativity.

'Steve Jobs took shrooms,' she says.

'And now he's dead,' I remind her. Willow ignores me. This is typical of our relationship.

I've never taken any drugs. Between my over-protective Chinese father and catastrophizing Jewish mother, plus that neuroscience course at university, I'd had the fear of God put in me at a young age and no hippie, dealer or university hallmate had ever made an offer of drugs that tempted me. Hypothetical hippies, usually, because also, people very rarely offered me drugs, period. Until now.

'It'll be good for you to get out of London,' she says. 'Get out of your head.'

I turn her down imperiously, but after we part ways I can't stop thinking about Willow's invitation. London *has* been bothering me lately: polluted, crowded, dirty. I'm still feeling fragile after bombing onstage at the Edinburgh Fringe. In short, I'm restless. To relax, I spend the weekend reading a 500-page book on psychedelics.

I discover that psilocybin, the naturally occurring psychedelic compound found in magic mushrooms, can increase the intensity of emotions, cause synaesthesia and distort our sense of time. Users also report feeling temporarily freed from their egos.

I think back to the weight of the loneliness I'd felt in Budapest. The anxiety of caring what people thought of me onstage in Edinburgh. Freed from my ego? That part sounded downright thrilling.

But still, magic mushrooms? I didn't know what to think any more. After all, I had started this year afraid of strangers and found out that fewer people were out to murder me than I had thought. Christ, I like improv now. I can't be sure of anything. I cannot always rely on my knee-jerk reactions, because it turns out I am often wrong.

In the book on psychedelics, I read that bad reactions can and do happen, but they're rare, usually caused by too much of a substance, or an anxiety-inducing environment, like a crowded nightclub or heaving street party.

'It's women only, in a secluded forest, away from the city,' Willow tells me in a message. 'That's why we chose it.'

Still, I hesitate.

'You only live once,' Willow writes. I refuse to bow to that sort of rationale. You also only have to die once.

But after a particularly lacklustre day in London, I spend a restless night tossing and turning, listening to sirens and loud street noise. I lie awake worrying about work deadlines and my tax bill. When dawn finally breaks I sit up and think: *I want to go to the forest.*

If I wanted the openness of this year to stick, then maybe I needed to apply this new openness to my real, everyday life.

'You're going to find out so much about yourself. The mushrooms dig up your unconscious desires and needs,'

Willow tells me, sounding like a talking woodland creature straight out of a fairytale, who has happened upon me in the forest. I'm just not sure if she's the good kind or the kind that's secretly trying to poison me.

'I'm so excited for you,' she adds.

I actively don't want to know what is buried in my subconscious, but a few days later I pack a rucksack full of biscuits, peaches and bug repellent and meet Willow at her car. Another girl is already there: Kai. She's leaning against the passenger door and eating a cucumber – straight up chomping on a whole one.

When Kai finds out that I've never done psychedelics before, she takes the cucumber out of her mouth.

'I'm so excited for you,' she says, putting her hand on my arm and looking searchingly into my face. The regularity with which that phrase keeps coming up is doing nothing for my nerves.

Kai has the face of a wise but fearsome goddess with long wild hair. She seems like she could carry you across a river if you lost your limbs in a war or nurse you back to health if you've been shot by an arrow. Like the lovechild of Katniss Everdeen and Bear Grylls. I like her immediately.

The last to arrive is Janet. A slim woman in a red business-casual dress and gladiator sandals shouldering a big rucksack and pulling a massive suitcase behind her.

We all hop into Willow's car: Kai takes the front seat, because even wise earth goddesses call shotgun if they arrive first. This leaves Janet and me in the back, her giant bag between us.

It starts almost immediately.

Janet starts talking as we pull on to the main road and she does not stop for the entire trip. By the end, I know the status of: her ex-boyfriend, her job, the job she wants to have, the two jobs she interviewed for last week that she didn't get, the man who lives in her building who is teaching her how to drive, the text that that man sent her before she left for a holiday ('Enjoy the sun!'), what this text might mean, the personal trainer she went on one date with, how she seduced him with her eyes, the YouTube video that taught her how to seduce him with only her eyes, how many children her sister has, that it's been four months since she had sex, that she hates her flatmate, that she loves the gym and that she loves Jordan Peterson.

Ordinarily, I like people who overshare. They can demolish awkward silences and create intimacy out of thin air. But not like this. In a group of strangers, there will always be one person you don't like. I don't make the rules. It's a law. Janet's Law.

Janet begins shouting about how her vagina needs a good workout and how she's going to secretly take her copper coil out so she can have a baby, probably with her unsuspecting ex-boyfriend. I can't take any more. Don't get me wrong, this is actually the most interesting thing she's said on the entire car ride. But I can't handle it. It's breaking my brain.

'Can we have some road trip music?' I ask Willow feebly as Janet gasps for air between thoughts. Willow puts on 'Tropical Brainstorm' by Kirsty MacColl and for a few blissful minutes there is respite.

Magic mushrooms are illegal in most countries. Which is fine because we drove to Portugal that evening, where they are legal. Not sure if you knew this, but if you try really hard, you can drive to Portugal from London in just a few hours, which is what we did. Portugal looks exactly like a British forest, though.

'I have to pee!' Janet bellows, ten minutes later.

After we hit up a rest area, the conversation gets deeper as we stretch our legs in the car park. Kai, Janet and I are all in our early thirties. Another law, this one called Fear-Mongering Fertility Biological Clock Panic Law, means we will inevitably discuss if and when we are having children (though not with each other). This one goes a bit differently than usual, though.

'When I took ayuahuasca in Peru, I had a vision of myself at thirty-five holding a perfect baby girl,' Kai says, 'so I just trust that the universe is going to take care of everything.'

I have nothing to say to this, as I rarely trust the universe with anything. Instead, I blurt out the first thing that pops into my head from a recent article I'd read.

'Pregnancy reprogrammes your brain,' I say.

Kai smiles at me, calmly.

'Tonight is going to reprogramme your brain.' She pats me on the back and it's only vaguely threatening.

Back in the car, Janet takes a deep breath and plunges back in, this time about the occasions when her dad will and won't eat meat. I have a very strong memory and am upset that I will carry this information with me until the end of my days.

As we get deeper and deeper into the countryside (closer to Portugal), I look out the window and think, 'I trust that the universe will take care of everything.'

Soon, the scenery becomes green, thick, foliage-y, magical. We're all staring out the windows, taking it in.

'This is forest as fuck!' Janet shouts in my face. Then she repeats it, for her Instagram story.

We pull into a clearing and Willow drives through tall grass until she reaches a parked truck. Evie, a Portuguese native, is waiting for us.

'Welcome,' Evie says and hugs each of us, one by one. She is dressed exactly like Cheryl Strayed in *Wild*: shorts and those signature boots. She gives off Mother Earth vibes.

It's cool, quiet and dark under the canopy of leaves. Eerily beautiful – the sort of place melancholy teenagers would go to lose their virginity in an indie film. We are walking through thick dry leaves, dappled light filtering through the green canopy above us, and there's not another soul around. Through the gaps in the trees, I can see only more forest.

'We have a hundred acres,' Evie says. 'We're all alone out here.'

Deep in the forest, it feels magical to be engulfed by nature. We walk for about ten minutes until we reach a clearing, where there is a giant tent and a man building a fire. Toby, Evie's husband, comes over to say hello. He's the one who foraged the mushrooms we're going to take tonight. He hands her the goods, wishes us luck and tells us that since there is no one around for miles, we should be safe. And then he drives off.

We set our bags down and Janet announces she wants to change into her psychedelic onesie.

Willow wanders off and starts twirling in the forest; Kai is assuming yoga poses on some fallen logs.

'I'm being bitten by mosquitoes!' I yell out to them.

'Mosquitoes have got to eat, too!' Willow calls back, pirouetting into a pile of leaves.

I blink and suddenly remember a troubling quote from the TV show *30 Rock*: 'Never follow a hippie to a second location.'

It's too late for me.

Later that night, settled in our campsite, Kai says we should all take a seat inside the tent, sit in a circle and state our intentions and fears.

Janet, wearing her shaman feather headdress, starts burning sage and waves it around my body to ward off bad spirits. I can't believe I'm witnessing this. The smoke surrounds me and I cough. Does Janet not know that *she* is the bad spirit? She leans across and starts rubbing oil on my forehead as we form our circle.

Kai goes first, talking about how she's had a rough year, transitioning into a new career. Evie resents her family and wants a release. Willow is doubting her recent move to Stockholm and wants clarity on the decision. Janet says, mysteriously, 'We are purging what no longer serves us,' with no further explanation.

It falls silent. They slowly turn to me.

'I'm . . .' My mind is rattling. What I really want to say is that I've opened up my world to new experiences and new people, but I'm not sure if I am properly learning from them. Or what I was supposed to be learning. Part of me still feels lost and anxious, despite all the challenges I've invited into my life this year and I don't know if I'm ever going to be the sort of person I hoped I could be.

Instead I say, 'I'm scared of a lot of things, which has been holding me back in my life . . . I guess Willow invited me here because I'm a closed-off person . . .'

'No, I invited you because you want to understand your social anxiety. To open up your mind. Psychedelics have been proven to help with that,' Willow says. 'Plus, I love you and I wanted to share this experience with you,' she adds.

'Oh,' I say. Frankly, I'm touched.

'I'm still kind of amazed you came,' Willow says. 'I never thought you'd say yes.' Me neither. I reach out to grab Willow's hand just as Janet claps her hands together. 'All right! Let's do this!' she shouts, standing up.

We take seats outside in a circle around the fire as the sun begins to set. Evie hands me a small mushroom, wrapped in cling film. I stare at it in my hands, my mind already whirring. I don't want to kill the peaceful vibe in the forest, but I'm apprehensive. I remind myself: a mycologist picked these. His friends have already eaten from this very batch and they are fine. Supposedly.

I look at Willow. She smiles, reassuringly.

Kai unwraps her mushroom. She starts to eat it. Willow does the same. I look around me. At the trees. At the big sky above. I unwrap it. It's been dehydrated, picked months ago from this very forest in Portugal, and is now a hard stub. My first thought is that it looks like the nub of an umbilical cord. Why? Why does my brain go here? How can I trust it on magic mushrooms?

Before thinking too hard, I break off a piece of the stub in my hand and chew a piece of it.

It's tough but tastes like something you'd want sprinkled over your spaghetti bolognese.

The sun is just beginning to set. The chatter slowly dies down, and as the sun sinks below the horizon the stars emerge big and bright in the clear sky. It is stunning. They are winking and I feel very, very small.

Janet has started talking again.

I lean back, staring at the sky, silently fuming at her inane chatter. Why can't we just be quiet for one minute and look at the stars? Why do I have to know that her dad is lactose intolerant, her aunt has coeliac disease and she ate pineapple for breakfast? Are you allowed to shush someone you just met? Or trap their voice in a shell and throw it into the sea?

Imagining this makes me laugh so hard that I start to cry. The shrooms are beginning to take effect.

Until Janet starts a monologue about the meaning behind the mysterious text her neighbour sent her (to reiterate, the text in question was, 'Enjoy the sun!'). I give up and dig around in my pocket for my headphones. I put on Laura Marling's song 'Wild Once'.

I pull up my coat collar to block Janet from my peripheral vision as Laura's voice drowns her out. I close my eyes. I'd read that bad trips tend to happen when you're afraid, when you're upset, when you don't trust the substances, when you don't feel safe.

The mushrooms really are in my brain now – fantastical colours and images sweep across the canvas in my mind. I have to trust that, whatever happens next, I can handle it.

Right now I am inside of the music. I am swimming through the melodies, through Laura's voice and the strumming of the guitar and I am floating through the black space between the notes. The most astonishing part of the entire experience is that I'm not scared.

More than any other time in my entire life, I am not in control. By choice. And I'm OK.

I am sinking slowly into the ground.

I open my eyes and look up again at the giant black sky. The stars are blinking and swaying to the melody. I . . . I am melting. I am the stars. I am the sky. I am the forest. I am a deer. I am a tick. I am everything. I am Laura Marling. I am Janet.

I stay there for a long time, with no concept of how much time is passing. My eyes grow heavy.

'The shrooms are telling you that you need to sleep,' Willow calls out to me. 'Go to sleep. The mushrooms come from this forest and they know what you need.' The woodland creature has spoken.

I nod, plod over to my sleeping bag in the tent and pull a beanie over my head. I feel myself being pulled into slumber and fall fast asleep, dreaming in Technicolor.

At 5 a.m., my bladder wakes me up. The sun has barely risen and after lots of zipper confusion and fumbling for my glasses, I finally stumble out of the tent. It's gloriously silent and beautiful with everyone else still asleep. Only trees and ground foliage and the light blue and orange sky. I walk towards a clearing. There's no one else around.

My shoes move softly through the leaves when I hear the rustle a few metres away. Was this the communing with wolves that I had always feared?

I look up.

And then I see him.

A deer. A stag. He's beautiful: red, with big antlers and brown eyes. Imposing. Staring straight at me.

We look at each other. He takes me in for a few seconds. I remain as still as possible, not wanting to scare him off. He pauses, for one more golden second, then he gallops off into the mist. Gone.

In the *Harry Potter* books, a 'patronus' is an advanced magic charm that wizards conjure to scare away evil Dementors. Harry Potter's patronus is a stag.

And I have just seen a stag in the forest at dawn.

Please don't misunderstand me. What I'm saying is this: I took magic mushrooms, Janet is my Dementor, a lone stag appeared, we locked eyes and now I am Harry Potter.

Sofa Jess had longed for adventures, though I'm not sure this is the kind she had ever imagined.

But encountering that lone stag in the forest was thrilling. Spine-tingling wonderful. So many things had to happen to lead both of us to the same spot at dawn, staring at each other in the woods, the trees silent around us.

Introverts crave closeness but often dislike putting themselves in situations that are likely to initiate new relationships.

But just by showing up and taking part, even if on this trip I hadn't, say, bonded with Janet, there was something enlivening about expanding my self-definition. Willow had said, 'I'm amazed that you came.' I was, too.

Janet had said, 'We are purging what no longer serves us.' Staying closed-off and saying no to things, merely because I was scared, was no longer useful to me. Staring at the sky, for those brief moments of silence, looking up at the stars, I'd felt like introvert and extrovert were labels that might not serve me any more.

I had already done so many things this year that I'd previously struck off as impossibilities. But I was still me. I still liked solace, I still needed to go home after lots of socializing, I still craved one-on-one coffee dates over loud parties in a crowded pub. I don't anticipate taking magic mushrooms in the forest again, but I'd taken a risk, and it had led me to one of the most magical moments the next morning.

On the way home later that day, we stop in a restaurant for lunch and a bad night's sleep appears to have stunned the chatter out of Janet. Then, she does something unexpected. She asks me a question.

'Jess, you're so far from home. Do you miss your family?'

'I . . . yeah, I do,' I say.

We talk for twenty minutes about both of us living far from our families.

Back in the car, Janet falls asleep. It's peaceful and I begin to think that I was wrong about Janet. She looks serene. Barely demented at all. She's not so bad. I could handle her, maybe I could even like her. Fleetwood Mac plays softly in the background.

Janet opens her eyes and raises her head, as if on cue.

'I have to poop!' she shouts in my ear.

I turn my body away from her and lean my head against the window, gazing out into the forest around us.

Expecto Patronum.

REDEMPTION
or
stand-up comedy,
round III

'That's so bad. It's inside of you. It's a stain on your soul. Oh yeah, you're fucked for a while now.'

I've just relayed the story of my Scottish humiliation to this woman. She is gratifyingly horrified, which I appreciate, especially since she's one of my favourite performers.

Sara Barron is a relatively new comedian, but this year she was nominated for the Edinburgh Fringe Best Newcomer Award. She's charismatic, with impeccable timing.

I seek her out because I couldn't end my year with such a huge, embarrassing failure onstage in that pub in Edinburgh. I didn't want my last memory of being onstage to be a Scottish girl flicking me a V.

I didn't want that to be the end. I wanted to rewrite my ending.

After surviving the woods with Janet, and staring up at the enormous black sky, I felt small, in a good way. Like I could take more risks and, no matter what, the sky wasn't going to fall down, so why not try again? But I needed to talk to one more person.

When I hear Sara on a radio interview saying that she used to suffer from nearly debilitating stage fright when she first tried stand-up comedy ten years ago in New York, I know I have to meet her. Had she really suffered from stage fright? She was one of the best performers I'd ever seen live. What had changed? I had to know.

Sara says that when she started to pursue comedy in London, she found out that if she gigged three times a week, her brain didn't have room to dread every single gig – that's what finally broke the back of her performance anxiety. That, and having a baby, which put everything in perspective (babies, fake deathbeds, whatever you need to get you through the day).

'I was showing up doing these disgusting open mic things all the time. And maybe the audience just thought I was a weird, older woman, but I felt like such a badass. I'd think: *none of you idiots can begin to know what I've been through*. I felt like such a hero – I've given birth!' Sara says.

Giving birth is not an immediate option for me. Besides, I'm putting that off for a year as per my bribe with my dad.

I tell Sara about how scared I am onstage.

'It's the weird intelligence of even the dumbest crowd. If they can smell your fear, you're not in charge,' Sara says.

'I'm not in charge ever,' I say.

'But you *could* be,' she says.

Sara tells me what she says someone else told her when she started out: that you're only as good as your last gig.

'And you're really in the shits right now. You have no perspective. That feeling will stay with you until you have another gig that goes OK,' Sara says.

Here we go again.

The Cavendish Arms is a comedy institution in Stockwell, South London. It's home to an infamous open-mic night called Comedy Virgins. Twenty comedians, five minutes each, all competing for one trophy at the end. Enough desperation to power Kylie Jenner's phone for eternity.

If your set goes over six minutes, they play 'Move Bitch (Get Out The Way)' by Ludacris to usher you off the stage. Whatever else happens, I cannot bear that sort of public shaming. Some people never recover from that kind of distress.

I bring Sam with me. I wouldn't normally, but another rule of the night is that if you want to perform, you have to bring a friend. And they have to stay the entire evening, watching the other new comedians. I could not inflict that on one of my fragile new friendships, so better to risk my marriage.

I'm here because Sara's right. The Edinburgh gig is a stain upon my soul. And this is my chance at redemption.

I want to puke.

On the night, the MC pulls names out of a hat to determine who goes next, so no one knows the running order (and so people can't tell their friends just to come for the second half).

After each set, if the audience likes the comedian, they yell, 'Buy them a drink!' This simple act makes the comedian eligible for the much-coveted trophy at the end of each show.

As the room fills up with comedians and their hostages, I take deep breaths. I've ditched the smart Oxford shirts and am in a T-shirt and jeans because this is who I really am.

Onstage, the MC waves the trophy in front of the audience. It's small, fitting in the palm of his hand. I want that tiny trophy. I see it as my personal redemption after winning the tragic Midnight Oil Award that triggered this year-long saga. I want it in my grubby little paws. I want to put it on my mantelpiece, should I ever be able to afford a flat with a mantelpiece, and when people would stop by, should I ever have people stop by, I'd say, 'Oh, this? This is just a small memento of the time a group of strangers made me their queen.'

The MC pulls the first name out of the hat.

'Please clap your hands for . . .'

Hot white fear runs through my body.

'DANIEL GILBERT!'

Right before the MC announces each name, I feel sick. As the night progresses, the odds of it being my name increase exponentially, but it never is me. This is torture. I've been hyperventilating for forty-five minutes already. How can they do this to us?

Ten comedians down, and the night is halfway through. I'm a wreck, my hair is tangled from the number of times I've run my hands through it, my eyeliner smeared, my lipstick long gone from chugging water to combat a dry mouth. I'm trying to remember my act. I'm sweating. *I have to be next*, I think as the MC calls the next name.

But I'm not. The MC draws the twelfth comedian out. And then the thirteenth.

Who is the queen of England and can she kill me now?

'Please clap your hands for . . .'

I'm so desensitized that I don't even recognize my own name. Sam claps me on the leg, hard. OH!

I bolt towards the stage. On the way up there, I try to do that thing where I wave my arms in the air like I'm really excited and cool and confident in myself and just a *fun* person but can only muster one limp arm.

I climb on to the stage and take the mic from the MC.

Here we go. Stain-scrubbing of the soul commences now.

Have you ever seen anything sadder than a woman weakly singing, '(Is This The Way To) Amarillo' by herself, *to herself*, onstage, to an audience full of apathetic millennials in nice trainers?

You have not.

Once on holiday, I accidentally drove down a pedestrian-only street in Italy. Old Italian ladies started hitting the car with their handbags, as Italian men slapped the windshield in anger and disappointment. I kept cry-yelling at them, 'OK BUT WHAT DO YOU WANT ME TO DO NOW? I HAVE NO CHOICE BUT TO KEEP GOING.'

This feels very similar, but this time around, in an exciting twist, I am warbling at a stony-faced crowd of twenty-somethings who are begging me to stop with their eyes. One woman in the front row actually covers her face with her hair to protect herself from my jokes.

I am drowning. I can't remember if I've told particular jokes. Everything has gone black.

I'm careening through my set at full speed when I finally, finally hear some laughter. The slightest titter from the audience as I'm describing the intense feelings I developed for Hugh Grant after watching *Four Weddings and A Funeral* as a child.

Eventually, I put the mic back into the stand and run back into the crowd to take my seat. Sam puts a reassuring arm around me. The reassuring arm of shame. But then—

'Buy her a drink!' a man behind me yells.

I have been saved! If you are only as good as your last show, this man is proof that this show wasn't a total failure. I'm stunned.

The night takes a weird turn. Each of the following comedians bomb harder than the one before. A woman comes on and the audience, myself included, can't tell if what she's saying are supposed to be jokes. She's followed by a man who tries to explain the deeper meaning behind rap lyrics, but forgets all of the lines. He holds his head in his hands, trying to remember, and dies, right there onstage. A woman comes on and pretends to be a sexy baby. Enough.

This room is a graveyard of crumpled up bucket lists.

Finally, it's time for the trophy ceremony. Tradition has it that at the end of the show the performers who the audience chose to 'buy a drink' all gather onstage and go through a humiliating 'clap off', where the audience applauds for their favourite performer, until the one who generates the most noise is declared the winner of the trophy.

There was a similar voting process at my high school for cheerleaders, except they had to cartwheel down the length of the gym in front of the entire school. I had vowed never to participate in something so humiliating, but I had not reckoned with the catastrophic stupidity that would come with age.

I'm so close to the trophy. It's me and four men competing, so now I also have to win to take down the patriarchy. I ball my fists. The MC gestures towards me like I'm a valuable vase he's trying to sell, encouraging the audience to clap.

But, what is this? The audience *is* clapping. For me. Had I really managed to do this? Had I managed to clinch the win on the most lacklustre comedy night in history and pocket that sweet, sweet golden trophy?

Well, no.

In real life, what happens is that even though you wear a shedload of NARS lipstick and mascara, you are the first one to be clapped off and are ultimately bested by a sixteen-year-old Jamaican teenager who made few jokes but who delivered a very convincing David Attenborough impression. He is crowned our champion.

You walk off the stage morosely and go home and take a long shower and eat spaghetti carbonara, realize the mouse in the kitchen cupboard is back and then you fall asleep dreaming of Scotland.

Paul once told me, 'The fear of rejection feels worse than the reality.'

I respectfully beg to differ.

But we *can* survive the rejection. It's like food poisoning. You feel fragile and utter shit and you don't want anyone to touch or look at you for about three days, but then you wake up, open the curtains, see the sun and realize you want to eat ramen and see how much water weight you lost while you were languishing.

To make myself feel better after the Cavendish Arms, I go see *Crazy Rich Asians* and quietly eat Maltesers. I was just one crazy, sad Asian, crying in the cinema.

In the film, at a fancy party thrown by a wealthy family, two women start making a big deal about some cactus.

'It only blooms at midnight once a year!' they shout, beckoning others to marvel at it.

I sit up in my seat.

That plant is my spirit animal.

For one night, in Piccadilly Circus, I was really, really good. I still have the video evidence. It shocks me whenever I watch it.

After the movie, I email my brother Aaron, who is a paleo-botanist (not the funny brother), and ask him to tell me more about this mystical plant from the film.

He writes back:

The Tan Hua 'orchid' (also known as the Night Blooming Cereus or the Queen of the Night) has white flowers that bloom once for a few days a year at night. The flowers die, but the cactus remains alive and blooms again next year.

I was never going to be the kind of performer who hits it out of the park every time. I don't want to spend my evenings watching hours of bad comedy for five stage minutes of bombing onstage. I'm not a natural performer.

But on certain nights, I can blossom. Admittedly, it was less of an ethereal transformation and more a rigorous process of aggressive grooming, mirror pep talks, hours of practice, mornings shouting into pillows, and fighting the desire to drop-kick my husband. But it was still blossoming, for me.

Recently, I watched a documentary about the first Norwegian woman to climb actual Everest. She tells the host Ben Fogle, 'I have that feeling and I can still use it. I can go and get that feeling if I need it.'

Even though comedy had twice stung me, when I think back to that first night onstage, I can see that poised version of myself; I can call upon her confidence when I need her the most. And if I start to feel too good about myself, I can revisit the Scotland gig and knock myself back down to earth.

There's something invigorating about doing something everyone else is afraid of. If everyone says, 'Don't go into the bedroom, there's a bear in there!' and you're like, 'It's fine, I can handle bears' – there's a power to that. Even when the bear mauls your leg and you are bleeding badly, at least you faced the magnificent fucker. Some people never see the bear. Some people never even make it into the bedroom.

Lily said that, for her, stand-up comedy was 50 per cent the most stressful thing she'd ever done and 50 per cent the most fun thing she'd ever done. For me it was more of an 85/15 split.

The best part for me has been the intimacy of friendships forged in the fire of public humiliation. I haven't had a work husband or wife since I met Sam and promptly made him my real-life husband, and my Ryanair relationship with Jaime was beautiful but fleeting. Now, in Lily and Vivian, I have two comedy wives.

When I text them about the Cavendish, Lily immediately replies: 'Everyone who wins the trophy on their first try goes on to be arrogant and disappointed.'

Everyone deserves a Lily in this life.

COME DINE
WITH ME
or
the dinner party

My year was nearly complete. The comedy had been performed, the strangers approached, the friend-dates conquered, the improv acted out, the Danube visited, the magic mushrooms ingested, the networking tolerated. I'd been humiliated, vindicated, elevated and had publicly bathed multiple times. I was beginning to think there was something wrong with me.

Eleven months. And now it was time.

For the finale: a dinner party at my flat that would bring together the people I'd met during my year in the literal and figurative wilderness.

A dinner party is social, unpredictable and requires juggling many things at once – all things introverts aren't crazy about. For me, it meant so many anxieties to be addressed in one evening: fear of cooking bad food (a rational fear – I regularly burn dinner), fear of being held hostage by guests (how do you have an exit stategy in your own home?), fear of throwing a party that is no fun (which means you are no fun), fear of being exposed by your own environment (what if you leave out your retainer?) and something truly horrifying: the mixing of various social groups.

There should be a word for the fear of combining your social circles. If the 'fear of long words', the cruelly named *Hippopotomonstrosesquippedaliophobia*, gets recognition, then so too should this fear.

Don't think you have it? Just imagine every person you know on Facebook in the same room together, asking each other how they know you. Your parents. Your colleagues. Your childhood best friends. Your flatmates. Your exes. Your friends who are too cool for *Eat Pray Love* and your friends who call *Eat Pray Love* their bible. Pious church-goers and polyamorous couples. Friends who saw *A Star is Born* five times in the cinema and your boss who calls it cliché tosh. Friends who think Adnan definitely did it and friends who won't associate with anyone who thinks he's guilty. You get it. Now imagine throwing a topic like Irish borders, a bad casserole and some alcohol into the mix.

Now how do you feel?

Just the thought of it makes me spiral because in that room I'd find out the answer to uncomfortable questions like: Am I a different person for all of these people? If so, which version will I be when we're all together? What if they like each other more than they like me? Who did I lie to about reading *1984* and who knows the truth?

I ask around to see if other people feel this way and men consistently tell me that they feel this anxiety at their stag dos.

'Dads, uncles, the lads, the lads' lads, work friends, childhood mates, brothers, football mates, your fiancée's brother – it's a nightmare,' one tells me. 'You don't know which version of yourself to dial up or dial down.'

I'm relieved to know I'm not alone in this, though I suspect many extroverts don't have this fear because they like hanging out in groups more in general. Then there are the psychopaths who throw out an invite to all seven hundred of their Facebook friends saying, 'Birthday drinks this Friday! The more, the merrier!' At least this is what I think, until Jori tells me she throws out invites like this and now I'm rethinking our entire friendship.

For my end-of-year finale, this can't be just any old dinner party. I have to imbue the night with a sense of occasion so people actually show up. My birthday isn't for a few months. The holidays are too busy. I know that what I can't say is, 'I've been doing a social experiment on myself (and sort of also you) for a year and I need to get you all in the same room, ply you with alcohol and watch the results unfold.'

Then it dawns on me. I have the ultimate key to getting British people to have dinner at my house. The trump card. The ace in the hole. The trick up my sleeve. A secret weapon.

Thanksgiving.

British people think Thanksgiving is a magical holiday because they don't get to have it. It's been glamorized by American movies where families always have enormous brick houses, sprawling back yards and kooky family members wearing cosy jumpers who fall asleep in beds piled high with an irrational number of crisp, luxurious pillows.

I, too, want this mythical Thanksgiving, but it does not actually exist. We just don't have that many pillows on our beds. But the British don't know that. I will entice them with mysterious puddings like pumpkin pie and sweet potatoes with mini-marshmallows.

It is the perfect bait.

It also means that I can have the meal at 2 p.m. instead of the evening. This relaxes me, slightly. The pressure of a full-on dinner is stressful. Lunch? Lunch isn't important. If I fail at lunch, people will live.

Wary after trying to plan my mass friend-date and being stood up by twenty women, I cast a wide net. I'm competing with weddings, holidays, birthdays and work trips. Trembling, I invite twenty-five people who I met this year.

The RSVPs roll in. Unfortunately, Paul, Vivian and Lily are out of town. But ten people say they can make it.

Jermaine and Toni, two other people from my comedy course. Toni's husband, Rob. Laura, Liz and Caroline from improv. Charles, my travel mentor. Benji, the psychiatrist-comedian and his girlfriend, Sylvia. And, of course, Sam.

Which means there really will be eleven people in my flat.

I count the number of plates I have. Five.

Reality sets in.

As I've never hosted a dinner party before, my frame of reference is the definitive dinner party show *Come Dine With*

Me. As I mentioned, before all of this began and I first moved to London and could not work, I was mystified and obsessed with this reality TV programme. During each episode, four to five strangers take turns hosting a dinner party in their homes for their fellow contestants over the course of one week. At the end of each evening, the contestants rate each other's nights (food quality and hosting prowess) in the back of black cabs on their way home. The contestant who wins the most points over the week takes home a prize of £1,000.

My favourite episode of *Come Dine With Me* is when a middle-aged man named Peter, who expected to win, discovers he has come in last place. He is livid at the winner. With a withering stare that flits between her and the camera, he delivers this monologue:

> 'Enjoy the money, I hope it makes you very happy. Dear Lord, what a sad little life . . . You ruined my night completely so you could have the money and I hope you spend it on getting some lessons in grace and decorum because you have all the grace of a dump truck reversing.'

This is the bar I've set for myself. If no one utters 'Dear Lord, what a sad little life . . .', then I'll consider the night a roaring success.

The *Come Dine With Me* dinner party format is strict: starter, main, dessert. Then a bad forced activity like karaoke or dancing. Why don't they ever show the contestants scream-crying to their mothers on the phone when the sauce isn't thickening? Surely it's the defining moment of any dinner prep.

This summer, Sam and I were eating dinner outside at the River Cafe, courtesy of a gift voucher my brother and his wife had given us as a Christmas present. It was a warm, balmy evening, just before sunset, when two wonderful things happened in quick succession. First, the waiter put down a plate of handmade pasta and truffles in front of me. And then I glanced up just as Nigella Lawson glided by our table, beaming at my pasta.

It was like the patron saint of delicious and decadent pasta had blessed my plate. I was giddy; it was like I'd been touched by an angel. The pasta was divine, and Nigella's approval was its crowning glory.

Nigella, as we all know, is the embodiment of cosiness, comfort and sophistication. The queen of dinner parties. The original domestic goddess. My hosting mentor had revealed herself to me.

But that was in the summer. When everything had seemed possible and this dinner party had seemed so far away.

When it comes time to planning my Thanksgiving dinner, my mentor is on the other side of the world. Nigella is on tour in Australia. It's almost as if she can't go around personally helping every anxious woman hosting a dinner party.

No matter. She smiled at my pasta, and so it is written. She will be my mentor in spirit. I pore over her website, books and television shows.

When I find a video she did in the US with her Thanksgiving tips, I sink my nails into it. In other words, I follow it to a tee with unhinged dedication.

'If you were to say to someone . . . "Can you bring a dessert?" I think they would be delighted,' Nigella says.

I text Laura, the girl with blue hair from my improv class: 'Bring your signature bake.'

Then I text my friend Toni, who was in my comedy course: 'Bring pumpkin pie.'

This was easy.

Elsewhere, Nigella says she often likes to foster a casual atmosphere by going barefoot at dinner parties. That I could do.

I study her books and take notes like a schoolgirl preparing for her A-Levels. I decide to make her Superjuicy Roast Turkey, and then am stunned into silence when I see her recipe for Coca-Cola Ham. Boiling ham in Coca-Cola? It is so decadent, so ludicrous, so unhealthy. So American. I add it to the menu.

Then, I order a bench that will seat more people. I arrange to borrow plates and cutlery from Hannah (new best friend) and her husband downstairs, who were invited but will be on holiday.

Crucially, I pretend to have everything under control, but in reality I have no idea what I'm doing.

And as the date creeps closer, I realize Nigella on a screen is not enough for me. I need a real-life mentor. Someone I can confess my fears to. Someone who can coach me through the practicalities of proper hosting. Someone I can possibly scream-cry to on the phone when the turkey is raw.

The journalist Dolly Alderton and I look very different on paper. And in 3-D. Dolly is six foot tall and blonde. I'm five two and brunette. She has shiny long hair and thick black eyelashes and wears flowy dresses: if you threw her in the clothes drier and tossed in a dirty dish towel used to change an engine's oil, then I might emerge an hour later, shrunken, crumpled, shyer, wobbly. More house elf, less supermodel.

In her memoir, *Everything I Know About Love*, Dolly's life is full of soirées, dinner parties, dates, dancing all night, music festivals and talking to strangers in pubs for fun. She regularly does all the things I had to have a quarter-life-crisis to try once.

Dolly fell in love with hosting dinner parties as a teenager and she says that she's happiest at the stove, shouting through to her friends and being responsible for everyone's wellbeing. I wouldn't know if that makes me happy because it's literally never happened.

Three days before my Thanksgiving dinner, I call Dolly.

Over the phone, while she's waiting at a train station, I explain my situation to her: I'm a shy introvert and I'm inviting ten people who don't know each other for a dinner party. And I'm a very average cook.

Dolly senses the urgency and fear in my voice and immediately transforms into my official guide. At a rapid pace, she begins firing off advice, as if I've just told her we need to diffuse a bomb and only she can talk me through it.

'OK, a good playlist is really important. I'm amazed at dinner parties where there's no music playing and the overhead lights are on. You need to have all the lamps on, lots of candles and you need to have a great playlist of music people love,' Dolly says.

I had not even thought of music or lighting. I know even less than I thought I did. I start writing down everything Dolly says verbatim. There is no time to waste.

'The best thing you can do, my love, is do all of it in advance. Do a cold starter, so you can pre-prep it on plates. For your main, do something slow-cooked,' she says.

'Do something in a tray or pot that you can leave. Don't do Ottolenghi side dishes – no one wants that. People just want comfort food, like lasagna. Do NOT do a risotto.'

I write 'risotto' with a big slash through it.

'Do a cheese board. Just get three cheeses, you don't need any more – one hard, one blue and one soft,' Dolly says. I will follow this advice exactly.

'Pudding-wise – don't do any fancy pudding. Just buy the pudding or get really nice ice cream so you don't have to do anything on the day or be away from your guests.'

Luckily, I'd already outsourced this to Laura and Toni.

When I admit to Dolly that actually this isn't just *a* dinner party, this is my first dinner party ever, I hear her take a deep breath.

'Do a Sainsbury's shop to come straight to your house a day or two before – make sure you have foil and loads of Fairy liquid. Leave all of the washing up until everyone's gone, have extra wine in the house even if people are bringing some,' she says. 'You do not want to run out of alcohol.'

This woman is a hero.

I confess my fear of how the other people will get on. How does she ensure that conversation flows?

'Before I host, I work out the different connections between different people. Sometimes hosts need to act like the social lubricant. Sometimes you need to be the person that says, "Oh, you were saying you want to go to Mexico this year", "Chris – you went to Mexico last Christmas" – stuff like that.'

Ah, Perpetua. This is Mark Darcy.

'People think that socially relaxed people don't think about stuff like that but before I go on a date I already have, like, five fallback funny stories to tell in case conversation falls flat.'

I'd never imagined that confident, outgoing people did this, unless they were going on late-night talk shows. It's comforting to imagine the most charming people I know telling themselves stories on their journeys over.

'It's so hard to imagine people we deem successful to be vulnerable,' Dolly says. 'When we see a perfect hostess, it's so hard to think of her doing a menu plan or thinking about what to talk about – but that's what people do.'

Dolly is one of these women who I deem to be successful and a perfect hostess. It's incredibly reassuring to hear her say this.

I want to run one more thing by her. Games. Despite being shy, I like party games because they can bond guests and can take the pressure off conversations, which actually exhaust me more. But when I ask her what game she would recommend playing, her tone changes.

'I'm so English, I hate any organized fun,' Dolly says.

Why do all British people say this? Aren't croquet, polo and football all organized fun? Why must all fun be chaotic?

'But wait a minute – we do a massive Christmas lunch every year, and we do play "Who's in the Bag?", which is a lot of fun.'

I consider this tacit approval of game playing and move on.

After we hang up the phone I make a menu list, then place an order for the ingredients with Sainsbury's along with all the extras Dolly had recommended. I buy two chairs from the charity shop so everyone will have a seat. I move a lamp from our bedroom into the living room so we don't have to use the overhead lights.

I flip through Nigella's *How to Be a Domestic Goddess* book and feel the need to invoke her spirit. I decide to bake her brownies. Just for me, oh so casual. I begin melting dark chocolate and butter together over the stove. I am barefoot, my hair is down, I am calm, the epitome of Zen in the kitchen. The mixture is gooey and smells amazing. I pour it into a pan and place it in the oven.

And burn the shit out of them.

The twelve-pound turkey arrives frozen, which is not what I had expected, and I nearly break my back carrying it upstairs. I realize that to get it to defrost in time, I have to submerge it in cold water and change the water every thirty minutes. It requires more attention than an infant.

I stress about a playlist but then find one called 'Nigellissima' that is full of sexy, jazzy Italian songs. It's perfect. (The Spotify user is Marc Roman – go subscribe immediately. You'll feel like you stepped into a summer night in Rome, wearing a backless silk dress, sipping a Negroni, minutes away from making love to an Italian named Giovanni. And crucially, not like you are massaging an oversized dead turkey baby with cold butter.)

Taking Dolly's advice to heart, I bake the Thanksgiving stuffing with sausage, apples, onions and mushrooms the day before. Charles, my travel mentor, can't have gluten, but I've made it with gluten-free bread. I'm feeling smug as I look at it, already prepped a full day before the party.

Together, Sam and I prep the giant turkey to cook the night before. There's a lot of yelling. After some elaborate manoeuvring we manage to shove the bastard in there, run cool water over Sam's inevitable oven burns and make up. Then, when I'm not looking, he peels a load of sweet potatoes I'd wanted to leave skins on, and I shout, 'YOU'RE RUINING EVERYTHING!' He storms out of the kitchen.

One of my guests texts me. He tells me his girlfriend is a gluten-free vegan. I scream.

On the day, I oversleep after staying up too late watching Nigella videos to calm down. There is no time to clean the flat, but I decide that I am not going to care about this. My Dutch neighbours hadn't cleaned their flat before they had us over for dinner, and I had revelled in this. It had put me at ease, as if I was family who had just dropped by. (I will tell myself anything to avoid hoovering the stairs.)

I throw everything lying around (clothes, books, magazines) into the study and close the door. Instead of making my bed, I shut the bedroom door behind me. My cleaning strategy involves lots of shut doors.

I am swiftly chopping root vegetables to roast in the oven when I hear the first buzzer. It's 2 p.m. Charles, my travel mentor, is standing on my front step with Liz, a girl I met at improv, and Jermaine, a comedian from my course.

Three people with nothing in common but me.

They will have to talk about me.

Hell hath begun.

I usher them upstairs, take their proffered bottles of wine and put them on the sofa with glasses of Prosecco. Our flat suddenly feels very full and very, very loud. Six more guests are on their way.

As I'm prepping the vegetables, I overhear Liz talking extensively about her trip to South America. Which is fine. Except she's explaining the sites of Bolivia to Charles, who has backpacked throughout the country. I think of Dolly's advice: I need to jump in and save Liz from embarrassment.

'My mother wants to have her ashes sprinkled on this trail in Bolivia – you would love it, it's gorgeous,' Liz says.

'Charles, haven't you been to Bolivia?' I shout from the kitchen.

'I have,' he says.

'And haven't you been on that trail?' I ask.

'Yep,' he says.

'What? Why didn't you say something?' Liz asks Charles, her hand to her mouth.

I can't take it. I shout, 'Where do you guys want your ashes sprinkled after you die?' from the kitchen.

They both turn to me.

'Because I'd like mine to be in Hawaii!' I say.

I am social lubricant. I am the pinnacle of Debrett's. I am Nigella.

It begins to pour, huge sheets of rain. I run around closing the windows. And then the door buzzes again. And again. People just keep coming.

Laura from improv arrives with no umbrella and her hair is soaking wet. She's carrying a cake she'd just baked and a bottle of Polish spirits. I take her upstairs to my bedroom and have to actually open the door and let her in so she can blow dry her hair. Now Laura knows my mode of organization, known as 'piles of clothes'. Damn it. But there's no time to care because downstairs, in the living room and kitchen area, there are people everywhere.

I run down. Sam is reheating the turkey and whipping up the vegan mashed potatoes. I take a look at my sweet potatoes covered in butter, sugar and marshmallows. The marshmallows have failed to form that camp-fire-y, charred glaze and are instead completely melted, the white dissolving into clumps among the orange sweet potatoes.

'It looks like I spat my toothpaste out in it,' Sam says.

I want to kill him. But there are too many witnesses.

Finally, when all the food is hot and on the table, I stand, bare feet planted (so casual, so calm), and assess my guests. Toni and her husband Rob are on the sofa, Liz is yelling about rugby, the others are engrossed in a conversation about jumpsuits. A few girls from improv are discussing our former class.

'Hey!' I say.

No one turns around.

'Hello! Hey! Hey! Hey!' I shout, waving a fork in the air. A few heads turn towards me. Toni is merrily still shouting at Liz in the corner.

'TONI!' I yell.

The room goes silent. Oh no. I have turned into a schoolteacher.

'Plates are here, cutlery is here and please help yourself!' I gesture towards the table. Is that how it's done? Is this how you do this? I've never done this before.

'We have turkey, we have stuffing, we have something called Coca-Cola ham.' As soon as I utter the words 'Coca-Cola ham' the room immediately 'oohs' and 'ahhs' with glee. It's like casting a spell.

'Charles, I made the stuffing with gluten-free bread,' I say. Casually but with a clear: Look at me, the perfect hostess. So prepared. So accommodating.

'Amazing. Quick question: are the sausages also gluten-free?' he asks.

'Why would sausages have gluten in them?'

There's a beat as we both realize: the sausages definitely have gluten in them (the casing), and he won't be able to eat the stuffing, which is my worst batch ever due to the rock-hard bread I'd purchased at the gluten-free bakery.

After everyone has helped themselves to the food, the eleven of us sit in a circle with our plates of food on our laps. This is the moment I had been waiting for. The moment I wasn't sure I could make happen.

In America, it's tradition for everyone at the Thanksgiving table to go around and say something they are grateful for. It is earnest and deeply American. And it's so in-line with everything I've learned from this year: opening up to people and diving into Deep Talk.

I remember right at the beginning of all this, what the School of Life teacher Mark had said: about how we plan dinner parties so meticulously, we make the food, we clean the house (sort of), we buy the booze, but don't take any care with the conversation. This was my effort to try a little. I didn't want only the normal, polite small talk or the biting humour to hide all emotions.

This is the moment. Sam and I had cooked for two days. We had defrosted the twelve-pound turkey in shifts. We had destroyed our kitchen and nearly our marriage.

But we'd also brought all of these people together, all strangers to one another. I'd met them or received guidance from them during this past year. I had not known most of them a year ago and if I had never attempted all this extroverting, none of them would be here right now, in this moment.

The rain was pouring. The candles were lit. I had *hygge*-d the hell out of the evening.

'There are two rules at Thanksgiving,' I say. 'Eat as much as you can and everyone says one thing they're grateful for.' I spot Charles, my American comrade in the corner, not eating gluten.

'Charles, why don't you go first?' I suggest (command).

'I'm grateful for old friends,' he says, raising his glass to Sam. 'And to meeting new people and good food.'

Next it's Toni's turn.

'I am grateful to live in a country with universal healthcare,' she says. (Toni briefly lived in America, and is obsessed with the NHS.) A few people say they are thankful for the food we've provided.

The circle reaches me. My moment. I look around at these faces that I didn't know a year ago.

'I'm thankful that I met most of you this year and that I did a lot of scary things that led me to a lot of amazing people,' I say. 'I invited each of you because I want to know you better but you are all already really special to me. You changed my year in a positive way. You changed me.'

I did it. I let myself be vulnerable.

It's Rob's turn.

'I am . . . thankful Nigella discovered how good Coca-Cola tastes with ham,' he says. I let him off the hook because Rob is British and he can't do sincere in public.

The final person to go is Jermaine.

'You guys already used up all the good ones,' he says. 'I'm thankful for . . . doors. It would be terribly drafty without them,' he says. And I can't argue with that. I am also grateful for doors, right now they are hiding all my mess.

I study Jermaine, my knife and fork still hovering in the air. Will he also say something real?

'But also I'm grateful to be here with all of you. You come to parties and sometimes they're fun and sometimes they're full of weirdos, but I think this is a great group of fun weirdos,' he says. He downs his beer to drown out his overt kindness.

Fun weirdos. The man sums it up perfectly.

A South African, two Geordies, a Romanian, one American, a Mackem, three English southerners, one Australian and a Northern Irishwoman come together.

And the food! The pescatarian ate two platefuls of ham. And the gluten-free vegan? I clocked her eating the pumpkin pie. See, this is what Thanksgiving is really about: breaking our diets and our ethics so we can partake in Coca-Cola ham.

As soon as the main course is over, I'm up clearing plates and head back to the kitchen alone. I turn up the music, switch on my own playlist and start blasting Marvin Gaye's 'Got To Give It Up'.

As I arrange the Dolly-steered cheeseboard, I sing the lyrics to myself: 'I used to go out to parties / And stand around / Cause I was too nervous / To really get down'.

Marvin Gaye *must* have been an introvert. He had, after all, written the anthem for introverts going to an extrovert's party.

Then I realize. I'm standing in the kitchen, alone with a cheeseboard, with my music on and a party going on outside that was *my* party. This is the dream. I am being social, but there are still moments to be alone. I am in the party and not in the party. I am Schrodinger's hostess. I have unlocked the code to having it all. I have my music, my favourite food and my hand-picked guests, but I get to leave the room whenever I want.

I grab the cake Laura brought, whipped cream, custard and Nigella's burnt chocolate brownies (I certainly wasn't going to eat them), vanilla ice cream, paper plates and lay it all out with the cheeseboard with gluten-free crackers and normal crackers.

I put a poached pear in the corner because I can't resist. I need to pay tribute to the show that had kept me company when I first moved to London. And that had inspired me to do this next bit.

'Do we want to play a game?' I ask, tentatively, to the group.

There's ambivalence in the air. Some blank stares.

Everyone wants to play the game, but no one wants to be the first to admit it. I have improv people in my home – and you're telling me they don't want to play a game?

Also, I had heard Toni earlier telling the group how much she hated games. She had poisoned the well.

I introduce the group to a game that my Venezuelan flat-mate in Australia had introduced to me at a Christmas house party: *papelitos*, meaning 'little pieces of paper' in Spanish. Everyone writes down five movies on the little pieces of paper, we throw them into a bowl, and then we have to get our teammate to guess the movie. We go through three rounds of guessing: one round with word descriptions only, one round where you are only allowed to say one word and one round of charades.

Everyone starts writing their movies on the pieces of paper. It's all going to plan.

'Organized fun is lame!' Toni yells drunkenly from the corner.

Oh no. Oh no, you don't.

I take a seat next to her and put my hand gently on her arm. I lean in closely.

'Enjoy the money, I hope it makes you very happy. Dear Lord, what a sad little life. You ruined my night completely so you could have the money and I hope you spend it on getting some lessons in grace and decorum because . . .'

No, I don't.

Instead, I say:

'Toni. Please. For the love of Thanksgiving. Do not heckle the game.'

She nods, slightly scared.

This is my *Come Dine With Me* and this is my shit activity and by God we will do it.

I pair her with her husband and we agree that he will do all of the acting and looking stupid, and she will do all the guessing. This appeases her.

The game begins. I've been grouped with Sylvia (gluten-free vegan) and Rob.

The competition gets heated. In one round, I'm trying to get Rob to guess the movie *About A Boy*. I think about the single word hint.

'Teenagerhood,' I say – and everyone loses their minds.

'That's not a real word!' they protest, pulling out their phones to check.

Guess what, suckers? It is. It is the condition of being a teenager and it is horrible.

Didn't matter, though, because Rob did not guess the movie correctly.

During *papelitos*, there's a lot of impassioned yelling, a lot of acting, a tight contest for the winner.

This, as it turns out, is all you need for a good time: invite friends, make them take off their shoes, stuff them with turkey and booze, and then make them act out *Die Hard III*.

Laura brings out her bottle of Polish hazelnut spirits. She pours shots and then adds whole milk to each one, as is tradition. We pass them around and down them. It tastes like necking a Ferrero Rocher.

And I realize I'm actually enjoying myself. In fact, before I know it, the afternoon is over. Eventually, people begin to gather their coats to go.

Finally, the last group leaves: Toni, Rob and Jermaine. I hug them, they head down our stairs and shut the door behind them.

I'm making my way back up my own stairs when I hear: 'That was GREAT!' Jermaine is speaking in the stairwell. Jermaine! It feels like the equivalent of him being in a taxi and giving me a nine out of ten on *Come Dine With Me*. (Literally no one gets given a ten.)

I collapse on the sofa next to the window.

I discovered that afternoon parties are the best because it meant that by 8.30 p.m. I was drinking decaf coffee and eating the rest of the pumpkin pie while watching *Friends* Thanksgiving reruns on the sofa with Sam.

I gathered ten (mostly) strangers for an elaborate meal in my home. Watching from afar, I saw new friendships forming. All of these people were a part of my year, but now they were also in each other's lives, even if just for this one afternoon. The eleven of us had a shared experience.

Like the moment when Jermaine made faux-love to a plate of ham to get his team to guess *Fifty Shades of Grey*. We all have to have that burned into our brains for ever.

It turns out that hosting is actually great if you're socially awkward because it makes the night feel like a blur and you always have something to do. Plus you can always go and hide in your own bedroom – it's not weird if you climb under the bed covers. Well, not as weird as if you climbed under someone else's bed covers at someone else's house.

INTROVERT.
EXTROVERT.

convert?

I'm having a drink at a bar in Islington with my new friend, Christie. I'd met her at a networking event I'd said yes to, instead of skipping out on, this year. Christie waves to someone she sees across the room. I look over – it's the comedian Sara Barron.

She starts when she sees me.

'This is my friend, Jess,' Christie says to Sara.

It takes Sara a second to recognize me – the woman scarred by her Edinburgh comedy gig who had sought out her help in recovery.

'But you said you didn't have any friends!' Sara exclaims, teasing but surprised. I nod.

'That was before,' I say.

The day after my dinner party, I come across an eerie sentence written by a psychologist in the *Guardian*:

overt is not necessarily constrained to a
ess'.

darkest moment on my sofa I'm not sure I
was 'constrained to a life of unhappiness'.

ally, maybe I did. Or at least I feared it. A little.

ometimes I feared it a lot.

It was that fear – fear that if I never changed I would never know what it was like to live a bigger life – that propelled me throughout this year, pushing me out of the house, on to the stage, into people's homes and into strangers' conversations.

I didn't even necessarily think I'd like a bigger life.

But I wanted to know what it was like. To be able to make a choice about what kind of life I had.

It's generally agreed that introversion is a natural trait. Some personality studies say that introversion is physiologically or even genetically based, while others report that introversion is 40–50 per cent heritable. But that line in the *Guardian* was written by a psychologist, Brian R. Little, who argues that our personalities are not fixed or exclusively determined by nature or nurture; instead, they can change as a result of action.

His research has uncovered the value in our 'personal projects', from the trivial (walking the dog) to the formidable (climbing Everest) to the interpersonal (trying to become a better listener). In his book, he writes, 'What you do can remake who you are – and it's a revelation that turns previous ideas about human personality on their heads.'

He says that we have 'free personality traits'. Free traits describe a behaviour or quality we take on when we need it (i.e. an introvert being more social when her work requires it or a shy person acting incredibly confident as the maid of honour at her best friend's wedding).

I think about being onstage at Union Chapel, in the spotlight, after all those years hiding from it. Watching myself in the video at my first stand-up comedy gig, controlled and confident. Walking into a room where I knew barely anyone and striking up a conversation with Paul. Trying on all of these free traits when I needed them to get through the year.

I met so many other introverts who were acting as extroverts over the course of these challenges. It surprised me, but it shouldn't have. We all have to give presentations and talk to strangers and be social sometimes if we want to succeed professionally. Richard, the charisma coach, figured it out early on. So did many of the journalists I met while networking. So had Benji, the psychiatrist who had also become a successful comedian. He had told me he was tired of being held hostage to his introversion and shyness (and he wound up being the pescatarian who ate ham at my flat on Thanksgiving).

That's because it's true: modern society favours extroverts. Extroverts are more likely to talk to strangers, are more social, go to more parties and are quicker to strike up new friendships. They are more likely to be appreciated and noticed at work. Of course I don't think we should all be extroverts. But the self-care trend has extroverts pursuing introvert activities to help them reflect and relax – so why shouldn't we introverts do the same? When we need to be loud and social and outgoing, we can steal their traits. We don't even have to be bitten by a radioactive extrovert to gain their powers.

Naturally, my sense of kinship and compassion still lies with my fellow introverts. I love you. In fact, most of the new friends I've made are introverts, because I'm naturally drawn to them. The quiet ones, also observing, who are witty and thoughtful and want to leave early with me. (It's just so hard to get you to hang out with me.)

So if modern society favours extroverts, what's an introvert to do? Or more specifically, what's an introvert unhappy with their lot to do? I'd spent most of my life telling myself I was one kind of person, not believing I could do things that I saw other people doing. Then I spent a year doing all of those things that petrified me. I know plenty of happy introverts who don't want to change and I have nothing but respect for them. But for me, having the ability to morph, to change, to try on free traits, to expand or contract at will offers me an incredible feeling of freedom and a source of hope.

I think a small part of me thought I'd do all these challenges, go through hell and emerge at the other end as the most socially savvy, articulate, gregarious social butterfly in the world. Or wind up hiding in a ditch. One or the other. But I am still who I was at the beginning of this year. But I know more now.

I took steps forward and I took steps back. My anxiety around public speaking will likely never go away, but now I know it isn't necessarily an obstacle.

When I visit Union Chapel again, this time once again in the audience for *The Moth*, I sit still, listening to a young woman tell the story about the first time she met the sister she never knew she had. I can't believe that had once been me up there. I watch and listen intently to the woman onstage who is speaking confidently, surely. But suddenly she stops. It's a long pause. She has forgotten her next line. She has lost her place. She takes a deep breath and slowly, measuredly, exhales, the air rushing into the mic. The audience, on the edge of their seats, exhales with her. She does not stutter, or rush, or run off the stage in tears. She stands still, waiting. And then her story comes back to her.

For years, I thought that if you were onstage at a big performance and you froze or messed up, you wouldn't be able to recover. But afterwards, in the bar, the woman is fine. She is better than fine. She is glowing. She doesn't seem embarrassed or ashamed. The worst had happened and she is overjoyed. Of course she is. Why had it taken me so long to believe that even when these things don't go perfectly, we can still survive?

Even when you face your biggest fears and it all goes as badly as it could possibly go, like when you declare your love for England onstage in Scotland.

People asked me so many times this year whether I was happier acting like an extrovert.

At times. In the best moments of improv, surrounded by warm, friendly faces, in a small classroom, just playing and being creative and laughing, I was indescribably happy. When I fell into a good conversation with a stranger that I had initiated, like with Claude on the Eurostar, I had the loveliest sense of unexpected kinship. When I wandered into the first bathhouse in Budapest and floated on my back, staring at the sky, with no plans to make or break, I felt free.

I loved learning about people and making connections, like having dinner with the storytellers at *The Moth* or over pie at book club, or even in the hospital with Pete, hearing about his Chinese grandparents while he took my father's blood pressure.

At the same time, as I ushered those final guests out of our flat after Thanksgiving dinner, I was so, so tired. How do extroverts get any work done? I genuinely do not know. How do they know what has happened to them without being alone to process it and fret about it and stay up all night thinking about it? How can they hear themselves think with all these new conversations in their head?

How do you sleep at night, extroverts?

A year of living like one was hard.

But now I have Lily and Vivian. I know that we will continue to meet up and workshop comedy together and if I ever do perform again, they will be there for me when I say the wrong thing onstage.

I know that a new friend is only two flights of stairs away, in my Dutch neighbour, Hannah.

I know that, when it comes to public speaking, I will always feel anxious and despairing, but if I practise and rehearse, then I can do it.

I know I have a new swimming and coffee pal in Abigail.

I know that it's worth it to have Deep Talk over Surface Talk and that even though people are wary of it, it brings you closer together.

I know that one small action sets off so many more. I met Paul at a networking event and his girlfriend recommended my comedy class, which led me to Lily and Vivian. Someone on Facebook recommended my improv course, which unlocked a whole side of me that I'd forgotten existed. Talking to a co-worker led me to that cosy book club.

In one evening, I set someone up with a literary agent, give someone dating advice and, on the way home, lead an elderly French couple to the right Tube station. On the underground, I help a woman on the escalator with her four bags of luggage. Normally I'd just want to, but would be too hesitant to get involved in someone else's affairs. The woman doesn't speak English, so instead of saying 'Thank you' she blows kisses at me as she waves and walks away. Perhaps, briefly, I get to be someone's Pete after all.

I learned a lot about loneliness. As an adult, sometimes if you're lucky, you have close friends from childhood near by, but when you move away from home or outgrow your old friends, you have to find your people. And it's so hard. It can take years. You have to actively go out and get them. You'll need them for when life gets dark or one of your loved ones has just gone into the operating room for major surgery and you're standing in the hospital corridor, scared out of your mind, and you really, really need someone to sit beside you. But once you have these friends, you get to keep them. Even if they move to, say, Paris or Poole, they're still yours. And everyone gets lonely. Everyone I met talked about it. It sneaks up on you, especially if you don't protect yourself from it.

Finding my voice and challenging myself to do intimidating things made me feel more confident. This is priceless in a world that can be scary, maddening and unfair. When there are fewer things we are scared of and fewer things that can control us, this can only be a good thing.

It was more than I could have ever hoped for when I started. I feel more in control of my life because I can extrovert. I can socialize in a room full of people I don't know. I can disrupt an entire theatre row if I really need to pee. I can get up and shout a question at a lecturer if I genuinely do not understand. I can befriend someone new, take their number and eventually feed them Coca-Cola ham in my house. I'm beginning to think I'm slowly becoming less of a shy introvert and slightly more of a gregarious introvert (grintrovert?).

This week, I happened to walk by that fancy gym. The one that had the competition that eventually led me to the sauna. I'd been avoiding it ever since the final weigh-in. I didn't like remembering who I had been that day. One of the trainers recognized me through the window and ran out to say hello as I did my best to speed quickly on by.

'Where've you been?' she asked.

Budapest, Edinburgh, strangers' houses, improv classes, on stages, on friend-dates.

'Oh, I've been around,' I said, mysteriously.

'You know who won the contest this year?' she asked.

'Who?' I asked.

'Portia,' she said.

I feel an overwhelming sense of relief. All is right in the world. I hadn't messed up the space – time continuum after all.

I'm about to head out the door to meet Hannah for coffee. Laura has texted asking if I want to take another improv course with her next month, and I've said yes. I'm reading the next book for our book club. Paul and his girlfriend are coming over for dinner next week. Sam and I are going to make Thanksgiving at ours an annual tradition. Claude and I are email pen pals now, and he always signs off, 'I hope that you are well and that you do nice things,' which I like very much. Lily and Vivian are trying to persuade me to perform comedy again. Probably I'll just go along to their gigs and cheer them on. And there's nothing wrong with that.

I have a tiny little social life. A new way to experience the world when I want to. I really like my comfort zone, but I also know I'll be OK if I leap into the unknown or the scary for a little while.

But if you see me at Glastonbury, please, take me gently by the hand and put me on the first bus home. I have been kidnapped and brought there against my will.

A NOTE ON INTROVERSION

Like Susan Cain in her book *Quiet: The Power of Introverts in a World That Can't Stop Talking* (which I can't recommend highly enough), in this book I address introversion from a cultural point of view.

In other words, I am working from the understanding that introverts, to paraphrase: seek solitude, concentrate well, are contemplative, dislike small talk, love one-on-one conversations, find long periods of socializing draining, and are often, though not always, shy and sensitive. And that extroverts are: highly sociable, risk-taking, relaxed in the spotlight, loud, enthusiastic, and enjoy large groups of people.

Traits associated with cultural introversion may come under different categories in the Big Five personality traits taxonomy (i.e. shyness may fall under 'neuroticism' and a risk-averse nature may fall under 'openness to experience').

Likewise, the Meyers-Briggs Personality Inventory describes introverts as individuals who obtain energy from contemplation or time alone, as opposed to extroverts, who gain energy from taking action or socializing. This book's interpretation of introversion is consistent with this definition, but also includes the aforementioned cultural traits associated with introverts.

If you are an introvert (or extrovert), some traits or tendencies I mention may apply to you, others may not. We are, as a rule, too complex for such simplification. And to quote Carl Jung, 'There is no such thing as a pure extrovert or a pure introvert – such a man would be in the lunatic asylum.'

I am not a trained psychologist or academic researcher, but throughout this book I reference research studies. For the sake of readability, the details of these studies and sources appear in the Notes section.

Many names and identifying details have been changed to protect the privacy of individuals who appear in this book. I have tried to remain faithful to the chronological details of the events detailed wherever possible.

NOTES

Introduction

one out of every two or three people is an introvert: Rowan Bayne, *The Myers-Briggs Type Indicator: A Critical Review and Practical Guide* (Chapman and Hall, 1995) and a brochure published by the Center for Application of Psychological Type: *Estimated Frequencies of the Types in the United States Population*, Center for Applications of Psychological Type Research Services (1996).

introverts, to paraphrase, concentrate well, relish solitude, *dislike small talk, love one-on-one conversations, avoid public speaking*: Susan Cain, *Quiet: The Power of Introverts in a World That Can't Stop Talking* (Crown Publishers, 2012), pp. 13, 269.

2 Talking to Strangers *or* New People

an effective treatment for social anxiety is a form of exposure therapy: A. Fang, A. T. Sawyer, A. Asnaani, S. G. Hofmann, 'Social Mishap Exposures for Social Anxiety Disorder: An Important Treatment Ingredient', *Cognitive and Behavioral Practices* 20 (2) (2013), 213–20. doi: 10.1016/j.cbpra.2012.05.003.

discovered that when people talk to strangers during their commutes, it makes them happier: N. Epley and J. Schroeder,

'Mistakenly Seeking Solitude', *Journal of Experimental Psychology: General*, 143(5), (2014), pp. 1980–99.

Introverts tend to hate chit-chat: several studies associate small talk with being draining for introverts, but this is summed up well in this article: Lindsay Dodgson, 'What Everyone Gets Wrong About Introverts', *Business Insider*, 11 May 2018. https://www.businessinsider.com/what-its-like-to-be-an-introvert-and-what-everyone-gets-wrong-2018–5?r=US&IR=T

Deep Self / Surface Self: 'How to Be Sociable' workshop taught at the School of Life and attended in London.

Deep Talk: discussed over the phone with Nicholas Epley; findings about how Deep Talk is less awkward than we think it will be, see M. Kardas, A. Kumar and N. Epley, 'Digging Deeper: Meaningful Conversations Are Surprisingly Pleasant', presented at the Society for Personality and Social Psychology Conference, Portland, OR (2019).

3 Shaking in the Spotlight *or* Stage Fright

Public speaking is an incredibly common fear – though introverts are significantly more likely than extroverts to suffer: Susan K. Opt and Donald A. Loffredo, 'Rethinking Communication Apprehension: A Myers-Briggs Perspective', *Journal of Psychology* 134, no. 5 (2000), pp. 556–70. See also Peter D. Macintyre and Kimly A. Thivierge, 'The Effects of Speaker Personality on Anticipated Reactions to Public Speaking', *Communication Research Reports* 12, no. 2 (1995), pp. 125–33.

when we are stressed our bodies also release cortisol, which interferes with our attention and short-term memory:

M. Biondi and A. Picardi, 'Psychological Stress and Neuroendocrine Function in Humans: The Last Two Decades of Research', *Psychotherapy and Psychosomatics* 68 (3) (1999), pp. 114–150.

See also: G. Matthews and L. Dorn, 'Cognitive and Attentional Processes in Personality and Intelligence', in *International Handbook of Personality and Intelligence*, edited by Donald H. Saklofske and Moshe Zeidner (Plenum Press, 1995), pp. 367–96; A. W. K. Gaillard, 'Stress, Workload, and Fatigue as Three Biobehavioral States: A General Overview', in P. A. Hancock and P. A. Desmond (eds), *Stress, Workload, and Fatigue* (L. Erlbaum, 2001); A. W. K. Gaillard and C. J. E. Wientjes, 'Mental Load and Work Stress as Two Types of Energy Mobilization', *Work and Stress*, 8 (2) (1994), pp. 141–52.

4 Heart Problems, a Real-Life Interlude

Evolutionary psychologists hypothesize that extroverts may handle stress better because they are better at handling rapid change and thinking on their feet: Nigel Barber, 'Do Extroverts Manage Stress Better?', *Psychology Today*, 5 June 2017, https://www.psychologytoday.com/gb/blog/the-human-beast/201701/do-extroverts-manage-stress-better

5 In Search of The One *or* Friend-Dating

research says that we have the most friends we'll ever have when we are twenty-nine: a survey of 1,505 Britons conducted by Genius Gluten Free found that twenty-nine-year-olds on average had eighty friends, the highest number of the participants surveyed (the average person had sixty-four).

while other studies say we start to lose friends after the age of twenty-five: K. Bhattacharya, A. Ghosh, D. Monsivais, R. I. M. Dunbar, K. Kaski, 'Sex Differences in Social Focus across the Life Cycle in Humans', *Royal Society Open Science* 3(4) (2016), 160097.

Introverts tend to value quality over quantity when it comes to relationships: C. L. Carmichael, H. T. Reis, P. R. Duberstein: 'In Your 20s It's Quantity, in Your 30s It's Quality: The Prognostic Value of Social Activity Across 30 Years of Adulthood', *Psychology and Aging*, 2015.

Studies show that we're spending more time online than ever before: an Ofcom study in the UK reported in their Communications Market Report that time spent online has doubled in the past ten years and that one quarter of Britons spend 40 hours online a week, largely on their mobile phones.

Social media is a huge part of the loneliness problem: Melissa G. Hunt, Rachel Marx, Courtney Lipson and Jordyn Young, 'No More FOMO: Limiting Social Media Decreases Loneliness and Depression', *Journal of Social and Clinical Psychology* 37 (10) (2018), pp. 751–68.

it's harder for men to make new friends: Jane E. Brody, 'The Challenge of Male Friendships', *New York Times*, 27 June 2016, https://well.blogs.nytimes.com/2016/06/27/the-challenges-of-male-friendships/

2.5 million British men have no close friends: research by the Movember Foundation found that 51 per cent of respondents, the equivalent of about two and a half million British men, have no close friends.

Rachel Bertsche went on fifty-two friend-dates in one year: Rachel Bertsche, *MWF Seeks BFF: My Yearlong Search for a New Best Friend* (Ballantine Books, 2011).

Brené Brown calls these friends 'move a body' friends: Brené Brown, 'Finding Shelter in a Shame Storm (and Avoiding the Flying Debris)', 21 March 2013, Oprah.com.

six to eight meetings: Ellen Hendriksen, *How to Be Yourself: Quiet Your Inner Critic and Rise Above Social Anxiety* (St Martin's Press, 2018).

on average, it takes fifty hours of time with someone before you consider them a casual friend and ninety hours before you feel comfortable upgrading them to 'friend': J. A. Hall, 'How Many Hours Does it Take to Make a Friend?', *Journal of Social and Personal Relationships* 36 (4) (2018), pp. 1278–96.

6 Crowd Control *or* Networking

Research has shown that it is our outer circle of acquaintances, also known as 'weak ties', that bring about the most change in our lives: M. Granovetter, 'The Strength of Weak Ties', *American Journal of Sociology* 78 (1973), pp. 1360–80, and his 1983 follow-up paper, 'The Strength of Weak Ties: A Network Theory Revisited' in *Sociological Theory* 1 (1983), pp. 201–33.

magnetism is 50 per cent innate and 50 per cent learned: the study was carried out by Professor Richard Wiseman, a psychologist at the University of Hertfordshire, who examined the theory of 'emotional contagion' and charisma in a public arena.

it takes four seconds to create an awkward silence: N. Koudenburg *et al.*, 'Disrupting the Flow: How Brief Silences in

Group Conversations Affect Social Needs', *Journal of Experimental Social Psychology* (2011), doi:10.1016/j.jesp.2010.12.006

Daisy Buchanan: Daisy Buchanan, *How to Be a Grown-Up* (Headline, 2007).

Emma Gannon: Emma Gannon, *The Multi-Hyphen Method* (Hodder & Stoughton, 2018).

7 The Wedding in Germany, a Real-Life Interlude

Researcher and public speaker Brené Brown says that connection is why we're here. That humans are neurobiologically built for it: Brené Brown, 'The Power of Vulnerability', June 2010, https://www.ted.com/talks/brene_brown_on_vulnerability

See also: C. Brené Brown, *Daring Greatly: How the Courage to Be Vulnerable Transforms the Way We Live, Love, Parent, and Lead* (Gotham, 2012).

'Some women don't need so much help with public speaking as with the self-doubt and self-loathing that hold them back from getting involved in it': Viv Groskop, *How to Own the Room* (Bantam Press, 2018).

8 Free-falling or Improvisation

Psychologists say that improv classes can help alleviate social anxiety and stress: Kathleen Toohill, 'So Funny, It Doesn't Hurt', *The Atlantic*, 11 September 2015, https://www.theatlantic.com/health/archive/2015/09/comedy-improv-anxiety/403933/

9 Everest *or* Stand-Up Comedy

Many comedians identify as introverts: G. Greengoss and Geoffrey F. Miller, 'Personality and Individual Differences', 47 (2) (2009), pp. 79–83.

40–60 per cent of the population identifies as shy: Steve Bressert, 'Facts About Shyness', *Psych Central* (2018), retrieved on 3 February 2019 from https://psychcentral.com/lib/facts-about-shyness/

public speaking is the number-one fear in America: Victoria Cunningham, Morty Lefkoe and Lee Sechrest, 'Eliminating Fears: An Intervention that Permanently Eliminates the Fear of Public Speaking', *Clinical Psychology and Psychotherapy* 13 (2006), pp. 183–93.

embarrassment is a healthy emotion because it signals to others that we care about the social code: M. Feinberg, R. Willer and D. Keltner, 'Flustered and Faithful: Embarrassment as a Signal of Prosociality', *Journal of Personality and Social Psychology*, 102 (1) (2012), pp. 81–97.

'Is this the way to Amarillo ...' I start to croon tentatively: '(Is This The Way To) Amarillo' written by Neil Sedaka and Howard Greenfield.

10 Talking to Men, a Real-Life Interlude

Research suggests that men are significantly lonelier than women: a poll by Eurostat which measured 'Persons who have someone to discuss personal matters by income quintile, household type and degree of urbanization' finds the situation is worst in France, where 12.24 per cent of respondents lack someone to confide in, and in Italy (11.9 per cent). See also 'Persons who have someone to ask for help by income quintile, household type and degree of urbanization' – the situation is worst in Italy, where 13.2 per cent of respondents lack someone to go to in difficulty, Luxembourg (12.9 per cent), the Netherlands (10.2 per cent) and Portugal (9.6 per cent).

That one third of men feel lonely regularly: as many as 35 per cent of men in Britain feel lonely at least once a week, while 11 per cent admit to suffering with the emotion every day, according to 2018 research conducted by the Commission by the Royal Voluntary Service.

one in eight men report that they have no one to discuss serious topics with: a YouGov survey for the Movember Research Foundation found that 12 per cent of men do not have a friend they would discuss a serious topic with (e.g. work worries, a health problem, money worries) and 51 per cent of men have two friends or fewer that they would open up to about a serious problem.

Loneliness: a 2010 report by the Mental Health Foundation found that the 18–34-year-olds surveyed were more likely than the over-55s to feel lonely often and to feel depressed because of loneliness. Research from the ONS in 2018, based on a survey of more than 10,000 adults, found that almost 10 per cent of people aged 16–24 were 'always or often' lonely – the highest proportion of any age group.

Also, according to the Mental Health Foundation, 42 per cent of respondents have felt depressed because they felt alone. This is higher among women (47 per cent, compared to 36 per cent of men), and higher among those aged 18–34 (53 per cent, compared to 32 per cent of those over 55).

(See: https://www.mentalhealth.org.uk/sites/default/files/the_lonely_society_report.pdf)

9 million people in Britain often or always feel lonely: according to a study by the Co-op and the British Red Cross in the UK across all adult ages, a greater number than the population of London are either always or often lonely.

massive demographic (the majority of which are men – male supporters outnumber women two to one in the UK): in 2016, Statista.com found that 67 per cent of respondents from the UK who stated they follow football were male: https://www.statista.com/statistics/658959/europe-football-fans-by-country-and-gender/

the researcher Arthur Aron who claimed he knew how to make two strangers fall in love: A. Aron *et al.*, 'The Experimental Generation of Interpersonal Closeness: A Procedure and Some Preliminary Findings', *Personality and Social Psychology*, 1997.

See also Mandy Len Catron, 'To Fall in Love with Anyone, Do This', *New York Times*, 9 January 2015, https://www.nytimes.com/2015/01/11/fashion/modern-love-to-fall-in-love-with-anyone-do-this.html

I wish more men could admit these things: one in three of us (30 per cent) would be embarrassed to admit to feeling lonely, according to the Mental Health Foundation.

See also C. Brené Brown, *Daring Greatly: How the Courage to Be Vulnerable Transforms the Way We Live, Love, Parent, and Lead* (Gotham, 2012).

I I La-La Land or Travelling Solo

one in two travellers think the best thing about travelling is getting out of their comfort zones: according to the travel trend forecaster Virtuoso®, 'Luxe Report Shares Five Must-Have Travel Experiences In The Coming Year' (2016).

12 **Scotch Courage** *or* Stand-Up Comedy, Round II

all I do is yell at myself in the mirror and emerge the exact same person: K. N. Ochsner, S. A. Bunge, J. J. Gross and J. D. I. Gabrieli, 'Rethinking Feelings: An fMRI Study of the Cognitive Regulation of Emotion', *Journal of Cognitive Neuroscience* 14 (8) (2002), pp. 1215–29.

13 **Introvert into the Woods** *or* A Real-Life Interlude

reading a 500-page book on psychedelics: Michael Pollan, *How to Change Your Mind: What the New Science of Psychedelics Teaches Us About Consciousness, Dying, Addiction, Depression, and Transcendence* (Penguin Press, 2018).

14 **Redemption** *or* Stand-Up Comedy, Round III

two women start making a big deal about some cactus: *Crazy Rich Asians*, screenplay written by Peter Chiarelli and Adele Lim.

15 **Come Dine With Me** *or* The Dinner Party

requires juggling many things at once – all things introverts aren't crazy about: M. D. Lieberman and R. Rosenthal, 'Why Introverts Can't Always Tell Who Likes Them: Multitasking and Nonverbal Decoding', *Journal of Personality and Social Psychology* 80 (2) (February 2001), 294–310.

'Enjoy the money … Take the money and get out of my property': *Come Dine With Me* contestant Peter Marsh, Channel 4, 4 January 2016.

Coca-Cola ham: Nigella Lawson, *Nigella Bites* (Chatto and Windus, 2001).

Super-juicy turkey: Nigella Lawson, *Nigella Christmas* (Chatto and Windus, 2008).

Brownies: Nigella Lawson, *How to Be a Domestic Goddess* (Chatto and Windus, 1998).

Dolly Alderton: Dolly Alderton, *Everything I Know About Love* (Fig Tree, 2018).

16 Introvert. Extrovert. Convert?

Some personality studies say that introversion is physiologic-ally or even genetically based: David G. Winter, *Personality: Analysis and Interpretation of Lives* (McGraw-Hill, 1996), pp. 511–16.

See also Susan Cain, *Quiet: The Power of Introverts in a World that Can't Stop Talking* (Crown Publishers, 2012) and Daniel Nettle, *Personality: What Makes You the Way You Are* (Oxford University Press, 2007).

introversion is 40–50 per cent heritable: Thomas J. Bouchard Jr and Matt McGue, 'Genetic and Environmental Influences on Human Psychological Differences', *Developmental Neurobiology* 54 (1)(2003), pp. 4–5.

our personalities are not fixed or exclusively determined by nurture or nature; instead, they can change as a result of action: Brian R Little, *Who Are You, Really?* (Simon & Schuster, 2017).

ACKNOWLEDGEMENTS

Thank you so much to my literary agent, the brilliant and kind Emma Finn. Thank you for taking a chance on me, for always giving me incredible editorial notes, for never forgetting to add an accent to 'Beyoncé' and for being such a wonderful friend to me.

Thank you to Darcy Nicholson, my genius editor who Marie Kondo'd the hell out of my book and to whom I am so grateful. I'm sorry for all the late-night emails – I can't promise you've received the last of them. Thank you to Allison Adler for being such a thoughtful editor. It's been such a pleasure to work with you two and your teams. Thank you, Hayley Barnes (I'm sorry for what I wrote about Geminis) and Emma Burton, for your enthusiasm, hard work and ideas. Thank you to Sophie Wilson for your eagle eyes.

Thank you to everyone who helped mentor me and everyone I interviewed: Stefan G. Hofmann, Nicholas Epley, David Litt, Rachel Bertsche, Richard Reid, Daisy Buchanan, Emma Gannon, Liam Brennan, Maria Rivington, Kate Smurthwaite, Phil Wang, Charles Knowlton, Sara Barron and Dolly Alderton. Thanks for your expertise and for helping me survive the madness.

Thank you to Nigella Lawson for your spell-binding recipes that won over my dinner-party guests and for patiently answering my question at your book talk about whether you were an introvert or an extrovert.

Thank you to Jori Thompson for being my best friend for so long and for your notes. Thank you to Chantal Haines and Lucy Handley for moral support and style guidance over tacos. Thank you, Sabine Handtke, for telling me to keep writing. Thank you, Tarn Rodgers Johns, for you know what. Thank you to Hannah van der Deijl (new best friend?) for taking the time to read this and give thoughtful feedback after you'd known me only a few weeks. You are all true best-friend material.

A special thanks to Kim Chi Kunn of Maison D'etre and Maison Bleu Canteen for always having ice for my iced lattes even in the dead of winter, but also for creating the cosiest refuge to write in. You're the best.

A big thank-you to the special class of friends who picked up on the hysterical tone of my text messages and late-night emails and gently offered, 'Would you like me to take a look?' I will be forever grateful to Jessica J. Lee, the best, kindest doppelganger a girl could ever hope for, who also takes me swimming; Julia Buckley, the fellow introvert hero who appeared out of thin air and introduced me to Alice; and Morgan Jackson – you are so funny, smart and generous, and wow, you make great chutney. Thank you all for taking the time to read excerpts and give thoughtful notes.

A massive thank-you to Rachel Kapelke-Dale. Without you, there would be no book, and also likely no writing and also a lot less fun. Thank you for long coffee sessions, frantic phone calls, nocturnal emails and for always being there for me. Thank you for being such a good friend for all these years and for being an amazing editor to me. This book wouldn't exist without your encouragement and pep talks under rainy awnings. You mean the world to me, and your hair looks great.

Thank you to my parents, my brothers and my grandparents – anything funny I have ever said or written probably came from one of you. Thanks especially to my parents, for always encouraging me, for always worrying about me and for telling me to go big.

A huge thank-you to 'Sam' – I'm so, so grateful I have you. Thank you for helping me survive this by cooking dinner for me, ironing my shirt before performances, reading my drafts, talking to me about this and nothing else all year, and so much more. Meeting you was one of the luckiest things that ever happened to me. There aren't enough words to express how much you mean to me.

Thank you to all the new, wonderful people I met as a result of this strange year, including but certainly not limited to: Rosie Luff, Cathryn Basden, Toia Mangakahia, Venus Wong, Sarah Biddlecombe, Meg Bowles, Benji Waterstones, Paul Stafford, Alice Adams and Paul Creasy.

I know I don't say it enough, but in the spirit of Deep Talk, here goes: I love you all so much.

Jessica Pan is a journalist whose work has appeared in the likes of the *Guardian*'s Weekend magazine, *Stylist*, *The Cut*, *Lenny Letter* and *Vice*. She has a BA in Psychology from Brown University. Jessica is also the co-author of the book *Graduates in Wonderland*, an epistolary memoir about living in Beijing and Paris. She previously worked as a TV reporter and magazine editor in Beijing and now lives in London.

Also by Jessica Pan, with Rachel Kapelke-Dale

Graduates in Wonderland